THE EUROPEAN UNION AND INTERNATIONAL INVESTMENT LAW

This book explores the interaction between the EU and international investment law, both at the internal level, namely within the EU internal market, and at the external level, ie in the context of its relations with third States.

The joint treatment of these dimensions reveals that the EU has assumed an ostensibly ambivalent attitude towards international investment law. At the internal level, it has consistently asserted that intra-EU international investment agreements (IIAs) are not compatible with EU law and has advocated their termination. At the external level, it has eagerly deployed IIAs to develop its post-Lisbon international investment policy.

The book finds that beneath this apparent ambivalence towards international investment law ultimately lies the EU's attempt to impose, both internally and externally, its own original model of regulation of cross-border investment. It then argues that the EU adopted this approach with a view to supporting its internal market, enhancing its external influence, and, ultimately, pursuing long-term 'federal aspirations'. Finally, the book identifies the legal and political obstacles that have curtailed the EU's efforts at both the internal and the external level.

Studies in International Trade and Investment Law: Volume 29

Studies in International Trade and Investment Law

Series Editors
Gabrielle Marceau
Krista Nadakavukaren Schefer
Federico Ortino
Gregory Shaffer

This series offers a forum for publication of original and scholarly analyses of emerging and significant issues in international trade and investment law – broadly understood to include the whole of the law of the WTO, the public international law of foreign investment, the law of the EU common commercial policy and other regional trade regimes, and any legal or regulatory topic that interacts with global trade and foreign investment. The aim of the series is to produce works which will be readily accessible to trade and investment law scholars and practitioners alike.

Recent titles in this series:

Public Procurement and Labour Rights: Towards Coherence in International Instruments of Procurement Regulation
Maria Anna Corvaglia

The China-Australia Free Trade Agreement: A 21st-Century Model
Edited by Colin Picker, Heng Wang and Weihuan Zhou

Regional Economic Integration and Dispute Settlement in East Asia: The Evolving Legal Framework
Anna G Tevini

The EU, World Trade Law and the Right to Food: Rethinking Free Trade Agreements with Developing Countries
Giovanni Gruni

Patent Games in the Global South: Pharmaceutical Patent Law Making in Brazil, India and Nigeria
Amaka Vanni

The Nationality of Corporate Investors under International Investment Law
Anil Yilmaz Vastardis

The Regulation of Product Standards in World Trade Law
Ming Du

Investors' International Law
Edited by Jean Ho and Mavluda Sattorova

Rethinking, Repackaging, and Rescuing World Trade Law in the Post-Pandemic Era
Edited by Amrita Bahri, Weihan Zhou and Daria Boklan

Flexible Regional Economic Integration in Africa: Lessons and Implications for the Multilateral Trading System
Timothy Masiko

International Investment Law: An Analysis of the Major Decisions
Edited by Hélène Ruiz Fabri and Edoardo Stoppioni

State Capitalism and International Investment Law
Edited by Panagiotis Delimatsis, Georgios Dimitropoulos and Anastasios Gourgourinis

The European Union and International Investment Law

The Two Dimensions of an Uneasy Relationship

Francesco Montanaro

•HART•
OXFORD • LONDON • NEW YORK • NEW DELHI • SYDNEY

HART PUBLISHING

Bloomsbury Publishing Plc

Kemp House, Chawley Park, Cumnor Hill, Oxford, OX2 9PH, UK

1385 Broadway, New York, NY 10018, USA

29 Earlsfort Terrace, Dublin 2, Ireland

HART PUBLISHING, the Hart/Stag logo, BLOOMSBURY and the Diana logo are trademarks of Bloomsbury Publishing Plc

First published in Great Britain 2023

A catalogue record for this book is available from the British Library.

A catalogue record for this book is available from the Library of Congress.

ISBN: HB: 978-1-50996-380-5
ePDF: 978-1-50996-382-9
ePub: 978-1-50996-381-2

Typeset by Compuscript Ltd, Shannon

Foreword

THE SUBJECTS COVERED by this book could not be more topical. On the one hand, the interplay between intra-EU BITs and EU law remains one of the most problematic expressions of the wider phenomenon generally referred to as 'fragmentation of international law'. Whether EU law may be reconciled with the pre-existing investment obligations binding EU Member States is a matter of heated debate. Investment arbitral tribunals, the European Commission and the CJEU have divergent views on this issue. The cleavage between the actors embroiled in this predicament has even grown after the issuance of a string of CJEU's judgments addressing various aspects of this matter. On the other hand, the emergence of the European Union as an actor in international investment lawmaking has also raised a panoply of questions. The first one concerns the delimitation of the European Union's competence in the field of foreign investment. Another debated issue was and still is what the international investment agreements concluded by the European Union should look like. Should they aim to change radically the international investment regime? Or should they limit themselves to address specific drawbacks thereof?

Needless to say, both these topics have attracted a great deal of scholarly attention. But this book, in my view, stands out from this large crowd, because it does not treat them as two distinct issues. Rather, it draws a link between them. The intra-EU BITs issue and the development of the EU international investment policy are respectively regarded as the 'internal' and the 'external' dimensions of the Union's action in the field of foreign investment.

With this in mind, the author then engages in an accurate and extensive analysis of both dimensions. In the section devoted to the 'internal' dimension, the book retraces almost twenty years of interaction between arbitral tribunals, the European Commission and the CJEU. In doing so, it explains that the debate about the (in)compatibility between EU law and intra-EU BITs is ultimately a debate between two irremediably divergent perspectives. In the section devoted to the 'external' dimension, it illustrates how the European Union has emerged as a driving force in the process of reform of the international investment regime.

The joint treatment of these matters leads the author to put forward his own original reading of the Union's action in the field of foreign investment. More specifically, he interestingly argues that the external and the internal dimensions are clear manifestations of the Union's attempt to assert internally and externally its own model of regulation of cross-border investment. The author, however, does not limit itself to suggest this captivating interpretation of the EU's action, but he also highlights the obstacles hindering the full implementation of this project.

In conclusion, this book, besides providing an exhaustive and well-written analysis of the 'internal' and 'external' dimensions Union's action in the field of foreign investment, offers an insightful reflection on the challenges stemming from the interaction between EU law and international investment law.

Giorgio Sacerdoti
Milan
14 July 2022

Acknowledgements

THIS BOOK IS the result of an extended effort, which started with my doctoral studies. I wrote my PhD thesis under the joint supervision of Professor Claudio Dordi and Professor Yves Nouvel and defended it in 2017. After a period of reflection, the persisting relevance and topicality of the subject of my doctoral studies led me to start the second leg of this journey. It was rather difficult because it implied a rethinking and restructuring of the initial manuscript. But I faced this daunting challenge with confidence because I could rely on the precious guidance of Professor Giorgio Sacerdoti, to whom I am infinitely grateful.

I also wish to thank Giuseppe Bianco, Viktoriia Lapa, Nicolò Nisi, and Federica Violi for agreeing to read and comment on the early drafts of the book.

My heartfelt gratitude also goes to my family for the unwavering, but discreet, support provided over the years and to Chiara for her admirable patience and constant encouragement.

Needless to say, all the views expressed in this book are strictly personal and do not reflect the position of the institution where I am currently working.

Contents

Foreword ... *v*
Acknowledgements ... *vii*
Table of Abbreviations ... *xiii*
Table of Cases ... *xv*
Table of Legislation ... *xxiii*

1. Introduction ... 1
I. The Focus and the Rationale for this Study ... 2
II. Setting the Scene: The European Union, EU Member States and International Investment Law ... 3
III. Book Structure ... 5

2. The Role of EU Member States and the EU in the Field of Foreign Investment ... 8
I. The Role of European States in the Creation of the International Investment Regime ... 8
II. Foreign Investment and the European Integration Process: The Foundational Phase ... 9
III. The Emerging Role of the European Community in the Field of Foreign Investment ... 12
IV. Towards the Allocation at the European Union Level of the Competence Over Foreign Direct Investment ... 14
V. The Commission's View on Article 207 TFEU ... 18
VI. Setting the Ground for the Development of the EU Foreign Investment Policy ... 19
A. Managing the Transition to EU IIAs and Investment Chapters ... 20
B. Dealing with the Financial Consequences of the Involvement of the EU in Investment Disputes ... 21
VII. Taking a Step Back: The Political Impracticability of the Commission's Extensive Interpretation of the Union's Competence Over Foreign Investment ... 24
VIII. A Rude Awakening: Opinion 2/15 and the Boundaries of the Union's Exclusive Competence Over Foreign Investment ... 26
A. The Union's Exclusive Competence Over Foreign Direct Investment ... 27

B. The Union's Competence Over Foreign Indirect Investment and Investor-State Dispute Settlement 28
C. The Union's Competence to Terminate EU Member States' BITs with Singapore 30
IX. The Consequences of Mixity 31
X. Conclusion 34

3. The Internal Dimension: The Relationship between EU Law and Intra-EU IIAs 36
I. Possible Areas of Tension between EU Law and Intra-EU IIAs 37
A. Different Approaches to the Regulation of Cross-Border Investment 37
B. Differences in the Content of Substantive Rules 38
C. Investment Protection Rules and EU Competition and State Aid Rules 40
D. Investment Protection and the EU's Climate Commitments 41
E. The Coexistence of Two Distinct Adjudicatory Bodies 42
II. Dealing with the Tensions between EU Law and Intra-EU IIAs: A Matter of Perspective 43
A. Ensuring the Autonomy and the Primacy of EU Law: The 'EU Law-Centred' Approach 43
B. The 'International Law-Centred' Approach: The Role of the Vienna Convention on the Law of Treaties 47
III. Clash of Paradigms: 'EU Law-Centred' Approach vs 'International law-Centred' Approach in Practice 50
IV. The 'EU Law-Centred' Approach in the Amicus Curiae Briefs of the European Commission in the Pre-*Achmea* Era 51
A. The 'EU Law-Centred' Approach and the Intra-EU BITs 52
B. The 'EU Law-Centred' Approach and the ECT 53
V. The International Investment Tribunals' View on the Relationship between EU Law and Intra-EU IIAs in the Pre-*Achmea* Era 54
A. The Relationship between the EU Judicial System and the ISDS Mechanisms Contained in Intra-EU BITs 54
B. The Relationship between Investment Protection Rules under Intra-EU BITs and EU Substantive Law 59
C. The Relationship between the EU Judicial System and the ISDS Mechanism Contained in the ECT 60
D. The Relationship between the EU Substantive Law and the Investment Protection Rules under the ECT 61
VI. The CJEU and the 'EU Law-Centred' Approach: The *Achmea* Judgment 62
A. Arbitral Tribunals and the Interpretation of EU Law 63

B. Ex Ante Control Over the EU Consistency of Arbitral Awards 65
C. Ex Post Control Over the EU Consistency of Arbitral Awards 66
VII. The Aftermath: The Debate on the Impact of the *Achmea* Judgment 68
VIII. Doubling-Down on the 'EU Law-Centred' Approach: The Commission's Communication of 19 July 2018 71
IX. Intra-EU Investment Arbitration after *Achmea*: The Arbitral Case Law's Perspective 72
X. The Member States' Declarations on the Legal Effects of the *Achmea* Judgment 75
XI. Are the 'Masters of the Treaties' Still in Charge? The Role of Member States' Declarations in Intra-EU Investment Arbitration 78
XII. The Return of the 'Masters of the Treaties': The Termination Agreement 82
XIII. The End of Intra-EU BITs? Appraising the Possible Effects of the Termination Agreement 84
A. The Material Scope of Application of the TA 85
B. The Effects Ratione Temporis of the TA 85
C. The TA and the Enforcement of Intra-EU Arbitral Decisions 86
XIV. Beyond *Achmea*: The CJEU's Bid for the Eradication of Intra-EU Investment Arbitration 87
A. The Enlargement of the *Achmea* Dictum 87
B. The CJEU's View on the Interplay between EU Substantive Law and Investment Protection Rules 91
XV. What's Next? Intra-EU Investment Arbitration under the ECT after *Komstroy* 91
XVI. Conclusion 95

4. The External Dimension: The EU as a Player in the Investment Treaty-Making Arena 97
I. The Initial EU's Approach to Investment Treaty-Making: Seeking Incremental Reform 98
A. The Fair and Equitable Treatment Clause 99
B. The Umbrella Clause 104
C. The Protection against Illegal Expropriation 107
D. Redefining the Relationship between General Interest Objectives and Investment Protection Rules: Clarificatory Rules, Hortatory Rules, Exception and Carve-out Mechanisms 115

E. The ISDS Mechanism in the Early Versions of the EU Investment Chapters 122
II. The Shift Towards Systemic Reform: The Investment Court System 128
A. The Persistent Discontent about the ISDS Mechanism in EU IIAs 128
B. Seeking Systemic Reform: The Investment Court System 130
C. Is Systemic Reform Enough? Domestic and EU Law-Based Challenges against CETA 137
D. The Investment Court System and the EU Legal Order: Opinion 1/17 139
E. The Modernisation of the ECT as a Further Example of Systemic Reform? 146
III. Conclusion 147

5. The External and the Internal Dimensions of the European Union's Action in the Field of Foreign Investment 149
I. The EU's Ambivalence Towards International Investment Law 149
II. The Obstacles Hindering the Full Implementation of the Union's Action in the Field of Foreign Investment 151
A. Legal and Political Obstacles at the Internal Level 151
B. Legal and Political Obstacles at the External Level 152
III. Conclusion 153

Postscript *155*
Bibliography *157*
Index *175*

Table of Abbreviations

ASEAN	Association of Southeast Asian Nations
BIT	Bilateral investment treaty
BITs	Bilateral investment treaties
BLEU	Belgium-Luxembourg Economic Union
CACs	Collective Action Clauses
CAFTA	Dominican Republic–Central America Free Trade Agreement
CETA	Comprehensive Economic and Trade Agreement
CFREU	Charter of Fundamental Rights of the European Union
CJEU	Court of Justice of the European Union
CPTPP	Comprehensive and Progressive Agreement for Trans-Pacific Partnership
CUSMA	Canada-United States-Mexico Agreement
EC	European Community
ECA	Economic Cooperation Agreement
ECPC	European and Community Patents Court
ECT	Energy Charter Treaty
ECHR	European Convention on Human Rights
ECtHR	European Court of Human Rights
EEC	European Economic Community
EFTA	European Free Trade Area
EPA	Economic Partnership Agreement
ETS	Emission Trading Scheme
EU	European Union
EUSFTA	European Union-Singapore Free Trade Agreement
EUSIPA	European Union-Vietnam Investment Protection Agreement
EUVIFTA	European Union-Vietnam Free Trade Agreement

EUVIPA	European Union-Singapore Investment Protection Agreement
FDI	Foreign direct investment
FET	Fair and equitable treatment
FIPA	Foreign Investment Promotion and Protection Agreement
FNC	Friendship Navigation and Commerce
FTA	Free Trade Agreement
FTC	Free Trade Commission
GATT	General Agreement on Tariffs and Trade
GATS	General Agreement on Trade in Services
ICJ	International Court of Justice
IIAs	International investment agreements
ICS	Investment Court System
ICSID	International Centre for Settlement of Investment Disputes
IPRs	Intellectual Property Rights
ISDS	Investor-State dispute settlement
MFN	Most-favoured nation
MIC	Multilateral Investment Court
NAFTA	North American Free Trade Agreement
NT	National Treatment
PACER	Pacific Agreement on Closer Economic Relations
RCEP	Regional Comprehensive Economic Partnership
REIO	Regional Economic Integration Organisation
TEU	Treaty on the European Union
TFEU	Treaty on the functioning of the European Union
TPP	Trans-Pacific Partnership
TRIPS	Trade-Related Aspects of Intellectual Property Rights
TTIP	Transatlantic Trade and Investment Partnership
UNCLOS	United Nations Convention of the Law of the Sea
WTO	World Trade Organization

Table of Cases

Court of Justice of the European Union

Adeneler and others v *ELOG (Ellinikos Organismos Galaktos)*, Case C-212/04, EU:C:2006:443 68

Amministrazione delle Finanze dello Stato v Simmenthal, Case 106/77, EU:C:1978:49 44

Annunziata Matteucci v Communauté française de Belgique and Commissariat général aux relations internationales de la communauté française de Belgique, Case 235/87 44

Ascendi Beiras Litoral e Alta, Auto Estradas das Beiras Litoral e Alta v *Autoridade Tributária e Aduaneira*, Case C-377/13, EU:C:2014:1754. 66

Commission of the European Communities v Ireland, Case C-459/03, EU:C:2006:345 .... 45–46, 57

Commission of the European Communities v Portugal, Case C-62/98, EU:C:2000:358 44

D. v Inspecteur van de Belastingdienst/Particulieren/Ondernemingen buitenland te Heerlen, Case C-376/03, EU:C:2005:424 59

Eco Swiss China Time Ltd v Benetton International NV, Case C-126/97, EU:C:1999:269 67

Elisa María Mostaza Claro v Centro Móvil Milenium SL, Case C-168/05, EU:C:2006:675 67

European Commission v European Food SA and Others, Case C-638/19, EU:C:2022:50 90

Federazione nazionale delle imprese elettrotecniche ed elettroniche (Anie) and Others v Ministero dello Sviluppo Economico, Gestore dei servizi energetici (GSE) SpA, joined Cases C-798/19 and C-799/18, EU:C:2021:280 .... 39–40, 70

Flaminio Costa v *ENEL*, Case 6/64, EU:C:1964:66 .... 1, 44

Germany v Council of the European Union, Case C-600/14, EU:C:1998:94 30

International Chemical Corporation v *Amministrazione Finanze*, Case 66/80, EU:C:1981:102 68

International Fruit Co. NV v Produktschap voor Groenten en Fruit, joined Cases 21 to 24/72, EU:C:1972:115 31

Internationale Handelsgesellschaft v Einfuhr- und Vorratstelle für Getreide und Futtermittel, Case 11/70, EU:C:1970:114 44

Klaus Konle v Austria, Case C-302/97, EU:C:1999:271 19
Kühne & Heitz v Productschap voor Pluimvee en Eieren, Case C-453/00, EU:C:2004:17 ....68, 72
Margarethe Ospelt and Schlössle Weissenberg Familienstiftung, Case C-452/01, EU:C:2003:493 19
Moldova v Komstroy LLC, Case C-741/19, EU:C:2021:655 88
NV Algemene Transport en Expeditie Onderneming van Gend & Loos v Netherlands Inland Revenue Administration, Case 26/62, EU:C:1963:1 ....1, 61
Opinion 1/00, EU:C:1992:189 45
Opinion 1/09, EU:C:2011:123 ....46–47, 58, 63–64, 141
Opinion 1/17, EU:C:2019:341 139–45
Opinion 1/20, not yet published 88
Opinion 1/76, EU:C:1977:63 44
Opinion 1/91, EU:C:1991:490 45
Opinion 1/92, EU:C:1992:189 45
Opinion 2/13, EU:C:2014:2454 ....46–47, 63, 68, 142
Opinion 2/15, EU:C:2017:376 ....5, 19, 25–31, 33, 35
Poland v PL Holdings Sàrl, Case C-109/20, EU:C:2021:875 ....70, 89
Robert Bosch GmbH v Hauptzollamt Hildesheim, Case 135/77, ECLI:EU:C:1978:75 92
Robert Fearon & Company Limited v Irish Land Commission, Case 182/83, EU:C:1984:305 19
S.C. European Food S.A, S.C. Starmill S.R.L., S.C. Multipack S.R.L and others v European Commission, joined Cases T-624/15, T-694/15 and T-704/15, ECLI:EU:T:2019:423 90
Slovak Republic v Achmea, Case C-284/16, EU:C:2018:158 ....62–63, 65–67, 140
Société Arcelor Atlantique et Lorraine and others v Premier ministre, Ministre de l'écologie et du développement durable and Ministre de l'économie, des finances et de l'industrie, Case C-127/07, EU:C:2008:728 41
SpA Eridania-Zuccherifici nazionali and SpA Società italiana per l'industria degli zuccheri v Minister of Agriculture and Forestry, Minister for Industry, Trade and Craft Trades, and SpA Zuccherifici Meridionali, Case 230/78, EU:C:1979:216 38
Staat der Nederlanden v Essent NV, Essent Nederland BV, Eneco Holding NV and Delta NV, joined Cases C-105/12 to C-107/12, EU:C:2013:677 27
Thomas Pringle v Ireland and Others, Case C-370/12, EU:C:2012:756 28

European Court of Human Rights

Bosphorus Hava Yolları Turizm ve Ticaret Anonim Sirketi v Ireland (2006) 42 EHRR 1 53

Permanent Court of International Justice

Certain German Interests in Polish Upper Silesia (Germany v Poland) [1926] PCIJ Rep Series A No. 7, 19 64

International Court of Justice

Aegean Sea Continental Shelf (Greece v Turkey), Judgment (19 December 1978), ICJ Rep. 1978 50

International Tribunal for the Law of the Sea

Southern Bluefin Tuna case (Australia and New Zealand v Japan), Decision on Jurisdiction and Admissibility (4 August 2000), ITLOS, Rep. of International Awards XXIII 50

Other jurisdictions

Conseil Constitutionnel (France)

Decision No 2017-749 DC 137–38

Bundesverfassungsgericht (Germany)

2 BvR 1368/16, 2 BvR 1444/16, 2 BvR 1482/16, 2 BvE 3/16 137

Bundesgerichtshof (Germany)

Slovak Republic v Achmea, I ZB 2/15 68

Oberlandesgericht Frankfurt am Main

Croatia v Raiffeisen Bank International AG, 26 SchH 2/20 88

Svea Hovrätt (Sweden)

CEF Energia BV v Italy, Case T-4236-19 87
Greentech Energy System A/S et al. v Italy, Case T-3239-19..........................87
Poland v PL Holdings S.à.r.l, Case T-8538–17...69

United Kingdom Supreme Court

Micula and others v Romania, 19 February 2020 [2020] UKSC 5 87

Arbitration awards

9REN Holding S.a.r.l v Spain, Award (31 May 2019), ICSID Case No ARB/15/15...78
Abaclat and others v Argentina (formerly Giovanna a Beccara and others v Argentine Republic), Decision on jurisdiction and admissibility (4 August 2011), ICSID Case No ARB/07/5......................121
Achmea B.V. v Slovak Republic, Award on jurisdiction, arbitrability and suspension (26 October 2010), UNCITRAL, PCA Case No 2008-13..52–53, 56–57, 59, 64
ADC Affiliate Limited and ADC & ADMC Management Limited v Hungary, Award (2 October 2006), ICSID Case No ARB/03/1...............111
Addiko Bank AG and Addiko Bank d.d. v Croatia, Decision on Croatia's jurisdictional objection related to the alleged incompatibility of the BIT with the EU *acquis* (12 June 2020), ICSID Case No ARB/17/37 79
AES Summit Generation Limited and AES-Tisza Erömü Kft v Hungary, Award (23 September 2010), ICSID Case No ARB/07/22.................... 40, 61
Alpha Projektholding GmbH v Ukraine, Award (8 November 2010), ICSID Case No ARB/07/16 109
Ambiente Ufficio SpA and others v Argentina (Ambiente Ufficio), Decision on jurisdiction (8 February 2013), ICSID Case No ARB/08/9...121
Antaris Solar GmbH and Dr. Michael Göde v Czech Republic, Award (2 May 2018) PCA Case No 2014-01.................................41, 72, 74
Antoine Goetz et consorts v Burundi, Award (10 February 1999), ICSID Case No ARB/95/3 111
Bayindir Insaat Turizm Ticaret Ve Sanayi A.S. v Pakistan, Award (27 August 2009), ICSID Case No ARB/03/29 ....39, 101
Belenergia S.A. v Italy, Award (28 August 2019), ICSID Case No ARB/15/40..80
Blusun S.A., Jean-Pierre Lecorcier and Michael Stein v Italy, Award (27 December 2016) ICSID Case No ARB/14/3 ....41, 53–54, 60
Cavalum SGPS S.A. v Spain, Reconsideration decision (10 January 2022), ICSID Case No ARB/15/34..92

CEF Energia BV v Italy, Award (16 January 2019), SCC 158/2015 .... 73, 78
Charanne and Construction Investments v Spain, Award (21 January 2016), SCC 062/2012 .... 60–61, 101, 109
Chemtura Corporation v Government of Canada, Award (2 August 2010), UNCITRAL 111
CME Czech Republic B.V. v Czech Republic, Partial Award (13 September 2001), UNCITRAL 111
CMS Gas Transmission Company v Argentina, Award (12 May 2005), ICSID Case No ARB/01/8 .... 101, 105
Compañiá de Aguas del Aconquija S.A. and Vivendi Universal S.A. v Argentina, Decision on annulment (3 July 2002), ICSID Case No ARB/97/3 64
Compañia del Desarrollo de Santa Elena S.A. v Costa Rica, Award (17 February 2000), ICSID Case No ARB/96/1 110
Continental Casualty Company v Argentina, Award (5 September 2008), ICSID Case No ARB/03/9 105
Cube Infrastructure Fund SICAV and others v Spain, Decision on jurisdiction, liability and partial decision on quantum (19 February 2019), ICSID Case No ARB/15/20 78
Eastern Sugar B.V. v Czech Republic, Partial Award (27 March 2007), SCC 088/2004 .... 36, 52–53, 55–56, 59
Eiser Infrastructure Limited and Energía Solar Luxembourg S.à r.l. v Spain, Final award (4 May 2017), ICSID Case No ARB/13/36 .... 51, 61
El Paso Energy International Company v Argentina, Award (31 October 2011), ICSID Case No ARB/03/1 109
Electrabel S.A. v Hungary, Award (25 November 2015), ICSID Case No ARB/07/19 .... 40, 53–54, 61–62
Eli Lilly and Company v Canada, Final award (16 March 2017), UNCITRAL, ICSID Case No UNCT/14/2 114
Eskosol S.p.A. in liquidazione v Italy, Decision on termination request and intra-EU objection (7 May 2019), ICSID Case No ARB/15/50 81
ESPF Beteiligungs GmbH, ESPF Nr. 2 Austria Beteiligungs GmbH, and InfraClass Energie 5 GmbH & Co. KG v Italy, Award (14 September 2020), ICSID Case No ARB/16/5 80
European American Investment Bank AG (EURAM) v Slovak Republic, Award on jurisdiction (22 October 2012), UNCITRAL 53, 56–59
Foresight Luxembourg Solar 1 S.Á.R1., et al. v Spain, Final award (14 November 2018), SCC 2015/150 73
Fynerdale Holdings BV v Czech Republic, Award (29 April 2021) PCA Case No 2018-18 82
Gami Investments Inc. v Mexico, Final award (15 November 2004), UNCITRAL 39
Georg Gavrilovic and Gavrilovic d.o.o. v Croatia, Award (25 July 2018), ICSID Case No ARB/12/39 72

Glamis Gold v United States of America, Award (8 June 2009), UNCITRAL 103
Green Power Partners K/S Sce Solar Don Benito Aps v Spain, Award (16 June 2022), SCC 2016/135........ 93
ICW Investments v Czech Republic, Award (15 May 2019), PCA Case No 2014-22........ 41, 78
Infracapital F1 S.à.r.l. and Infracapital Solar B.V. v Spain, Decision on respondent's request for reconsideration regarding the intra-EU objection and the merits (1 February 2022), ICSID Case No ARB/16/18...... 92
Infrastructure Services Luxembourg S.à.r.l. and Energia Termosolar B.V. (formerly Antin Infrastructure Services Luxembourg S.à.r.l. and Antin Energia Termosolar B.V.) v Spain, Award (15 June 2018) ICSID Case No ARB/13/31 72
International Thunderbird Gaming Corporation v Mexico, Award (26 January 2006), UNCITRAL 103
Jan Oostergetel and Theodora Laurentius v Slovak Republic, Decision on jurisdiction (30 April 2010), UNCITRAL 55
Joy Mining Machinery Ltd v Egypt, Award on jurisdiction (6 August 2004), ARB/03/11........ 105
Marfin Investment Group v Cyprus, Award (26 July 2018), ICSID Case No ARB/13/27 72
Marvin Roy Feldman Karpa v Mexico, Award (16 December 2002), ICSID Case No ARB(AF)/99/1 .... 39, 110
Masdar Solar & Wind Cooperatief U.A. v Spain, Award (28 September 2018) ICSID Case No ARB/14/1489-491........ 39
Metalclad Corporation v Mexico, Award (30 August 2000), ICSID Case No ARB(AF)/97/1 111
Methanex Corporation v United States of America, Decision of the Tribunal on petitions from third persons to intervene as 'amici curiae' (15 January 2001), UNCITRAL 123
NextEra Energy Global Holdings B.V. and NextEra Energy Spain Holdings B.V. v Spain, Final award (31 May 2019), ICSID Case No ARB/14/11........ 79
Noble Ventures Inc. v Romania, Award (12 October 2005), ICSID Case No ARB/01/11........ 39, 105
Occidental Petroleum Corporation and Occidental Exploration and Production Company v Ecuador, Award (1 July 2004), LCIA Case No UN3467 .... 39, 101, 109
OperaFund Eco-Invest SICAV PLC and Schwab Holding AG v Spain, Award (6 September 2019), Case No ARB/15/20 79
Philip Morris Brands Sàrl, Philip Morris Products S.A. and Abal Hermanos S.A. v Oriental Republic of Uruguay, Award (8 July 2016), ICSID Case No ARB/10/7........ 110

Pope & Talbot Inc. v Government of Canada, Interim Award (26 June 2000), UNCITRAL,....................109
Portigon AG v Spain, Dissenting Opinion by Giorgio Sacerdoti (2022) ICSID Case No ARB/17/15 (not published yet – on file with the author) 94
Postova Banka a.s. and Istrokapital SE v Greece, Award (9 April 2015), ICSID Case No ARB/13/8 121
PSEG Global et al. v Turkey, Award (19 January 2007), ICSID Case No ARB/02/5....................101
Raiffeisen Bank International AG and Raiffeisenbank Austria d.d. v Croatia, Decision on respondent's jurisdictional objections (30 September 2020), ICSID Case No ARB/17/34....................88
Rockhopper Italia S.p.A., Rockhopper Mediterranean Ltd, and Rockhopper Exploration Plc v Italy, Decision on the intra-EU jurisdictional objection (29 June 2019), ICSID Case No ARB/17/14.......79–80
RREEF Infrastructure (G.P.) Limited and RREEF Pan-European Infrastructure Two Lux S.à r.l. v Spain, Decision on jurisdiction (6 June 2016), ICSID Case No ARB/13/30....................51, 60, 62
Rupert Joseph Binder v Czech Republic, Award on jurisdiction (6 June 2007), UNCITRAL 56
RWE AG and RWE Eemshaven Holding II BV v Kingdom of the Netherlands, ICSID Case No ARB/21/4....................88
RWE Innogy GmbH and RWE Innogy Aersa S.A.U. v Spain, Decision on jurisdiction, liability and certain issues of quantum (30 December 2019), ICSID Case No ARB/14/34 79
Saluka v Czech Republic, Partial Award (17 March 2006), UNCITRAL.......101
Sevilla Beheer B.V. and others v Spain, Decision on jurisdiction, liability and principles of quantum (11 February 2022), ICSID Case No ARB/16/27....................92
SGS Société Générale de Surveillance S.A. v Pakistan, ICSID case No ARB/01/13, Decision on jurisdiction (6 August 2003) 105
SGS Société Générale de Surveillance S.A. v Philippines, Decision of the tribunal on objections to jurisdiction (29 January 2004), ICSID Case No ARB/02/6....................49, 105
SolEs Badajoz GmbH v Spain, Award (31 July 2019), ICSID Case No ARB/15/38....................79
Suez Sociedad General de Aguas de Barcelona S.A.and Vivendi Universal S.A. v Argentina, Award (19 May 2005), ICSID Case No ARB/03/19......... 123
Técnicas Medioambientales Tecmed S.A. v Mexico, Award (29 May 2003), ICSID Case No ARB(AF)/00/2....................101, 111
The PV Investors v Spain, Final award (28 February 2020), PCA Case No 2012-14....................80
Total S.A. v Argentina, Decision on liability (27 December 2010), ICSID Case No ARB/04/01 .... 39, 101, 111

United Utilities (Tallinn) B.V. and Aktsiaselts Tallinna Vesi v Estonia, Award (21 June 2019), ICSID Case No ARB/14/24 78
UP (formerly Le Chèque Déjeuner) and C.D Holding Internationale v Hungary, Award (9 October 2008) ICSID Case No ARB/13/35.................73
Vattenfall AB and others v Germany, Decision on the *Achmea* issue (31 August 2018), ICSID Case No ARB/12/12 ....54, 73–74
Voltaic Network GmbH v Czech Republic, Award (15 May 2019), PCA Case No 2014-20..78
WA Investments Europa Nova Ltd. v Czech Republic, Award (15 May 2019), PCA Case No 2014-19...78
Waste Management Inc. v Mexico, ICSID Case No ARB(AF)/00/3, Award (30 April 2004) 109, 111
Watkins Holdings S.à.r.l. and others v Spain, Award (21 January 2020), ICSID Case No ARB/15/44 .... 50, 78

Table of Legislation

EU Treaties

Charter of Fundamental Rights of the European Union [2012] OJ C326 .... 16, 39, 144–45
Draft Treaty establishing a Constitution for Europe [2003] OJ C169 .... 14, 15
Treaty establishing the European Economic Community, not published 1, 5, 10, 44, 58
Treaty of Amsterdam amending the Treaty on European Union, the Treaties establishing the European Communities and certain related acts [1997] OJ C340 12
Treaty of Lisbon amending the Treaty on European Union and the Treaty establishing the European Community [2007] OJ C306 .... 4, 15, 17, 18, 35, 97
Treaty of Nice amending the Treaty on the European Union, the Treaty establishing the European Community and certain related acts [2001] OJ C80/1 12
Treaty on European Union (Maastricht Treaty) [1992] OJ C191 .... 5, 11, 35
Treaty on the European Union (consolidated) [2016] OJ C 202 .... 27, 32, 42–43, 57, 68, 75, 89, 98, 150
Treaty on the functioning of the European Union (consolidated) [2016] OJ C202 .... 1, 15–19, 26–31, 38, 40–43, 46–47, 52, 57–58, 60, 62, 65–66, 68–69, 75, 88–90, 93, 138, 140

EU external agreements

Agreement between the European Union and Japan for an Economic Partnership [2018] OJ L330 34
Agreement on the European Economic Area [1994] OJ L1 45
Comprehensive Economic and Trade Agreement (CETA) between Canada, of the one part, and the European Union and its Member States, of the other part [2017] OJ L11 .... 25–26, 31–33, 54, 92, 100, 102–04, 106, 113–15, 117–22, 127–34, 137–45, 152–53

Economic Partnership Agreement between the CARIFORUM States, of the one part, and the European Community and its Member States, of the other part [2008] OJ L289 ....99, 117
Energy Charter Treaty [1998] OJ L69/26.... 4, 6, 14, 36, 39–40, 49, 53–54, 60–62, 70–81, 85, 87–89, 91–96, 146–47, 151
Europe Agreement establishing an association between the EC, EC Member States, and Hungary [1993] OJ L47 13
Europe Agreement establishing an association between the EC, EC Member States, and Poland [1993] OJ L348 13
Europe Agreement establishing an association between the EC, the EC Member States, and Romania [1994] OJ L357 13
Europe Agreement establishing an association between the EC, the EC Member States, and the Slovak Republic [1994] OJ L359. 13
Framework Agreement on Comprehensive Partnership and Cooperation between the European Union and its Member States, of the one part, and the Socialist Republic of Vietnam, of the other part [2016] OJ L329 117
Free trade Agreement between the European Union and its Member States, of the one part, and the Republic of Korea, of the other part [2011] OJ L127 ....98–99, 117, 120, 122
Free trade Agreement between the European Union and the Republic of Singapore [2019] OJ L294.... 24, 26, 28, 31, 34, 117–18, 127–28
Free Trade Agreement between the European Union and the Socialist Republic of Vietnam [2020] OJ L186 ....25, 34, 117–18, 129
Investment protection agreement between the European Union and the Republic of Singapore, not published......34, 102–04, 106–07, 113–14, 117–22, 130–34, 152
Investment protection agreement between the European Union and the Socialist Republic of Vietnam, not published.... 34, 102–04, 106, 113–15, 117–21, 130–34, 152
Multilateral Agreement between the European Community and its Member States, the Republic of Albania, Bosnia and Herzegovina, the Republic of Bulgaria, the Republic of Croatia, the former Yugoslav Republic of Macedonia, the Republic of Iceland, the Republic of Montenegro, the Kingdom of Norway, Romania, the Republic of Serbia and the United Nations Interim Administration Mission in Kosovo on the establishment of a European Common Aviation Area [2006] OJ L285......45
Stabilisation and Association Agreement between the EC, EC Member States and Croatia [2005] OJ L26....13
Strategic Partnership Agreement between the European Union and its Member States, of the one part, and Canada, of the other part [2016] OJ L329....117

Trade Agreement between the European Union and its Member States, of the one part, and Colombia and Peru, of the other part [2012] OJ L354 120

EU secondary legislation

Decisions

Council Decision (EU) 2017/38 on the provisional application of the Comprehensive Economic and Trade Agreement (CETA) [2017] OJ L11 32–33

Directives

Council Directive 88/361/EEC of 24 June 1988 for the implementation of Article 67 of the Treaty [1988] OJ L178 11
Directive 2003/87/EC of the European Parliament and of the Council of 13 October 2003 establishing a scheme for greenhouse gas emission allowance trading within the Community and amending Council Directive 96/61/EC [2003] OJ L275 41
Directive 2009/28/EC of the European Parliament and of the Council of 23 April 2009 on the promotion of the use of energy from renewable sources and amending and subsequently repealing Directives 2001/77/EC and 2003/30/EC [2009] OJ L140 39

Regulations

Council Regulation (EU) 2015/1589 of 13 July 2015 laying down detailed rules for the application of Article 108 of the Treaty on the Functioning of the European Union [2015] OJ L248 40
Regulation (EU) 2018/842 of the European Parliament and of the Council of 30 May 2018 on binding annual greenhouse gas emission reductions by Member States from 2021 to 2030 contributing to climate action to meet commitments under the Paris Agreement and amending Regulation (EU) No 525/2013 [2018] OJ L156 42
Regulation (EU) 2021/1119 of the European Parliament and of the Council of 30 June 2021 establishing the framework for achieving climate neutrality and amending Regulations (EC) No 401/2009 and (EU) 2018/1999 [2021] OJ L243 42
Regulation (EU) No 1219/2012 of the European Parliament and of the Council of 12 December 2012 establishing transitional arrangements for bilateral investment agreements between Member States and third countries [2012] OJ L351 20–21

Regulation (EU) No 182/2011 of the European Parliament and of the Council of 16 February 2011 laying down the rules and general principles concerning mechanisms for control by Member States of the Commission's exercise of implementing powers [2011] OJ L55 23
Regulation (EU) No 912/2014 of the European Parliament and of the Council of 23 July 2014 establishing a framework for managing financial responsibility linked to investor-to-state dispute settlement tribunals established by international agreements to which the European Union is party [2014] OJ L257 22–24

EU interistitutional agreements

Framework Agreement on relations between the European Parliament and the European Commission [2010] OJ L304 18

National legislation

Italy

Decree-Law (*Decreto Legge*) no. 91 of 24 June 2014 39
Law (*Legge*) No 116 of 11 August 2014 39

France

French Constitution 138

Belgium

Belgian Constitution 139

Other international agreements

Angola-Brazil BIT 122
2004 United States Model BIT 100, 125
2012 United States Model BIT 101, 112, 125
Argentina-Netherlands BIT 108
ASEAN Comprehensive Investment Agreement 112
ASEAN-Hong Kong China SAR Investment Agreement 101
ASEAN-India Investment Agreement 112
Australia-China FTA 124
Australia-Japan EPA 112, 126
Australia-Malaysia FTA 122
Australia-Mexico BIT 125
Australia-Poland BIT 104
Australia-Singapore FTA 113
Austria Model BIT 108
Austria-Algeria BIT 104

Austria-Croatia BIT 49, 100
Austria-Slovak Republic BIT 56–57
Bangladesh-Italy BIT 100
Belgium-Luxembourg Economic Union -Colombia BIT 112
Belgium-Luxembourg Economic Union -Croatia BIT 49
Belgium-Luxembourg Economic Union -Hungary BIT 82, 108
Belgium-Luxembourg Economic Union -Latvia BIT 42
Belgium-Luxembourg Economic Union -Madagascar BIT 125
Belgium-Luxembourg Economic Union -Peru BIT 125
Belgium-Luxembourg Economic Union –Poland 75
Belgium-Luxembourg Economic Union -Romania BIT 42
Belgium-Luxembourg Economic Union-Poland BIT 75
Belize-UK BIT 104
Benin-Canada BIT 112, 125
Brazil-Chile BIT 122
Brazil-Malawi BIT 112
Brazil-Mozambique BIT 122
Bulgaria-France BIT 82
Burundi-Germany BIT 104
Canada Model FIPA 113
Canada-Armenia BIT 113
Canada-Cameroon BIT 124
Canada-Côte d'Ivoire BIT 125
Canada-Czech Republic BIT 116, 124
Canada-Guinea BIT 37, 115
Canada-Korea IIA 101
Canada-Moldova BIT 115
Canada-Nigeria BIT 125
Canada-Senegal BIT 125
Canada-United States-Mexico Agreement 101–02
Colombia-Korea FTA 112
Colombia-Peru BIT 124–25
Colombia-Spain BIT 108
Colombia-United Kingdom BIT 112
Comprehensive and Progressive Agreement for Trans-Pacific
    Partnership 101–02, 109, 116, 126
Congo-Switzerland BIT 122
Convention on the Recognition and Enforcement of Foreign
    Arbitral Awards 58
Cyprus-Greece BIT 72
Czech Republic-Ireland BIT 108
Czech Republic-Netherlands BIT 36, 55
Denmark-Indonesia BIT 122
Denmark-Bolivia BIT 108

Dominican Republic–Central America Free Trade Agreement 116
Egypt-France BIT 100
Estonia-Netherlands BIT 78
Finland-Morocco BIT 108
Finland-Romania BIT 100
France Model BIT 108–09
France-Hungary BIT 82, 85
France-Kuwait BIT 100
France-Latvia BIT 42
France-Romania BIT 85
France-Russia BIT 100
France-Slovak Republic 37
France-Slovenia 37
France-Uganda BIT 100
Germany Model BIT 104, 109
Germany-Indonesia BIT 122
Germany-Iran BIT 122
Germany-Pakistan BIT 9
Germany-Poland BIT 37, 42
Germany-Romania BIT 37
Hungary-Spain BIT 108
India Model BIT 101, 112
India-Mexico BIT 125
International Centre for Settlement of Investment Disputes Convention, Regulations and Rules 58, 70, 72–74, 87, 90–91, 97, 124–26, 131–32
Iran-Slovak Republic BIT 105
Israel-Japan BIT 105, 109
Italy Model BIT 108–09
Italy-Jordan BIT 104
Italy-Russia BIT 108
Laos-Netherlands BIT 116
Lithuania-Netherlands BIT 108
Lithuania-Poland BIT 82
Mexico-Slovak Republic BIT 124
Mexico-United Kingdom 124
Netherlands-Oman BIT 108
Netherlands-Romania BIT 48
Netherlands-Slovak Republic BIT 55, 62–64, 66, 68–71, 76, 82
Netherlands-Slovenia BIT 82
New Zealand-Taiwan Province of China Economic Cooperation Agreement 116, 124
North American Free Trade Agreement 100, 103, 109, 113, 115, 123

OECD, Third Revised Decision of the Council concerning National Treatment, OECD/LEGAL/0263 12
Pacific Agreement on Closer Economic Relations Plus........ 101, 109, 116
Panama-United Kingdom BIT 108
Poland-UAE BIT 108
Regional Comprehensive Economic Partnership........ 101
Romania-Spain BIT 82
Romania-Sweden BIT 40, 90
Rwanda-United States BIT 115, 124–25
South Korea-Vietnam FTA 125
United Nations Convention on Transparency in Treaty-based Investor-State arbitration ('Mauritius Convention on transparency') 124
Vienna Convention on the Law of Treaties........ 47–50, 95, 155

Other documents

Decision 1/2021 of the CETA Joint Committee [2021] OJ L59........ 132–33
Joint Interpretative Instrument on the Comprehensive Economic and Trade Agreement (CETA) between Canada and the European Union and its Member States [2017] OJ L11 .... 103, 117, 143
Multi-party interim appeal arbitration arrangement pursuant to Article 25 DSU, 27 March 2020, 7112/20 WTO 61 150
NAFTA Free Trade Commission, Notes of Interpretation of Certain Chapter Eleven Provisions, 31 July 2001........ 100
Working procedures for appellate review, WT/AB/WP/6........ 131

1

Introduction

THE ROLE OF the European Union in the international legal order and the relationship between international law and EU law have long been objects of debate. Much of the controversy stems from the protean nature of the EU.[1] The EU is, before anything else, an economic union.[2] It ultimately rests upon an international treaty, which has been remodelled through subsequent treaty amendments.[3]

However, the EU has traditionally been portrayed as a *sui generis* legal entity. In the famous words of the Court of Justice, the Community (currently EU) constituted from its very beginning a 'new legal order of international law'.[4] Indeed, the Union differs from 'classic' international law in several respects. First, the principles of primacy and direct effect, though not entirely alien to the international legal order,[5] have acquired unprecedented prominence in the context of the EU legal order.[6]

Second, EU institutions have acquired over time extensive powers on a wide range of matters – the list of exclusive and shared competences is currently much longer than that contained in the original Treaty of Rome.[7]

[1] J Odermatt, *International law and the European Union* (Cambridge University Press, 2021) 10–21.

[2] Even in its foundational phase, the European construct was described as 'the highest form of international integration', even though at that time only constituted a 'customs union plus'. G Schwarzenberger, *The Frontiers of International Law* (Stevens & Sons, 1962), 280; N Perdikis, 'Trade Agreements: Depth of Integration' in JD Gaisford and WA Kerr (eds), *Handbook on International Trade Policy* (Edward Elgar, 2007) 108.

[3] The Treaty establishing the European Economic Community.

[4] *NV Algemene Transport en Expeditie Onderneming van Gend & Loos v Netherlands Inland Revenue Administration*, Case 26/62, EU:C:1963:1.

[5] See the two seminal European Court of Justice's judgments where these principles were affirmed for the first time: Case 26/62, (above n 4); *Flaminio Costa* v *ENEL*, Case 6/64, EU:C:1964:66.

[6] O Spiermann, 'The Other Side of the Story: An Unpopular Essay on the Making of the European Community Legal Order' (1999) 10 *European Journal of International Law* 766, 787; Odermatt (n 1) 11. These principles have placed individuals at the heart of the EU legal machinery, whereas, in the international legal order, they generally do not possess direct power of action. International investment law and human rights law are the most notable exceptions to this rule. See K Parlett, *The Individual in the International Legal System* (Cambridge University Press, 2011) 10–26.

[7] ibid.

Third, the EU, though devoid of its own army,[8] is an important player in international affairs and exercises external powers across a variety of matters.[9]

In sum, the EU, though built upon international law foundations, possesses several municipal legal order features.[10] The similarities with domestic constitutional legal orders have been emphasised so much that the EU has often been likened to a federal state in the making[11] or a 'case of federalism without federation'.[12] Now, the issue of whether the EU legal order constitutes an 'ordinary' legal order of international law or a *sui generis* legal order is not only theoretical. Quite the contrary, the way in which one conceptualises the EU and EU law affects its interaction with international law.

I. THE FOCUS AND THE RATIONALE FOR THIS STUDY

This study focuses on a specific area of the broader debate on the EU and international law. It explores the interaction between the Union and the treaty-based international investment regime and examines the EU's attitude towards international investment law. The guiding questions include: does the EU regard international law as a threat, as an instrument to extend its influence or both? To what extent do EU constitutional constraints affect the Union's action in the field of foreign investment? How did other players respond to the emergence of a more proactive role of the Union in the foreign investment domain?

The encounter between these two systems is particularly interesting and topical, for both the international investment regime and the EU, after enjoying widespread support for quite some time, have recently faced a heavy backlash.[13] The discontent towards the two systems brought about disruptive events, such as Brexit[14] and the decision of several states to abandon or curtail the

[8] It is worth recalling that the Treaty of Paris of 1952 establishing the European Defence Community never entered into force. However, after the US withdrawal from Afghanistan and the outbreak of the Russian-Ukrainian conflict, the debate on the creation of a European army regained steam.

[9] R Schütze, *Foreign Affairs and the EU Constitution – Selected Essays* (Cambridge University Press, 2014) 49–50.

[10] J Crawford and M Koskenniemi, 'Introduction' in J Crawford and M Koskenniemi (eds), *The Cambridge Companion to International Law* (Cambridge University Press, 2012) 12; Odermatt (n 1) 29.

[11] AM Sbragia, 'The European Community: A Balancing Act' (1993) 23 *Journal of Federalism* 23, 24.

[12] Federalism in this context has been understood not only as 'a political strategy designed to achieve a federal goal', but they also as the 'process of building Europe'. M Burgess, *Federalism and the European Union: The Building of Europe 1950–2000* (Routledge, 2002) 29.

[13] See generally B Bugarič, 'The Populist Backlash Against Europe' in F Bignami (ed), *EU Law in Populist Times* (Cambridge University Press, 2019); CE De Vries, *Euroscepticism and the Future of European Integration* (Oxford University Press, 2018); C Balchin, K Chung, A Kaushal and M Waibel (eds), *The Backlash Against Investment Arbitration: Perceptions and Reality* (Kluwer Law Internationl, 2010).

[14] On 31 January 2020, the UK officially withdrew from the EU.

ISDS system.[15] But it has also opened up the prospect for change. On the one hand, the calls for reforming the ISDS system have culminated in the ongoing UNCITRAL Working Group III discussion on the reform of international investment law. On the other hand, the EU institutions launched in 2021 the 'Conference on the Future of Europe',[16] which ended in May 2022 with the adoption of a report outlining the priorities for the reform of the EU.[17]

II. SETTING THE SCENE: THE EUROPEAN UNION, EU MEMBER STATES AND INTERNATIONAL INVESTMENT LAW

Although (Western) European states were the engine of the European integration process and, at the same time, substantively contributed to the creation of the international investment regime,[18] the relationship between these two systems initially raised little interest. During its first three decades of existence, the European integration process focused more on other aspects of international economic integration, most notably trade in goods. Hence, the EU legal order and international investment law ran for a long time on distinct tracks with little or no possibility of crossing each other.

However, as the European construct morphed into a more complex entity, this situation was bound to change. The developments ushering in a new phase in the relationship between the EU legal order and the international investment regime gradually emerged over a period of almost two decades. The trigger point was the full liberalisation of capital movements within the EU internal market at the beginning of the nineties. This bridged the gap between the free circulation of capital and the other (much more developed) EU fundamental freedoms.[19] Besides its relevance for the completion of the internal market, this development had a highly symbolic value in that it signalled the interest of the Union toward the promotion and protection of capital flows. It also foreshadowed what came next, namely the gradual emergence of the Union's role in the field of foreign investment. Indeed, just as the establishment of a customs union at the internal level required the Community to deal with the external reflections thereof,[20] the internal liberalisation of capital flows preluded the development

[15] See M Langford, D Behn and OK Fauchauld, 'Backlash and State Strategies in International Investment Law' in T Aalberts and T Gammeltoft-Hansen (eds), *The Changing Practices of International Law* (Cambridge University Press, 2018) 78–84.

[16] Joint Declaration of the European Parliament, the Council and the European Commission on the Conference on the future of Europe – Engaging with citizens for democracy – Building a more resilient Europe, [2020] OJ C91 I.

[17] Conference on the future of Europe – Report on the final outcome, 2022.

[18] Tellingly, the first of these agreements came into existence upon the initiative of a European state: the Federal Republic of Germany.

[19] J Snell, 'Free Movement of Capital: Evolution as a Non-Linear Process' in P Craig and G De Burca (eds), *The Evolution of EU Law* (Oxford University Press, 2021) 579–585.

[20] P Strik, *Shaping the Single European Market in the Field of Foreign Direct Investment* (Hart Publishing, 2014) 68.

of an external competence of the Union in the foreign investment domain. In exercising this external competence, as we shall see in chapter two, the Union has initially relied on an implicit legal basis. Only after the Lisbon Treaty went into force, it gained explicit powers in the field of foreign investment.

Another crucial event was the broadening of EU membership, which added a further layer of possible interaction between EU and international investment law. Between 2004 and 2007, several Central and Eastern European states joined the Union. In 2013, Croatia also became an EU Member. These new Member States brought with them a long history of investment relations with the Union and with its existing Member States. Their accession, however, was not accompanied by specific arrangements addressing the relationship between EU law and the investment treaties concluded with EU Member States before the EU enlargement. As a result, 'old' and 'new' EU Member States found themselves simultaneously bound by EU law, intra-EU BITs and the ECT (hereafter also cumulatively referred to as intra-EU IIAs).

Due to the combination of these factors, IIAs have become an object of contention and an instrument to exercise the Union's foreign power. The interaction between the EU and the international investment regime takes place at the internal level, namely within the internal market, and at the external level, ie, in the context of the relations with non-EU states. Thus, the EU's action in this field has both an internal and an external dimension.[21]

However, when designing and implementing its action at either level, the Union does not act in isolation. Its choices may impinge on the expectations, the spheres of competence, and the interests of a wide range of actors, such as EU Member States, the investment arbitral community, and non-EU Member States.

There is a sizeable body of literature covering the interplay between the EU and the international investment regime. However, legal scholarship has thus far examined the two dimensions of this relationship separately. This book provides a contribution to the existing literature by combining the analysis of both dimensions. The joint treatment of these issues would in turn shed some light on how the two dimensions relate to and affect each other.

When analysing the internal dimension, this book contrasts the way in which arbitral tribunals and EU institutions construed the relationship between intra-EU IIAs and EU law. In particular, it illustrates that the CJEU and the European Commission have traditionally regarded intra-EU IIAs as incompatible with EU law, while arbitral tribunals have generally denied the existence of a conflict between these two sets of rules.

[21] In this regard, it has been noted that '[i]n its internal aspect, that is viewing relations between the member states themselves, the Community is an organism for collective exercise of sovereignty in matters over which competence is transferred to the Community by treaty. In its external aspect, the Community functions as an international organisation, entering into treaties in matters within its competences'. R Gardiner, *Treaty Interpretation* (Oxford University Press, 2015) 129; see also Odermatt (n 1) 29.

When looking into the external dimension, this study investigates how the Union has eagerly deployed IIAs to develop its post-Lisbon EU international investment policy. In particular, it shows that the Union, though a newcomer in investment treaty-making, has sought to put forward and spread its specific reform strategy.

The joint analysis of these two dimensions reveals a certain ambivalence by the EU towards international investment law. This book argues that behind this ambivalence lies a rather coherent plan. That is to say, the Union seeks to impose both internally and externally its own model of regulation of foreign investments. Internally, this endeavour consists in subjecting cross-border investment exclusively to EU law, thereby getting rid of intra-EU IIAs. In contrast, externally, the Union aspires to replace the existing IIAs between Member States and non-EU Member States with EU IIAs and investment chapters included in comprehensive economic agreements. This book claims that EU institutions took this stance with a view to reasserting the Union's internal powers, enhancing its external influence and, ultimately, pursuing its long-term 'federal aspirations'.

This approach, however, did not play out as expected because of several legal and political obstacles. This book thus argues that such obstacles are partly linked to the structure and the functioning of international investment law and EU law. Moreover, these obstacles are also a consequence of the tarnished reputation of IIAs and, to a lesser extent, of the ailing popular support for the EU.

III. BOOK STRUCTURE

A full account of the interaction between the EU and the international investment regime requires diving into both systems. Accordingly, this book is structured as follows.

Chapter two recounts the steps leading to the emergence of the Union's role in the field of foreign investment and its implications. It starts by outlining the pre-Maastricht Treaty setting, when Member States played a crucial role in the international investment regime, while the then EEC stayed on the sidelines. It then shows how the liberalisation of capital flows within the internal market led the EEC to adopt a new approach in this field. In this new context, the EU, directly or through its Member States, deployed international investment arrangements as an instrument of foreign policy, particularly in the context of East-West relations. The account then illustrates that the long-awaited establishment of an express competence of the Union over foreign direct investment raised more questions than it answered. Finally, this chapter delves into how the CJEU addressed such questions in Opinion 2/15 and discusses the implications of such decision.[22]

[22] Opinion 2/15, EU:C:2017:376.

Chapter three is devoted to the 'internal' dimension of the relationship between the EU and international investment law. It specifically examines the questions raised by intra-EU IIAs. As a preliminary point, it shows that the interplay between EU law and intra-EU IIAs may be addressed from both EU law and international law perspectives. It shows that, from the outset, the European Commission has regarded intra-EU IIAs and the intra-EU application of the Energy Charter Treaty (ECT) as a threat to the functioning of the internal market and the very foundations of the EU legal order. This 'EU law-centred' approach, based on a broad reading of the principle of autonomy of the EU legal order,[23] is then contrasted with the 'international law-centred' approach taken by investment tribunals. An approach that has generally led arbitral tribunals to deny that intra-EU IIAs are inconsistent with EU law. This chapter then discusses how the CJEU and EU Member States intervened in this debate. It shows that the court has consistently embraced the 'EU law-centred' approach, while EU Member States, at least initially, have been somewhat reluctant to do so. Finally, it discusses the shortcomings of the 'EU law-centred approach' and its possible implications on the role of the EU in investment treaty-making.

Chapter four navigates the external dimension of the relationship between the EU and international investment law.

The first part of the chapter analyses the Union's initial approach to investment treaty-making by dissecting the content of the early versions of EU IIAs and investment chapters included in EU comprehensive economic agreements. More specifically, it examines the main investment protection rules, the exception mechanisms and the investor-state dispute settlement system against the general investment treaty practice background. In light of this analysis, this chapter shows that an 'incremental' reformist approach initially informed the investment chapters of the EU trade and investment agreements.[24] The analysis then illustrates how its constitutional constraints and its complex political structure led the Union to modify its approach to investment treaty-making. In particular, drawing on the existing literature,[25] it argues that the EU embraced a systemic reform strategy by proposing the establishment of the ICS and the MIC. Last, it discusses the persistent opposition to EU IIAs and investment chapters even after the shift to the systemic reform approach, focusing on how

[23] Further attention will be devoted to this principle in the following chapters. For the moment it is sufficient to say that it is an unwritten principle of EU law, whose primary function is to preserve the fundamental characteristics of the EU legal order, most notably the direct effect and the primacy of EU law. See P Koutrakos, 'The Autonomy of EU Law and International Investment Arbitration' (2020) 88 *Nordic Journal of International Law* 41, 44; C Contartese, 'The Autonomy of the EU Legal Order in the ECJ's External Relations Case Law: From the "Essential" to the "Specific Characteristics" of the Union and Back Again' (2017) 54 *Common Market Law Review* 1627, 1631–1632.

[24] A Roberts, 'Incremental, Systemic, and Paradigmatic Reform of Investor-State Arbitration' (2018) 112 *American Journal of International Law* 410, 410–411.

[25] ibid.

this enduring discontent has often been translated into questions of compatibility with the legal order of EU Member States and with the EU legal order.

Chapter five seeks to piece the puzzle together. This chapter explains the EU's ambivalence toward international investment law. It argues that this approach allows the Union to affirm its own regulation model of cross-border investment and curtail the role of EU Member States as investment rules setters. In doing so, the Union seeks to strengthen the internal market, amplify its external influence and, ultimately, pursue its federal aspirations. Finally, it seeks to identify the obstacles that have so far hindered the full implementation of the Union's plan at both the internal and the external levels.

2

The Role of EU Member States and the EU in the Field of Foreign Investment

I. THE ROLE OF EUROPEAN STATES IN THE CREATION OF THE INTERNATIONAL INVESTMENT REGIME

CURRENTLY, THE INTERNATIONAL investment regime appears as a thick constellation of international agreements,[1] including more than 2,300 BITs and around 320 treaties containing investment provisions.[2]

The system has been traditionally based on bilateral treaties[3] due to the failure of the various projects aiming to establish a multilateral investment system.[4]

The success of these treaties is ascribable to their content, which is deemed to provide more extensive and 'efficient' protection of foreign investment than international customary rules on foreign property.[5] More specifically, BITs combine three main features. First, they have an extensive scope of material application,[6] which normally covers both foreign direct investments, namely investments that create a lasting interest in an enterprise resident in another economy,[7] and portfolio investments (also known as 'indirect investment'),

[1] This phenomenon has been famously defined as the 'treatification' of international investment law. JW Salacuse, 'The Treatification of International Investment Law' (2007) 13 *Law and Business Review of the Americas* 155, 163–166.

[2] See for updated statistics the UNCTAD website, investmentpolicy.unctad.org/international-investment-agreements.

[3] Salacuse (n 1) 156–157.

[4] These attempts include the Havana Charter establishing the International Trade Organisation (ITO), the 1967 OECD Draft Convention on the Protection of Foreign Property, and Multilateral Investment Agreement (MAI). See R Toye, 'The International Trade Organisation' in M Daunton, A Narlikar and RM Stern (eds), *The Oxford Handbook on the World Trade Organisation* (Oxford University Press, 2012) 96–97; G Sacerdoti, 'Havana Charter' in R Wolfrum (ed), *Max Planck Encyclopedia of International Law* (Oxford University Press, 2013); SW Schill, *The Multilateralisation of International Investment Law* (Cambridge University Press, 2009) 35–40; 49–58.

[5] JW Salacuse and NP Sullivan, 'Do BITs Really Work: An Evaluation of Bilateral Investment Treaties and their Grand Bargain' (2005) 46 *Harvard International Law Journal* 67, 68–69; M Sornarajah, *Resistance and Change in International Law on Foreign Investment* (Cambridge University Press, 2015) 307–308.

[6] UNCTAD, 'Bilateral investment treaties 1995–2006: trends in investment rule-making', 2007, 10; M Sornarajah, *The International Law on Foreign Investment* (Cambridge University Press, 2010) 190–197.

[7] IMF, 'Balance of Payments Manual' (2010) 86.

ie, short-term investment in the form of bonds, notes, and other financial instruments.[8] Second, BITs provide for a wide range of investment protection rules. Some of these rules are unknown to customary international law, such as free transfer clauses, whose main objective is to liberalise inward and outward capital transfers. Some others, such as the expropriation and the fair and equitable treatment (FET) clauses, are based on the customary international rule on the minimum standard of treatment.[9] Third, BITs feature a dispute settlement mechanism that grants a direct right of action to individual investors. This mechanism, however, long remained dormant, and it was only with the emergence of the so-called arbitration without privity doctrine that investor-state arbitration – along with the entire system of foreign direct investment protection – made a real leap forward.[10] According to this doctrine, in fact, the investor-state dispute settlement clauses contained in BITs should be construed as expressing the consent of the contracting states to submit investment disputes to arbitration.[11]

European states were the first to perceive the possible advantages arising from such treaties. As is well known, in 1959 the Federal Republic of Germany was the first to enter one of these agreements.[12] The other European states soon followed suit.[13] At the end of the 1990s, Western European states were parties to 49 per cent of all the BITs existing at that time.[14] Twenty years later, seven of the first ten states to have concluded more BITs were Western European.[15] A large share of these agreements was struck with Central and Eastern European countries.[16]

II. FOREIGN INVESTMENT AND THE EUROPEAN INTEGRATION PROCESS: THE FOUNDATIONAL PHASE

At the outset, the European integration process primarily focused on the liberalisation of trade in goods. The Treaty of Rome essentially established a customs union, where foreign direct and indirect investment only played a marginal role. At the internal level, the treaty provision on free circulation of capital merely

[8] ibid 91.

[9] See A Orakhelasvili, 'The Normative Basis of the "Fair and Equitable Treatment": General International Law on Foreign Investment' (2008) 46 *Archiv des Völkerrechts* 74, 76–89; A Reinisch and C Schreuer, *International Protection of Investments: The Substantive Standards* (Cambridge University Press, 2020) 5–11.

[10] Sornarajah (n 5) 139–146.

[11] ibid; C Schreuer, L Malintoppi, A Reinisch and A Sinclair, *The ICSID Convention: a Commentary* (Cambridge University Press, 2009) 191.

[12] Germany-Pakistan BIT.

[13] The US began to negotiate this type of agreement only after shelving for good the ailing Friendship, Navigation and Commerce Treaty programme. See JK Vandevelde, *The First Bilateral Investment Treaties: U.S. Postwar Friendship, Commerce and Navigation Treaties* (Oxford University Press, 2017) 539–542. Friendship, Commerce and Navigation Treaties differed from BITs in that they covered a wider range of matters.

[14] UNCTAD, 'Bilateral investment treaties – 1959–1999' (2000) 16.

[15] ibid 18–19.

[16] ibid 17.

imposed on Member States the obligation to *progressively* remove obstacles to the movement of capital to the *extent* necessary for the functioning of the internal market.[17] Thus, the liberalisation and the protection of cross-border capital flows was only partially ensured by the provisions on the freedom of establishment. It is worth reminding that the freedom of establishment allows EU citizens and entities to start and conduct a stable economic activity in a Member State other than the state of origin. It thus prevents all types of hindrances, including, but not limited to, direct and indirect discrimination, to the establishment of foreign direct investment and the conduct of foreign direct investment operations.[18] The constraints stemming from such provision, however, did not prevent Member States from keeping in place rather pervasive capital control mechanisms for over 30 years.[19]

In the foundational period, foreign investment also played a marginal role in the context of the then EEC common commercial policy, which only encompassed various issues relating to trade in goods regulation and liberalisation.[20] Indeed, the Community's only initiative in the field of foreign investment was the proposal for the establishment of a European investment guarantee agency in the context of the European export policy.[21]

However, in view of the increasing financialisation of Member States' economies and the impending launch of the European Monetary Union, foreign investment gradually acquired greater importance in the context of the European integration process. At the internal level, the Community gradually introduced

[17] Article 67 of the Treaty establishing the EEC reads as follows: 'Member States shall, in the course of the transitional period and to the extent necessary for the proper functioning of the Common Market, progressively abolish as between themselves restrictions on the movement of capital belonging to persons resident in Member States and also any discriminatory treatment based on the nationality or place of residence of the parties or on the place in which such capital is invested. Current payments connected with movements of capital between Member States shall be freed from all restrictions not later than at the end of the first stage.' See S Hindelang, *The Free Movement of Capital and Foreign Direct Investment: The Scope of Protection in EU Law* (Oxford University Press, 2009) 32–34.

[18] P Strik, *Shaping the Single European Market in the Field of Foreign Direct Investment* (Oxford, Hart Publishing, 2014) 26.

[19] The EEC's approach was consistent with the cautious approach to capital flows liberalisation taken in the post-World War II era. See J Ruggie, 'International Regimes, Transactions, and Change: Embedded Liberalism in the Postwar Economic Order' (1982) 36 *International Organisation* 379, 395–396.

[20] Art 113 of the Treaty establishing the European Economic Community reads as follows: '[a]fter the expiry of the transitional period, the common commercial policy shall be based on uniform principles, particularly in regard to tariff amendments, the conclusion of tariff or trade agreements, the alignment of measures of liberalisation, export policy and protective commercial measures including measures to be taken in cases of dumping or subsidies' (English translation). For the sake of completeness, it should be noted that in this period the Community was also empowered to conclude association agreements. See R Schütze, *Foreign Affairs and the EU Constitution – Selected Essays* (Cambridge University Press, 2014) 238.

[21] This proposal was eventually rejected by the Member States. See JR Basedow, *The EU in the Global Investment Regime* (Routledge, 2017) 200.

more stringent rules on capital circulation.[22] The first step in this direction was the Commission's White Paper on completing the internal market, which included the free movement of capital among the Community's key priorities.[23] Subsequently, Directive 88/361/EC imposed on Member States the obligation to repeal restrictions on the free movement of capital within the internal market. Finally, with the entry into force of the Maastricht Treaty, the liberalisation of capital flows was enshrined in EU primary law. Article 73b of the Treaty introduced the obligation to remove all restrictions on the movement of capital and payments not only between Member States but also, unlike the other fundamental freedoms, between Member States and third states.[24] In addition, Article 73c entrusted the Council with the power to 'adopt measures on the movement of capital to or from third countries involving direct investment'.[25]

The liberalisation of capital movements within the EC internal market occurred at a time when momentous changes were brewing in the international trading system. In particular, the ambitious negotiating agenda of the GATT Uruguay Round foretold an overall expansion of the scope of international trade disciplines. Against this background, the Commission proposed a comprehensive reform of the common commercial policy.[26] In its view, the future common commercial policy should cover a wider range of matters, including foreign investment, trade in services, and intellectual property issues.[27] This proposal however did not meet with the favour of Member States.[28] Consequently, the Treaty of Maastricht did not amend the rules defining the scope of the common commercial policy, which remained confined to the various aspects of the regulation and liberalisation of trade in goods.[29]

[22] J Snell, 'Free Movement of Capital: Evolution as a Non-Linear Process' in P Craig and G De Burca (eds), *The Evolution of EU Law* (Oxford University Press, 2011) 551.

[23] European Commission, Completing the internal market: white paper from the Commission to the European Council, COM (85) 310, 32–33.

[24] Art 73b of the Maastricht Treaty stipulated that: '[w]ithin the framework of the provisions set out in this Chapter, all restrictions on the movement of capital between Member States and between Member States and third countries shall be prohibited. Within the framework of the provisions set out in this Chapter, all restrictions on payments between Member States and between Member States and third countries shall be prohibited'.

[25] Relying on the new wording of these treaty provisions, the CJEU put the free circulation of capital on a par with the other fundamental freedoms. See Snell (n 22) 552.

[26] Conference of the representatives of the governments of the Member States, CONF-UP 1788/91, 1991, 16, 28–29: See J Basedow, 'A Legal History of the EU's International Investment Policy' (2016) 17 *Journal of World Investment and Trade* 734, 748; see M Krajewski, 'External Trade Law and the Constitution Treaty: Towards a Federal and More Democratic Common Commercial Policy?' (2005) 42 *Common Market Law Review* 91, 111.

[27] ibid.

[28] ibid 112.

[29] Art 113 of the Treaty establishing the European Community, as amended by the Maastricht Treaty, stipulated that the common trade policy included 'tariff changes, the conclusion of tariff and trade agreements, the standardisation of liberalisation measures, export policy and trade defence measures, including those to be taken in cases of dumping and subsidisation'. W Shan, 'Towards a Common European Community Policy on Investment Issues' (2001) 2 *Journal of World Investment* 603, 607; J Ceyssens, 'Towards a Common Foreign Investment Policy? – Foreign Investment in the European Constitution' (2005) 32 *Legal Issues of Economic Integration* 259, 260.

III. THE EMERGING ROLE OF THE EUROPEAN COMMUNITY IN THE FIELD OF FOREIGN INVESTMENT

The Commission was clearly unsatisfied with this state of things, because the contours of the common commercial policy prevented the then European Community from developing comprehensive foreign trade and investment policies. Thus, it doggedly sought to assert a broader reading of the EC common commercial policy. In the proceedings for Opinion 1/94,[30] the Commission, relying on a teleological argument, contended that Article 113 of the EC Treaty explicitly gave the Community the power to conclude the GATS.[31] The Court, however, partially rejected this view. More specifically, it held that the Union possessed external exclusive competence only with respect to the GATS rules governing the mode of service provision that closely resembled trade in goods, namely cross-border provision of services.[32]

In the context of the proceedings for Opinion 2/92,[33] the Commission argued that Article 113 of the EC Treaty[34] conferred on the Community the competence to conclude the Third Revised OECD Decision on the obligation of national treatment,[35] an instrument dealing with the operations of foreign-controlled enterprises and affecting FDI activities.[36] But also in this case the Court did not uphold the Commission's view.[37] However, it found that the Community possessed external competence only over some of the matters covered by the Decision.[38]

In summary, the Court's case law clearly indicated that an enlargement of the EC Common commercial policy could not be achieved through interpretative means, but it required an amendment of Article 113 of the EC Treaty. The Treaty of Amsterdam first amended such a provision by establishing a procedure under which the Community could be empowered to negotiate and conclude 'agreements on services and intellectual property'.[39] Subsequently, the Treaty of Nice further eased the conditions under which the Community could exercise its external competence in these fields.[40]

[30] Opinion 1/94, EU:C:1994:384.

[31] ibid, para 36.

[32] ibid, paras 44–47. See P Pescatore, 'Opinion 1/94 on "Conclusion" of the WTO Agreement: is There an Escape from a Programmed Disaster' (1999) 36 *Common Market Law Review* 387, 396–399.

[33] Opinion 2/92, EU:C:1995:83.

[34] ibid, para 28.

[35] OECD, Third Revised Decision of the Council concerning national treatment, OECD/EGAL/0263.

[36] Opinion 2/92 (n 33).

[37] ibid.

[38] ibid.

[39] Art 109s, Treaty of Amsterdam.

[40] Art 133, Treaty of Nice.

These amendments, however, failed to introduce foreign investment among the matters falling within the scope of the CCP,[41] despite the Commission's insistence to this effect. Hence, the Community could only boast an implicit, limited and shared competence in such a field[42] stemming from other Treaty provisions, particularly those on free circulation of capital that, as noted above, also apply to the relations between Member States and third states.[43] Relying on this limited competence, the Community inserted investment liberalisation obligations in a wide range of international instruments, such as cooperation agreements, partnership agreements, and free trade agreements.[44] Moreover, although the Community lacked the power to negotiate and conclude treaties containing post-establishment commitments,[45] it nonetheless played a rather proactive role in this field.[46]

First, the Community sought to encourage EC Member States to conclude BITs with Eastern and Central European states by including specific provisions to this effect in the association agreements with such states,[47] and it did so with some success. Between 1990 and 1999, the number of treaties concluded between EC Member States and the former Soviet bloc's countries grew steadily.[48]

Second, and more importantly, it was the driving force behind the negotiation of the Energy European Charter and the Energy Charter Treaty.[49] The Charter's negotiations, involving several European states and the soon-to-be-extinct

[41] JA Bischoff, 'Just a Little Bit of Mixity? The EU's Role in the Field of Foreign Investment Protection Law' (2011) 48 *Common Market Law Review* 1527, 1536; D Leczykiewicz, 'Common Commercial Policy: The Expanding Competence of the European Union in the Area of International Trade' (2005) 6 *German Law Journal* 1673, 1673–1678.

[42] In the Commission's view, this setting was far from ideal, for the Community could not effectively exercise its residual competence in the field of investment liberalisation 'while the Member States continue to conclude bilateral treaties on investments'. European Commission, Report on the operation of the Treaty of the European Union, SEC (95) 731 final, 58.

[43] Shan (n 29) 609. Strik (n 18) 75.

[44] Shan (n 29) 616–617.

[45] Bischoff (n 41) 1536; Ceyssens (n 29) 268; Shan (n 29) 615–616.

[46] J Touscoz, 'The Role of the European Union in the Framework of the Energy Charter Treaty' (1997) 2 *European Foreign Affairs Review* 23, 29. See European Council, Presidency Conclusions, Bulletin EU 12-1994; European Parliament, Resolution on investments in countries of Central and Eastern Europe and the guarantees for those investments, A3-0162/92.

[47] See Opinion of Advocate General Wathelet in C-284/16, EU:C:2018:158, para 40. See, eg, Art 72 Europe Agreement establishing an association between the EC, EC Member States, and Hungary; Art 73 Europe Agreement establishing an association between the EC, EC Member States, and Poland, [1993] OJ L348; Art 74, Europe Agreement establishing an association between the EC, the EC Member States, and Romania; Art 74 Europe Agreement establishing an association between the EC, the EC Member States, and the Slovak Republic; Art 85 Stabilisation and Association Agreement between the EC, EC Member States and Croatia.

[48] UNCTAD (n 14) 7–17. As a result of the three enlargements, there were about 200 intra-EU BITs. See T Fečak, *International Investment Agreements and EU Law* (Kluwer Law International, 2016) 371–372. For an in-depth analysis of the effects of FDI on the economy of such states see N Bandelj, *From Communists to Foreign Capitalists: The Social Foundations of Foreign Direct Investment in Postsocialist Europe* (Princeton University Press, 2011) 16–28.

[49] J Kleisterkhamp, 'Investment Protection and EU Law: The Intra-EU and Extra-EU Dimension of the Energy Charter Treaty' (2012) 15 *Journal of International Economic Law* 85, 86. The negotiation process started with the European Council's Conclusions of June 1990 mandating the

Soviet Union, started in Brussels in July 1991. Adopted in The Hague a few months later, the Charter was a non-binding political document, which set out the guiding principles for future energy cooperation between the members and foreshadowed the negotiation of an international treaty embedding such principles.[50] After its adoption, negotiations continued until December 1994, when 49 states and the European Community signed the ECT in Lisbon. The treaty is a complex instrument encompassing both trade and investment issues. The provisions on international trade in energy products and electricity transit are complementary to the multilateral international trade system.[51] The rules on promotion and protection of international investment,[52] on the other hand, are akin to those contained in BITs.[53]

IV. TOWARDS THE ALLOCATION AT THE EUROPEAN UNION LEVEL OF THE COMPETENCE OVER FOREIGN DIRECT INVESTMENT

In the overall climate of optimism surrounding the European integration process,[54] particularly between the 1990s and the early 2000s, this setting was destined to be short-lived. Proposals for the reform of the common commercial policy surfaced once again during the negotiation of the Constitutional Treaty. The Praesidium included foreign direct investment in the EU common commercial policy 'in recognition of the fact that financial flows supplement trade in goods and today represent a significant share of commercial exchanges'.[55] This innovation reflected the Commission's view that the establishment of a comprehensive external competence over foreign investment constituted the necessary completion of the internal competence on free movement of capital.[56]

Commission to examine the Dutch Government's proposal to create a European energy network. In February 1991, the Commission, building on the Dutch proposal, advanced the idea of a European Energy Charter. See Conclusions of the European Council, 25 and 26 June 1990, 13.

[50] Touscoz (n 46) 24.

[51] See Y Selivanova, 'The Energy Charter and the International Energy Governance' in Y Selivanova (ed), *Regulation of Energy in International Trade Law: WTO, NAFTA, and Energy Charter* (Kluwer Law International, 2011) 377–378.

[52] See K Hobér, 'Investment Arbitration and the Energy Charter Treaty' (2010) 1 *Journal of International Dispute Settlement* 153, 154–164; T Wälde, 'Investment Arbitration under the Energy Charter Treaty – From Dispute Settlement to Treaty Implementation' (1996) 12 *Arbitration International* 429, 439–464.

[53] T Wälde, 'International Investment under the 1994 Energy Charter Treaty – Legal, Negotiating and Policy Implications for International Investors within Western and Commonwealth of Independent States/Eastern European Countries' (1995) 29 *Journal of World Trade* 5 9; JW Salacuse, 'The Energy Charter Treaty and the Bilateral Investment Treaty Regimes' in T Wälde (ed), *The Energy Charter Treaty: an East-West Gateway for Investment and Trade* (Kluwer Law International 1996) 328–329.

[54] See G Majone, *Rethinking the Union of Europe Post-Crisis: Has Integration Gone Too Far?* (Cambridge University Press, 2014) 60–63.

[55] Draft Articles on external action in the Constitutional Treaty, European Convention, CONV 685/03, 52. Strik (n 18) 78.

[56] Ceyssens (n 29) 270.

Moreover, such a competence would have endowed the Community with greater 'bargaining power' in pursuing the agenda of liberalisation of cross-border capital flows and creating a multilateral system for investment protection.[57] Last, it would have restored symmetry between the internal and external competences of the Union in the field of cross-border investment and ensured, at least in principle, greater degree of consistency in the conduct of foreign investment policy.[58]

The Praesidium's proposal, although vehemently criticised, eventually appeared in Article III-315 (1) of the draft Constitutional Treaty.[59] The Constitutional Treaty, however, never entered into force.

This traumatic event put on hold the prospect of reshaping the boundaries of Common commercial policy, but it did not mark the end of the Community's action in the field of foreign investment. In 2006, the Council adopted the Minimum Platform on Investment[60] for the negotiation with third countries of free trade agreements containing rules for the liberalisation of capital flows.[61]

More importantly, after a period of reflection, Member States, upon the initiative of the German Presidency of the Council, launched an intergovernmental conference to amend the EC Treaty. The work of the Conference culminated in the conclusion of the Lisbon Treaty, which, though it abandoned the constitutional rhetoric of its predecessor, preserved many of the innovations contained therein.[62] One of the elements of continuity between these two treaties is the establishment of a Union's competence in the field of foreign investment. Indeed, Article 207 TFEU replicates the wording of Article III-315 of the Constitutional Treaty and thus includes foreign direct investment in the scope of the EU CCP.[63] The Union thus eventually acquired an express exclusive competence over foreign direct investment.

[57] This objective was never completely abandoned despite the striking failure of the Multilateral Agreement on Investment and of the other multilateral initiatives. See Ceyssens (n 29) 269–270. Multilateral Agreement on Investment – Draft Consolidated Text, DAFFE/MAI(98)7/REV1.

[58] A Dimopoulos, 'The Common Commercial Policy after Lisbon: Establishing Parallelism Between Internal and External Economic Relations?' (2008) 4 *Croatian Yearbook of European Law and Policy* 101, 118.

[59] This provision reads as follows: '[t]he common commercial policy shall be based on uniform principles, particularly with regard to changes in tariff rates, the conclusion of tariff and trade agreements relating to trade in goods and services, and the commercial aspects of intellectual property, foreign direct investment, the achievement of uniformity in measures of liberalisation, export policy and measures to protect trade such as those to be taken in the event of dumping or subsidies'. See Krajewski (n 26) 104–105.

[60] The Minimum Platform on Investment was adopted by the Council in November 2006. Council of the European Union, Doc. 15375/06, 27 November 2006. See N Maydell, 'The European Community's Minimum Platform on Investment or the Trojan Horse of Investment Competence' in A Reinisch and C Knahr (eds), *International Investment Law in Context* (Eleven Publishing, 2007), 75.

[61] W Shan and S Zhang, 'The Treaty of Lisbon: Half-Way Toward a Common Investment Policy' (2011) 21 *European Journal of International Law* 1049, 1051.

[62] Y Devuyst, 'The Constitutional and Lisbon Treaties' in E Jones, A Menon and S Weatherill (eds), *The Oxford Handbook of the European Union* (Oxford University Press, 2012) 166.

[63] S Meunier, 'Integration by stealth: how the European Union gained competence over foreign direct investment', EU Working Papers, RSCAS 2014/66, 10.

This important innovation, however, did not soothe the debate on the contours of the Union's competence over foreign investment.[64]

First, there was a great deal of discussion about whether the phrase 'foreign direct investment' under Article 207 TFEU should be construed as referring to all types of foreign investment, ie, direct and indirect investments (also known as portfolio investments).[65]

Furthermore, this provision did not dispel all doubts about whether the Union can conclude international agreements containing rules applicable to the post-establishment phase.[66] Some commentators argued that the 'new' Article 207 TFEU, read jointly with Article 206 TFEU, would only cover the pre-establishment phase, because the latter provision only refers to the 'gradual abolition of restrictions [...] on foreign direct investment'.[67] The proponents of the restrictive reading of Article 207 TFEU also relied on Article 345 TFEU, which states that the EU Treaties 'shall in no way prejudice the rules in Member States governing the system of property ownership'. According to this view, Article 345 TFEU precludes the Union from negotiating agreements containing post-establishment provisions and, in particular, expropriation clauses[68] because they affect the regulation of private property in the Member States.

The opposite approach was based on a literal interpretation of Article 207 TFEU.[69] As this provision does not expressly distinguish between pre- and post-establishment phases, it has been argued that the competence of the Union would encompass both phases. The proponents of this view also maintain that Article 345 TFEU, if read together with the right to property under Article 17 CFREU, does not prevent the Union from undertaking post-establishment commitments.[70]

[64] A Reinisch, 'The EU on the Investment Path – *Quo vadis Europe*? The Future of EU BITs and Other Investment Agreements' (2014) 12 *Santa Clara Journal of International Law* 111, 115.

[65] Bischoff (n 41) 1537–1539; F Ortino and P Eeckhout, 'Towards an EU Policy on Foreign Direct Investment' in A Biondi, P Eeckhout and S Ripley (eds), *EU Law After Lisbon* (Oxford University Press, 2012) 314–315. R Baratta, 'La politica commerciale comune dopo il trattato di Lisbona' (2012) 26 *Diritto del Commercio Internazionale* 403, 411; PJ Cardwell and D French, 'The European Union as a Global Investment Partner: Law, Policy and Rhetoric in the Attainment of Development Assistance and Market Liberalisation?' in C Brown and K Miles (eds), *The Evolution in Investment Treaty Law and Arbitration* (Cambridge University Press, 2011) 206; PC Müller-Graff, 'The Common Commercial Policy Enhanced by the Reform Treaty of Lisbon?' in A Dashwood and M Maresceau (eds), *Law and Practice of EU External Relations: Salient Features of a Changing Landscape* (Cambridge University Press, 2011), 191.

[66] Bischoff (n 41) 1538; Cardwell and French (n 65) 207.

[67] Dimopoulos (n 58) 115; T Eilmansberger, 'Bilateral Investment Treaties and EU Law' (2009) 46 *Common Market Law Review* 383, 395; M Bungenberg, 'Going Global? – The EU Common Commercial Policy after Lisbon' in C Herrmann, M Krajewski and J Terhechte (eds), *European Yearbook of International Economic Law* (Springer, 2010) 144.

[68] ibid.

[69] A Reinisch, 'The Division of Powers Between the EU and its Member States "After Lisbon"' in M Bungenberg, J Griebel and S Hindelang (eds), *European Yearbook of International Economic Law – Special Issue: International Investment Law and EU Law* (Springer, 2011) 52. *cf* Bischoff (above n 41) 1540.

[70] Ortino and Eeckhout (n 65) 320.

These issues are not merely theoretical. They are crucial in determining whether the EU has a comprehensive competence in the field of foreign investment. Consequently, they affect the choice of the procedure governing the conclusion and ratification of future EU international agreements. If an agreement only covers matters falling within the exclusive competence of the Union, it can be concluded exclusively by the European Union ('EU-only agreement'). The Union may also conclude international agreements without the intervention of its Member States, if the agreement contains provisions governing both matters of exclusive competence of the Union and matters where both the Union and the Member States are competent. Such agreements, however, may also be facultatively concluded as mixed agreements (so-called 'facultative mixity').[71] The adoption of the mixed agreement procedure is, by contrast, mandatory for international agreements covering matters falling within the competence of the Union as well as matters falling within the exclusive competence of the Member States.[72]

If the Union acts alone when concluding treaties that cover matters included in the common commercial policy, the procedure follows the rules laid down in Articles 207 and 218 TFEU. Therefore, the Commission, the Council and the European Parliament jointly participate in the treaty-making process.[73] In the context of the EU common commercial policy, the Council generally acts by qualified majority. However, unanimous approval is required for the negotiation and conclusion of international agreements on trade in services, foreign direct investment, and commercial aspects of intellectual property 'where such agreements include provisions for which unanimity is required for the adoption of internal rules'.[74] The unanimity requirement also applies to agreements on trade in cultural and audiovisual services, and international agreements on trade in social, education and health services, 'where these agreements risk seriously disturbing the national organisation of such services and prejudicing the responsibility of Member States to deliver them'.[75]

The Lisbon Treaty granted to the European Parliament a greater role in the negotiation and the conclusion of international agreements falling within the CCP.[76] The European Parliament directly intervenes in the decision-making

[71] M Klamert and N Maydell, 'Lost in Exclusivity: Implied Non-Exclusive External Competences in Community Law' (2008) 13 *European Foreign Affairs Review* 493, 493–494.

[72] A Rosas, 'The European Union and Mixed Agreements' in A Dashwood and C Hillion (eds), *The General Law of EC External Relations* (Sweet & Maxwell, 2000) 203–204.

[73] See generally I Bosse-Platière, 'Les instruments juridiques des relations extérieures de l'Union européenne après le Traité de Lisbonne' in AS Lamblin-Gourdin and E Mondielli (eds), *Le droit des relations extérieures de l'Union européenne après le Traité de Lisbonne* (Brussels, Bruylant, 2013); C Cellerino, 'EU Common Commercial Policy in Context: Opportunities and Challenges of a Changing Landscape' (2015) 29 *Diritto del Commercio Internazionale* 783, 805.

[74] Art 207(4), TFEU.

[75] ibid.

[76] J Maupin, 'Where Should Europe's Investment Path Lead? Reflections on August Reinisch, "*Quo vadis Europe?*"' (2014) 12 *Santa Clara Journal of International Law* 183, 200–201.

process by approving, inter alia, agreements establishing a specific institutional framework by organising cooperation procedures, agreements with substantial financial implications for the Union, and agreements covering matters where the applicable internal decision-making procedures require consent by the European Parliament.[77]

The enhanced role of the European Parliament is further evidenced by the fact that the Commission is under the obligation to inform the latter about 'the progress of negotiations'.[78] The Framework Agreement on relations between the Commission and the European Parliament fleshes out this duty of information by stating that the European Parliament should be informed 'in sufficient time for it to be able to express its point of view if appropriate, and for the Commission to be able to take Parliament's views as far as possible into account'.[79]

On the other hand, when the Union cannot act or does not intend to act alone in case of international agreements covering exclusive and shared competence matters, it resorts to the mixed agreements procedure. This is a two-tiered procedure, under which the Union and its Member States ratify a given treaty respectively in accordance with the EU Treaties and their domestic constitutional requirements.[80]

V. THE COMMISSION'S VIEW ON ARTICLE 207 TFEU

A few months after the entry into force of the Lisbon Treaty, the Commission issued the Communication 'Towards a comprehensive European international investment policy' to design its new investment policy.[81] This Communication outlined an ambitious treaty negotiation agenda, according to which '[t]he Union should go where its investors would like to go'.[82] In the short term, the Commission planned to include foreign investment in the then ongoing talks with India, Canada and Singapore.[83] In the medium term, it also planned to negotiate investment agreements with states with which the Union had traditionally had rather complex trade and political relations, such as China and Russia.[84]

[77] See M Krajewski, 'The Reform of the Common Commercial Policy' in A Biondi, P Eeckhout and S Ripley (eds), *EU Law After Lisbon* (Oxford University Press, 2012) 308–310; Baratta (n 65) 415–417.

[78] Art 207 TFEU. See Krajewski (n 77) 309.

[79] Framework Agreement on relations between the European Parliament and the European Commission.

[80] G Van der Loo, 'Less is more? The role of national parliaments in the conclusion of mixed (trade) agreements', CLEER Papers, 2018/1, 15.

[81] European Commission, Towards a comprehensive European international investment policy, COM (2010) 343 final, 7. See N Pigeon, 'La *soft law* dans la construction de la politique européenne en matière d'investissements internationaux' (2014) 577 *Revue de l'Union Européenne* 201 (2014).

[82] European Commission (n 81).

[83] ibid 7.

[84] ibid.

As such an ambitious plan was likely to encounter a wide range of external political obstacles, the Commission initially sought to flatten at least the internal ones. The Communication unequivocally stated that the Union possessed exclusive competence both over foreign direct investment and indirect investment.[85] The former directly stemmed from Article 207 TFEU, while the latter was based on Article 3(2) TFEU.[86] That is to say, the competence over indirect investment was deemed necessary to ensure consistency between the development of EU investment policy and the TFEU's rules on capital and payments.[87]

The European Commission also clarified that it intended to negotiate IIAs and investment chapters of comprehensive economic agreements[88] containing liberalisation commitments and investment protection rules.[89] To support this view, the European Commission specifically stated that Article 345 TFEU did not preclude the negotiation of international agreements containing expropriation clauses. Notably, it held that such provision 'does not have the effect of exempting expropriation measures from the fundamental rules of the Treaty, including those on freedom of establishment and free movement of capital'.[90]

In sum, the Commission asserted a broad reading of the Union's 'new' competence in the field of foreign investment, which sought to overcome the division of competences between EU Member States and the EU existing in the pre-Lisbon phase. To put it simply, the European Union, in the Commission's view, possessed exclusive external competence on foreign direct and indirect investment.

VI. SETTING THE GROUND FOR THE DEVELOPMENT OF THE EU FOREIGN INVESTMENT POLICY

With the establishment of the new competence over foreign (direct) investment, the Union was also called upon to deal with the implications of its future agreements containing investment provisions.

[85] ibid 8.

[86] Art 3 (2) TFEU reads as follows: '[t]he Union shall also have exclusive competence for the conclusion of an international agreement when its conclusion is provided for in a legislative act of the Union or is necessary to enable the Union to exercise its internal competence, or in so far as its conclusion may affect common rules or alter their scope'.

[87] European Commission (n 81) 8.

[88] European Commission, Global Europe: competing in the world, COM (2006) 567. This trade strategy was adopted in the wake of the multilateral trading system crisis. See M Cremona, 'Shaping EU Trade Policy Post-Lisbon: Opinion 2/15 of 16 May 2017' (2018) 14 *European Constitutional Law Review* 231, 232.

[89] European Commission (n 81) 5.

[90] ibid 8. The Commission relied on the CJEU case law affirming this principle. See *Margarethe Ospelt and Schlössle Weissenberg Familienstiftung*, C-452/01, EU:C:2003:493, para 24; *Klaus Konle v Austria*, C-302/97, EU:C:1999:271, para 38; *Robert Fearon & Company Limited v Irish Land Commission*, Case 182/83, EU:C:1984:305, para 7.

A. Managing the Transition to EU IIAs and Investment Chapters

The European Union's new role in the field of foreign investment raised the question of how to handle the existing EU Member States' IIAs. To deal with this issue, the Commission published the draft Regulation establishing transitional arrangements for bilateral investment treaties between Member States and third countries (hereinafter also referred to as 'Grandfathering Regulation'). This proposed piece of legislation pursued one main goal: it sought to ensure that the existing and future Member States' IIAs would be consistent with EU law and EU policies.[91] Accordingly, the draft Regulation established a notification and authorisation procedure, under which the Commission had the power to grant or deny the authorisation to keep Member States' BITs in force depending on the fulfilment of the following conditions.[92] First, Member States' IIAs should not be at variance with EU rules other than those governing the division of competences between Member States and the Union. Second, they should not overlap with international agreements concluded by the Union, unless the latter contains an instrument to deal with this overlap. Third, they should not hinder the implementation or development of the Union's policies relating to investment.

The Commission could always withdraw such authorisation if one of the conditions listed in Article 6 of the draft Regulation were no longer satisfied.[93]

Finally, the negotiation of new treaties and the amendment of existing ones were also subject to the notification and authorisation by the European Commission.[94]

The far-reaching review powers attributed to the Commission,[95] however, did not make it into the final text of the Grandfathering Regulation, for they were unpalatable for both the European Parliament and the Member States.[96] The adopted text of the Grandfathering Regulation still imposes on Member States an obligation to notify the BITs concluded before 1 December 2009 or before their accession,[97] but grants to the Commission narrower powers of review.[98]

[91] A Perfetti, 'Ensuring the Consistency of the EU Investment Policy Within the EU External Action: The Relevance of Non-Trade Values' in G Sacerdoti, P Acconci, M Valenti and A De Luca (eds), *General Interests of Host States in International Investment Law* (Cambridge University Press, 2014) 318.

[92] Art 5 draft Regulation of the European Parliament and the Council establishing transitional arrangements for bilateral investment agreements between Member States and third countries, COM (2010) 344 final.

[93] Art 6 draft Regulation (n 92).

[94] Art 7, 8, 9 draft Regulation (n 92).

[95] A Dimopoulos, 'Creating an EU Investment Policy: Challenges for the Post-Lisbon Era of External Relations' in PJ Cardwell (ed), *EU External Relations Law and Policy in the Post-Lisbon Era* (TMC Asser Press – Springer, 2012) 419.

[96] Reinisch (n 64) 120; J Kleinheisterkamp, 'European Policy Space in International Investment Law' (2012) 27 *ICSID Review – Foreign Investment Law Journal* 416, 425–427.

[97] Art 2, Reg 1219/2012 of the European Parliament and of the Council of 12 December 2012 establishing transitional arrangements for bilateral investment agreements between Member States and third countries.

[98] Since the entry into force of the Regulation, Member States have notified some 1,360 BITs to the Commission. European Commission, Report on the application of Regulation (EU) No 1219/2012

First, the Commission can only assess 'whether one or more of their provisions constitute a serious obstacle to the negotiation or conclusion by the Union of bilateral investment agreements with third countries, with a view to the progressive replacement of the bilateral investment agreements notified pursuant to Article 2'.[99] Thus, unlike the Commission's proposal, the approved regulation does not contain a requirement of compatibility with EU law. The elimination of such ground of review, however, does not seem to preclude the Commission from initiating an infringement procedure against a Member State that refuses to renegotiate or terminate a BIT obstructing the achievement of an EU policy objective.[100]

Second, the notification under Article 2 of the Regulation 1219/2012 does not trigger a compulsory authorisation procedure, as the Commission's power of review is merely discretional ('may').

It is also worth noting that the Regulation stipulates that Member States are required to take appropriate action to ensure that their IIAs do not hinder the negotiation and the conclusion of IIAs by the EU with third states.[101] The same provision then says that this duty should be performed 'with a view to the progressive replacement' of Member States' IIAs.[102]

Finally, the approved text of the Grandfathering Regulation kept the authorisation procedure for the conclusion of new IIAs or the amendment of existing ones.[103] Such an authorisation can be denied if an IIA or an amendment to an existing IIA is inconsistent with EU rules other than those governing the allocation of competences between the Union and Member States or with the EU external action principles and objectives.[104] Moreover, the authorisation can also be denied when a Member State intends to start negotiations with a third state with which the Union also plans to negotiate or is already negotiating an IIA.[105]

B. Dealing with the Financial Consequences of the Involvement of the EU in Investment Disputes

A further consequence of the Union's direct participation in international agreements containing investment provisions is that this might sooner or later trigger

establishing transitional arrangements for bilateral investment agreements between Member States and third countries, COM (2020) 134 final, 2.

[99] Art 5, Reg 1219/2012 (n 97).

[100] Kleinheisterkamp (n 96) 426.

[101] Art 6, Reg 1219/2012 (n 97).

[102] ibid.

[103] See Art 7, Reg 1219/2012 (n 97). *Cf* Art 7, draft Regulation (n 92). Member States have thus far submitted 304 requests of authorisation to negotiate new BITs or amend existing ones – 241 of which were upheld – and 76 requests of authorisation to conclude new treaties. European Commission (n 98) 3–4.

[104] Art 9, Reg 1219/2012 (n 97).

[105] ibid.

international responsibility and give rise to financial consequences to be allocated between Member States and the Union. Managing such consequences is not particularly difficult when investment claims challenge a measure adopted by the Union in the exercise of one of its exclusive competences. In such circumstances, there is no doubt that the Union should bear in full the consequences thereof. But what about the measures taken by EU Member States to comply with EU law? How should financial responsibility be allocated when the EU and its Member States exercise a shared competence? Furthermore, which of the two has legal standing in investment disputes? To address all such questions, in the Communication on EU international investment policy, the Commission suggested that the Union would also act as a respondent in investment disputes originating from alleged Member States' violation of EU IIAs and investment chapters.[106] The main downside of this approach, however, is that it may cause moral hazard problems.[107] If the Union acted as a respondent and bore the financial consequences for its own violations and those of the Member States, the latter would have little or no incentive to avoid such violations.

The Commission thus revised this position when tabling the 2012 draft Regulation on financial responsibility.[108] This proposal stipulated that the financial responsibility stemming from the violation of EU trade and investment agreements does not exclusively lie with the Union, but with the 'author' of the illegal treatment. This approach eventually made it into the final text of the Regulation.[109] The approved text establishes that the Union is financially responsible for the violations of EU IIAs and investment chapters,[110] which are imputable to its institutions or bodies, while Member States bear the financial consequences of their conduct except when they act to comply with EU law.[111] Put differently, the Union assumes the consequences stemming from the adoption by a Member State of a measure that is inconsistent with EU IIAs and investment chapters, but consistent with EU law. This is because it would be unfair to drop upon Member States the unfavourable effects associated with the adoption of a measure that is mandated by EU law.[112] Member States, however,

[106] European Commission (n 81) 10.

[107] A Dimopoulos, 'The Involvement of the EU Investor-State Dispute Settlement: A Question of Responsibility' (2014) 51 *Common Market Law Review* 1671, 1676.

[108] Reg 912/2014 of the European Parliament and of the Council of 23 July 2014 establishing a framework for managing financial responsibility linked to investor-to-state dispute settlement tribunals established by international agreements to which the European Union is party.

[109] ibid.

[110] It is worth noting that the text of the Regulation exclusively refers to the 'classic' ISDS system, as it was enacted before the creation of the ICS (see ch 4).

[111] Art 3, Reg 912/2014 (n 108). For the thorough analysis of the origins of such principle see E Leinarte, 'The Principle of Independent Responsibility of the European Union and its Member States in the International Economic Context' (2018) 21 *Journal of International Economic Law* 171, 174.

[112] Dimopoulos (n 107) 1679.

are nonetheless responsible if they violate EU IIAs and investment chapters by enacting measures to repeal a prior EU-inconsistent measure.[113]

The 'author-of-the-measure' rule also generally determines whether the Union or the Member States should act as a respondent in a given investment dispute. This principle straightforwardly applies when the allegedly illegal treatment is afforded by the Union.[114] Thus, if an investment dispute arises from a measure adopted by the Union, the Commission is called upon to represent and defend the Union in that dispute.

On the other hand, the process of identification of the respondent is slightly more complex when it comes to treatments afforded by EU Member States. The default rule is that Member States are called upon to act as respondents when they are the author of the challenged measure(s).[115] However, the Commission may nonetheless act as a respondent if, after consulting with the affected Member State, the latter renounces to act as a defendant[116] or the Commission itself decide to act as respondent within 45 days from the initiation of the investment dispute.[117] The Commission may adopt such decision if either the Union would (partly or fully) bear the financial consequences arising from an investment dispute in accordance with the abovementioned apportionment criteria or the investment dispute also concerns treatment afforded by an EU institution or body.[118] Such a decision shall be adopted in accordance with Article 4 of Regulation 182/2011.[119] The Commission has thus a certain degree of discretion when formulating such a decision, but it shall nonetheless 'take into utmost account' the opinion delivered by a committee composed of Member States' representatives.

Furthermore, the Union may also decide to act as a respondent in an investment dispute arising out of a Member State's measure, if it concerns a legal issue that constitutes the object of a WTO dispute in which the European Union is already involved.[120] The Commission adopts this decision in accordance with the examination procedure outlined in Article 5 of Regulation 182/2011. This procedure differs from the one under the abovementioned Article 4 in that the committee of Member States' representatives issues an opinion that is binding on the Commission.

In any event, both the Union and the Member States have duties of information and cooperation when taking part in arbitration proceedings. On the one hand, Member States shall share all the relevant information with the

[113] Art 3, Reg 912/2014 (n 108).
[114] Art 4, Reg 912/2014 (n 108).
[115] See Arts 9 and 10, Reg 912/2014 (n 108).
[116] Art 9, Reg 912/2014 (n 108).
[117] ibid.
[118] ibid.
[119] ibid.
[120] ibid.

Commission and allow the Commission's representatives to join the delegation representing the Member State in the context of the arbitration.[121] On the other hand, when the Union acts as a respondent in a dispute where a Member State would bear part of the financial responsibility, the Commission shall keep the Member State affected by the dispute duly informed and cooperate with it.[122] Furthermore, it is also incumbent upon the Commission of the obligation to defend the interest of the Member State concerned in the course of the dispute.[123] The latter obligation may be at variance with the Commission's duty to defend the Union's interest under certain circumstances. If such a conflict arises, however, it seems reasonable to presume that the Commission should solve it by prioritising the protection of the Union's interest.

Finally, it should be noted that, when the Union acts as a respondent in a dispute in lieu of a Member State, the Union may partially or totally shift on the latter the financial consequences of the award or the settlement in accordance with the procedure under Article 19 of the Regulation on financial responsibility.[124]

To sum up, the Regulation on financial responsibility adopts a qualified version of the 'author-of-the-measure' principle to deal with the issues arising from the Union and Member States' participation in investment disputes. This criterion is not per se problematic, but it may be hard to square with the rules on international responsibility, particularly those on attribution of international wrongdoings.[125]

VII. TAKING A STEP BACK: THE POLITICAL IMPRACTICABILITY OF THE COMMISSION'S EXTENSIVE INTERPRETATION OF THE UNION'S COMPETENCE OVER FOREIGN INVESTMENT

As noted above (see section V), the Commission envisaged many potential partners to develop its international investment policy. These included states with which the Union was already negotiating trade agreements, such as India, Canada, and Singapore.[126] While the negotiations with India ran ashore in 2012,[127] the talks with Canada and Singapore progressed steadily.

[121] Art 10, Reg 912/2014 (n 108).

[122] Art 11, Reg 912/2014 (n 108).

[123] ibid.

[124] Art 19, Reg 912/2014 (n 108).

[125] Dimopoulos (n 107) 1683–1684; C Contartese and L Pantaleo, 'Division of Competences, EU Autonomy and the Determination of the Respondent Party: Proceduralisation as a Possible Way-Out?' in E Neframi and M Gatti (eds), *Constitutional Issues of EU External Relations Law* (Nomos, 2018) 442; P Palchetti, 'The Allocation of International Responsibility in the Context of Investor-State Dispute Settlement Mechanisms Established by EU International Agreements' (2017) 28 *European Business Law Review* 185, 186.

[126] Council of the European Union, Modification of the negotiating directives for the EU-India negotiations towards Broad-based Trade and Investment Agreement, 14 July 2011, 12839/11 EXT 1 (partially declassified on 23 October 2015); Council of the European Union, Modification of the negotiating directives for an Economic Integration Agreement with Canada, 14 July 2011, 12838/11 EXT 2 (15 December 2015); Council of the European Union, Modification of the negotiating directives for the EU-Singapore negotiations towards a Free Trade Agreement, 14 July 2011, 12840/11

This was just the beginning. Between 2011 and 2013, the Union embarked on the negotiation of several trade and investment agreements, including those with Vietnam, Morocco, Tunisia, and the US.[128] Moreover, on 15 October 2013, the Council adopted the negotiating directives for a comprehensive investment agreement with China.[129]

As the negotiations with third countries progressed, the Commission's approach to the delimitation of the Union's competence in the field of foreign investment became a major bone of contention. This question surfaced with the European Parliament's Resolution of 6 April 2011, which noted 'with concern' that the scope of the Union's international investment policy comprised both exclusive and shared competences.[130]

Shortly thereafter, EU Member States also started to voice their concern about the extensive reading of the Union's newly introduced competence in the field of foreign investment. In June 2014, upon initiative of the Committee for European Affairs of the Dutch House of Representatives, the chairs of the competent committees in the EU Member States' Parliaments wrote an open letter to the then EU Commissioner for trade, Karel De Gucht.[131] The letter clearly stated the view that the EU comprehensive economic agreements at the time still under negotiation 'should be considered as mixed agreements, since they contain provisions that concern policy areas which are within the competences of the member states'. One year later, during an Interparliamentary meeting on the commercial policy of the European Union in Paris, the representatives of EU Member States' Parliaments were united in claiming the mixed nature of these 'new' EU comprehensive economic agreements.[132] All these initiatives signalled a widespread discontent of Member States' Parliaments with the initial Commission's approach.[133]

(23 October 2015). It should be noted that the FTA with Singapore was a back-up solution adopted in response to the failure of the negotiation with a group of ASEAN countries. The stumbling block was the emergence of political difficulties with some of the negotiating parties, particularly Myanmar. See European Parliament, 'Driving trade in the ASEAN region – Progress of FTA negotiations', Briefing, 2016, 5.

[127] The *Enrica Lexie* incident also played an important role in forestalling the talks. See European Parliament, 'India and prospects for closer EU ties', Briefing, 2017, 5.

[128] See European Commission, Overview of the FTA and other negotiations, 2020.

[129] Council of the European Union, Council decision authorising the opening of negotiations on an investment agreement with the People's Republic of China, 8 October 2013, 14091/13. China and the EU reached an agreement in principle on the Comprehensive Agreement on Investment (CAI) on 30 December 2020. The agreement contained investment promotion rules and was devoid of an investor-State dispute settlement mechanism. The European Parliament put on hold the ratification of the CAI by adopting a resolution in May 2021.

[130] European Parliament, Resolution of 6 April 2011 on the future European international investment policy, P7_TA (2011) 0141,12.

[131] Letter to Mr de Gucht, Letter in the framework of the political dialogue: the role of national parliaments in free trade agreements, 25 June 2014.

[132] Interparliamentary meeting on the commercial policy of the European Union, Paris, 17 June 2015.

[133] D Kleimann and G Kübek, 'The Signing, Provisional Application, and Conclusion of Trade and Investment Agreements in the EU: The Case of CETA and Opinion 2/15' (2018) 45 *Legal Issues of Economic Integration* 13, 16.

Given the mounting political pressure, the Commission decided to play it safe. In 2015, after completing the negotiation with Singapore,[134] the Commission sought a CJEU's Opinion pursuant to Article 218 TFEU. More specifically, the Court was asked to clarify which components of the EUSFTA fell within the exclusive competence of the Union, in the Union-Member States' shared competence, and in the exclusive competence of the states.[135]

When the Court issued its opinion, the EU-Singapore FTA consisted of 17 chapters covering five broad areas. First, it included a wide range of market access rules ranging from commitments on non-tariff barriers and trade in goods to the establishment of new economic activities. Second, it devoted an entire chapter to intellectual property protection. Third, it sought to establish a level playing field between the two contracting parties by including specific chapters on competition and anti-dumping issues. Fourth, it covered 'non-trade' issues in the chapter concerning sustainable development and trade. Last, it included an investment chapter containing substantive investment protection rules and an investor-state dispute settlement mechanism.

Pending the CJEU's decision, the Commission took an even more cautious stance with respect to the ratification of the CETA. Only six days after announcing that the CETA would be concluded as an 'EU-only' agreement,[136] the Commission went back on its word to address Member States' remonstrations and opted for the mixed agreements procedure. In taking this step, Commissioner Cecilia Malmström stated that '[f]rom a strict legal standpoint, the Commission considers this agreement to fall under exclusive EU competence. However, the political situation in the Council is clear, and we understand the need for proposing it as a "mixed" agreement, in order to allow for a speedy signature'.[137] This decision is undoubtedly relevant in that it signals that the Commission itself gradually abandoned the idea that it could act alone when concluding comprehensive economic agreements.[138]

VIII. A RUDE AWAKENING: OPINION 2/15 AND THE BOUNDARIES OF THE UNION'S EXCLUSIVE COMPETENCE OVER FOREIGN INVESTMENT

The Court eventually issued its Opinion on the EUSFTA on 16 May 2017.[139] This Opinion was first and foremost expected to provide guidance regarding the

[134] European Commission, 'EU and Singapore conclude investment talks', Press release, 17 October 2014.

[135] Request for an opinion submitted by the European Commission pursuant to Art 218(11) TFEU.

[136] European Commission, 'European Council endorses Commission's priorities', Press release, 29 June 2016.

[137] European Commission, 'European Commission proposes signature and conclusion of EU-Canada trade deal', Press release, 5 July 2016.

[138] This choice has been criticised because it seems to suggest that the ratification procedure for 'EU-only' agreements does not ensure sufficient democratic scrutiny. M Dony, 'Quel avenir pour la politique commerciale commune de l'Union européenne' (2017) *Revue trimestrielle de droit européen* 189, 196–197.

[139] Opinion 2/15, EU:C:2017:376.

ratification of such an agreement, but it was also likely to be relevant for other EU trade and investment agreements.

After carefully examining the single chapters of the EUSFTA, the Court concluded that the provisions governing trade in goods, services, sustainable development, and intellectual property, fell within the exclusive competence pursuant to Article 3 TFEU and Article 207 TFEU.[140]

Having clarified this, the CJEU then went on to assess whether the EU possessed the competence to enter investment-related commitments.

A. The Union's Exclusive Competence Over Foreign Direct Investment

The Court started by noting that Article 207 TFEU, read jointly with Article 3(1) TFEU, granted to the Union exclusive competence over foreign direct investment only. Thus, Article 207 TFEU could not be construed as referring to both direct and indirect investment.[141] In the Court's view, foreign direct investment also satisfied the 'link with trade' requirement under Article 207 TFEU.[142] More specifically, the Court held that

> any EU act promoting, facilitating or governing participation [...] in the management or control of a company carrying out an economic activity is such as to have direct and immediate effects on trade between that third State and the European Union, whereas there is no specific link of that kind with trade in the case of investments which do not result in such participation.[143]

Then, contrary to what the Council argued in the course of the proceedings, the Court found that Article 207 TFEU conferred on the Union the power to undertake obligations relating both to the pre- and post-admission phases of foreign direct investment.[144] In this respect, it is also worth highlighting that the Court dismissed the claim that the provisions contained in the investment chapter impinged on the EU Member States' exclusive competence in the field of property law.[145] Relying on the conclusions reached in the *Essent* judgment,[146] the Court held that the principle of neutrality of the Union vis-à-vis national rules on this matter did not exempt Member States from the application of EU law. In fact, in the Court's view, Article 345 TFEU

[140] Of particular interest is the section of the Opinion devoted to assessing the Union's competence to undertake commitments relating to sustainable development. In dealing with this issue, the Court noted that the EU common commercial policy, being part of the EU's external action, shall be conducted in accordance with its principles and pursue its objectives. Thus, as sustainable development features among such objectives pursuant to Art 21 TEU, the Union possessed exclusive competence to undertake commitments relating to this matter. Opinion 2/15 (n 139) para 141–147.

[141] ibid, paras 81–83.

[142] ibid, para 36.

[143] ibid, para 84.

[144] ibid, para 85.

[145] ibid, para 107.

[146] *Staat der Nederlanden v Essent NV, Essent Nederland BV, Eneco Holding NV and Delta NV*, joined Cases C-105/12 to C-107/12, EU:C:2013:677, paras 29 and 36.

> seeks solely to make any nationalisation or expropriation decisions subject to limits which are intended to guarantee investors that such a decision will be adopted under equitable conditions and in compliance with general principles and fundamental rights, in particular with the principle of non-discrimination.[147]

B. The Union's Competence Over Foreign Indirect Investment and Investor-State Dispute Settlement

Once it established that Articles 3(1) and 207 TFEU only conferred on the Union the competence over foreign direct investment, the Court turned to consider whether the Union possessed competence over indirect investment pursuant to Article 3(2) TFEU. Under this provision, the exclusive competence of the Union to enter into an international agreement can arise from a legislative act of the Union or when it 'is necessary to enable the Union to exercise its internal competence, or in so far as its conclusion may affect common rules or alter their scope'. Key to the interpretation of this provision is the phrase 'common rules'. According to the Commission, the 'common rules' referred to in Article 3(2) TFEU also included EU primary law. In its view, this interpretation was supported by the CJEU's judgment in the *Pringle* case,[148] where the Court found that Article 3(2) TFEU prevented Member States from entering into an international treaty among themselves 'which might affect common rules or alter their scope'.[149] Therefore, in line with its Communication on the EU comprehensive international investment policy, it stated that Article 3(2) TFEU read in light of the provisions on the free movement of capital and payments conferred on the Union exclusive external competence on portfolio investments.[150]

The Court, however, rejected this view. Relying on its previous case law, it found that the definition of 'common rules' referred to in Article 3(2) TFEU only includes EU secondary legislation.[151] It then went on to note that the power to enter into an international agreement covering indirect investment could not be drawn from a specific piece of EU legislation.[152] Nor was the EUSFTA necessary to enable the Union to exercise an internal competence.[153]

[147] Opinion 2/15, para 107.
[148] *Thomas Pringle v Ireland and others*, C-370/12, EU:C:2012:756.
[149] Opinion of Advocate General Sharpston in Opinion 2/15, EU:C:2013:242, para 356.
[150] European Commission (n 81) 8.
[151] Opinion 2/15 (n 139) paras 232–234. See G De Baere, *Constitutional Principles of EU External Relations* (Oxford University Press, 2008) 44. As pointed out by Advocate General Sharpston, if one were to take the Commission's view, the Union would end up gaining exclusive competence 'even where the internal competence underlying the Treaty provision on which it relies has not been exercised'. Opinion of Advocate General Sharpston (n 149) para 357.
[152] Opinion 2/15 (n 139) para 236.
[153] ibid, para 237. Cremona (n 88) 249.

Having established that the Union does not enjoy exclusive competence over indirect investment pursuant to Article 3(2) TFEU, the Court turned to consider whether there was another legal basis that could justify the Union's action in this field. This provision was Article 216 TFEU, according to which the Union may exercise external competence in a given field when it is necessary to pursue one of the objectives set out in the Treaties. Despite their apparent similarities, Article 3(2) TFEU and Article 216 TFEU serve different functions.[154] The former establishes the exclusive competence of the Union to conclude an international agreement when this is 'the only means to exercise an internal EU competence'. The latter empowers the Union to enter into an international agreement insofar as it is necessary to achieve 'within the framework of the Union's policies, one of the objectives referred to in the Treaties'.[155] The objective pursued by the Union in the case at hand is that embedded in Article 63 TFEU, namely liberalising capital flows and payments from and to third countries. In other words, the conclusion of international agreements containing rules on indirect investments, such as the EUSFTA, was necessary for the implementation vis-à-vis third countries of the project of capital liberalisation enshrined in Article 63 TFEU. As the free movement of capital and payments falls within the shared competences of the Union, the Court concluded that the EUSFTA could not be entered into by the Union alone, but it should be concluded as a mixed agreement.[156]

Moreover, the Court found that the Union had no exclusive competence to enter into the EUSFTA, because the latter contained an investor-state dispute settlement system. In the Court's view, the Union could not act alone, for this mechanism grants investors the power to remove a wide range of disputes from the jurisdiction of Member States' courts.[157] The Court thus distanced itself from Advocate General Sharpston, who opined that the allocation of the competence to introduce dispute settlement mechanism depended on and followed the division of substantive competences.[158]

In reaching these conclusions, the Court seemed to imply that whenever an international agreement governs shared competence matters, the Union must resort to the mixed agreement procedure.[159] This approach, however, disregarded the fact that an international agreement covering the same matters as the EUSFTA could be facultatively entered into as an EU-alone or a mixed treaty. At face value, this judgment could even be considered as marking the demise of the

[154] I Govaere, 'Setting the International Scene: EU External Competence and Procedures Post-Lisbon Revisited in the Light of Opinion 1/13' (2015) 52 *Common Market Law Review* 1277, 1289.

[155] E Neframi, 'Article 216(1) TFEU and the Union's Shared External Competence in the Light of Mixity: *Germany v Council (COTIF)*' (2019) 56 *Common Market Law Review* 489, 508.

[156] Opinion 2/15 (n 139) para 244.

[157] ibid, para 292.

[158] Opinion of Advocate General Sharpston (n 149) para 523.

[159] P Hainbach, 'The CJEU's Opinion 2/15 and the Future of EU Investment Policy and Law-Making' (2018) 45 *Legal Issues of Economic Integration* 199, 207; Cremona (n 88) 251.

notion of 'facultative mixity' (see section IV). Yet, in its subsequent judgment *Germany v Council (OTIF)*,[160] the Court sought to nuance and clarify these findings. In particular, it observed that Opinion 2/15 required the involvement of EU Member States because 'there was no possibility of the required majority being obtained within the Council for the Union to be able to exercise alone the external competence that it shares with the Member States in this area'.[161]

C. The Union's Competence to Terminate EU Member States' BITs with Singapore

The Court finally assessed whether the EU possessed the competence to terminate the BITs between EU Member States and Singapore pursuant to Article 9.10 of the EUSFTA.[162] In this regard, it is worth recalling that Advocate General Sharpston[163] argued that Member States, not the Union, enjoyed exclusive competence to terminate bilateral investment treaty relations with Singapore.[164] In her view, the establishment of a Union's exclusive competence over foreign investment did not imply the allocation at the Union's level of the power to terminate previous investment treaty relations between Member States and Singapore. She suggested that Article 351 TFEU should govern the relationship between EU law and the obligations stemming from investment treaties between Singapore and EU Member States.[165] This implied that, although EU Member States were under no direct obligation to terminate these treaties, they were nonetheless required to 'do their utmost' to ensure consistency between the pre-existing treaties and EU law.[166]

Advocate General Sharpston's approach, however, did not persuade the CJEU, which dealt with this issue by resorting to the principle of 'functional

[160] *Germany v Council of the European Union*, C-600/14, EU:C:1998:94.

[161] ibid, para 68.

[162] Opinion 2/15 (n 139) para 246. Art 9.10 EUSFTA reads as follows: '[u]pon the entry into force of this Agreement, the agreements between Member States of the Union and Singapore [...] including the rights and obligations derived therefrom, shall cease to have effect and shall be replaced and superseded by this Agreement'.

[163] Opinion of Advocate General Sharpston (n 149) para 386.

[164] ibid, para 398.

[165] ibid, para 389. Art 351 TFEU reads as follows: '[t]he rights and obligations arising from agreements concluded before 1 January 1958 or, for acceding States, before the date of their accession, between one or more Member States on the one hand, and one or more third countries on the other, shall not be affected by the provisions of the Treaties. To the extent that such agreements are not compatible with the Treaties, the Member State or States concerned shall take all appropriate steps to eliminate the incompatibilities established. Member States shall, where necessary, assist each other to this end and shall, where appropriate, adopt a common attitude. In applying the agreements referred to in the first paragraph, Member States shall take into account the fact that the advantages accorded under the Treaties by each Member State form an integral part of the establishment of the Union and are thereby inseparably linked with the creation of common institutions, the conferring of powers upon them and the granting of the same advantages by all the other Member States'.

[166] J Klabbers, *Treaty conflict and the European Union* (Cambridge University Press, 2008) 122–123.

succession'.[167] Under this principle, the Union assumes Member States' international obligations insofar as they relate to matters that have been included within the exclusive competence of the Union through an amendment of the EU treaties.[168] This principle, in the Court's view, finds its corollary in Article 2 TFEU, under which Member States can enact legally binding acts in areas of Union's exclusive competence only if the latter empowers them to do so.[169]

The Court also added that Singapore had clearly no interest in preserving the existing investment treaty relations with EU Member States. In fact, Article 9.10 EUSFTA, if anything, signalled its unequivocal will to terminate the BITs with EU Member States.[170]

Therefore, the Court concluded that the competence to agree upon a provision such as Article 9.10 EUSFTA should be allocated in accordance with the principles established earlier in the Opinion. Thus, the EU was competent to undertake such an obligation to the extent that it related to 'the commitments concerning foreign direct investment contained in the bilateral investment agreements entered into between Member States and the Republic of Singapore'.[171] But it shared with the Member States the competence to terminate pre-existing BITs containing provisions on foreign indirect investment.[172]

IX. THE CONSEQUENCES OF MIXITY

The Commission's decision to ratify CETA as a mixed agreement and the conclusions reached by the CJEU in Opinion 2/15 accommodated Member States' requests for greater participation of Member States' Parliaments in the ratification process of new EU comprehensive economic agreements. The shift towards mixity, however, implies at best a prolongation of the ratification process, because the two-tiered procedure governing the ratification of these treaties is inevitably lengthier than that applicable to 'EU-alone' international agreements. The former requires a couple of years, whilst the latter generally takes a couple of months.[173] Moreover, the ebbs and flows of national politics might even wreak havoc on the ratification process. This risk is then worsened by the fact that, under EU law, there is no explicit obligation for Member States

[167] This was famously stated in the *International Fruit* case. See *International Fruit Co. NV v Produktschap voor Groenten en Fruit*, joined Cases 21 to 24/72, EU:C:1972:115, para 18.

[168] Schütze (n 20) 110. On the limited character of this succession see also P Pescatore, 'La Cour de justice des Communautées européennes et la Convention européenne des droits de l'homme' in F Matscher and H Petzold (eds), *Protecting Human Rights: The European Dimension* (Heymann, 1988) 441, 450.

[169] Opinion 2/15 (n 139) para 250.

[170] ibid, paras 253–254.

[171] ibid, para 252.

[172] ibid, para 256.

[173] Kleimann and Kübek (n 133) 24.

to ratify mixed agreements. Nor can such an obligation be inferred from the duty of sincere cooperation under Article 4(3) TEU.[174]

Given the difficulties associated with the ratification of mixed agreements, the Council, upon proposal of the Commission, allowed the provisional application of CETA just a few months after the decision to conclude CETA as a mixed agreement.[175] The provisional application of a treaty or part of it occurs when the latter starts producing legal effects before the completion of the ratification procedure and its entry into force.[176] The contracting parties are of course free to determine the moment from which provisional application starts, but this generally coincides with the date of adoption or signature.[177] Conceptually speaking, it is inappropriate to consider the provisional application of a treaty as a provisional entry into force,[178] because the agreement on the provisional application of a treaty is at the same time autonomous from and complementary to the main treaty.[179] Nonetheless, a treaty on provisional application is effective and enforceable pursuant to the *pacta sunt servanda* rule.[180] Thus, Article 25 VCLT constitutes an exception to Article 18 VCLT, under which, before the entry into force of a treaty, the contracting parties are only required not to defeat its object and purpose.[181]

In the EU context, the provisional application of international treaties cannot supersede the division of powers between Member States and the Union. Thus, it generally covers matters falling within the exclusive or shared competence of the Union.[182] In crafting the decision on the provisional application of CETA, the Council was particularly cautious, not least because at the time

[174] G Van der Loo and R Wessel, 'The Non-Ratification of Mixed Agreements: Legal Consequences and Solution' (2017) 54 *Common Market Law Review* 735, 744.

[175] Council Decision 2017/38 on the provisional application of the Comprehensive Economic and Trade Agreement (CETA).

[176] Art 25 VCLT stipulates that '[a] treaty or a part of a treaty is applied provisionally pending its entry into force if: (a) the treaty itself so provides; or (b) the negotiating States have in some other manner so agreed'.

[177] A Aust, *Modern Treaty Law* (Cambridge University Press, 2013) 172.

[178] D Mathy, 'Article 25' in O Corten and P Klein (eds), *The Vienna Convention on the Law of Treaties – A Commentary* (Oxford University Press, 2011) 646–647; ME Villiger, *Commentary on the 1969 Vienna Convention on the Law of Treaties* (Martinus Nijhoff, 2009) 354; G Gaja, 'The Diverse Legal Effects of the Provisional Application of Treaties' (2022) 105 *Rivista di Diritto Internazionale* 753, 756–757.

[179] D Vignes, 'Une notion ambiguë: la mise en application provisoire des traités' (1962) 18 *Annuaire française de droit international* 181, 192; P Picone, *L'applicazione in via provvisoria degli accordi internazionali* (Jovene, 1973) 215.

[180] Mathy (n 178) 652; Villiger (n 178) 354.

[181] It has been suggested that the relationship between Arts 18 and 25 VCLT is that of *lex generalis* and *lex specialis*. A Quast Mertsch, 'Provisional Application of Treaties and the Internal Logic of the 1969 Vienna Convention' in MJ Bowman and D Kritsiotis (eds), *Conceptual and Contextual Perspectives on the Modern Law of Treaties* (Cambridge University Press, 2018) 314, 320.

[182] Van der Loo and Wessel (n 174) 754; A Suse and J Wouters, 'Exploring the Boundaries of Provisional Application: The EU's Mixed Trade and Investment Agreements' (2019) 53 *Journal of World Trade* 395, 403.

the CJEU had not delivered Opinion 2/15 yet. In particular, it made clear that only the components of the agreement governing matters over which the Union has exclusive competence would be provisionally applied.[183] It thus excluded the provisional application of the most controversial elements of the treaty, such as investment protection rules covering both foreign direct and indirect investment, investment liberalisation commitments relating to indirect investment, and the investor-state dispute settlement mechanism. Notwithstanding this, Germany, Poland and Austria claimed they had the right to terminate provisional application under Article 30.7(3) c) CETA in accordance with the EU procedures.[184] These statements raised the question of whether individual Member States could terminate the provisional application of CETA. While the termination by individual Member States is arguably consistent with Article 25 VCLT, it is more difficult to reconcile it with the Council's decision on the provisional application of CETA. Although this decision does not specify which body is entitled to terminate it in case of failure of the ratification process at the national level,[185] it seems more reasonable to confer such a power on the body, namely the Council, which adopted the decision on provisional application.[186]

The case of CETA, however, shows that even the provisional application of a mixed agreement is only a band-aid solution when deeper doubts and concerns hinder the ratification of a treaty. Indeed, if the ratification process of a mixed agreement fails at national level, the provisional application of an international agreement will end.[187] That is why, after a short period of reflection, the Commission proposed a new architecture for the future EU trade and investment agreements. A Commission's document leaked in August 2017 revealed that the Union would split the comprehensive economic agreements, at the time under negotiation, into two separate agreements.[188] On the one hand, it would act alone when negotiating FTAs governing matters of EU's exclusive competence, such as commitments to the liberalisation of trade in goods and services. On the other hand, IIAs containing investment protection rules and the investor-state dispute settlement mechanism would be concluded as mixed agreement.

Since the Council did not immediately endorse its approach, the Commission in the Communication of 13 September 2017 explained that the recommendation to open negotiations for trade agreements with Australia and New Zealand did not include investment protection and ISDS rules, because 'the debate on the best architecture for EU trade agreements and investment

[183] Recital No 4, Council Decision (EU) 2017/38 (n 175); European Commission, Proposal for a Council Decision on the Provisional Application of CETA, COM (2016) 470.

[184] Council of the European Union, Statements to the Council minutes, 13463/1/16 REV 1, 14–15.

[185] Council of the European Union, Statements to the Council minutes (n 184) 14.

[186] *Commission v Council (US Air Transport Agreement)*, Case 28/12, EU:C:2015:282, para 44. Van der Loo and Wessel (n 174) 754; Suse and Wouters (n 182), 409; Van der Loo (n 80) 29–31.

[187] ibid, 29.

[188] Document circulated among EU ambassadors, see www.politico.eu/wp-content/uploads/2017/08/COM-proposal-splitting-trade-deals.pdf. See Kleimann and Kübek (above n 133) 32.

protection agreements must be completed and the Commission stands ready to discuss this further with the Council and the European Parliament'.[189] A few months later, the Commission announced the finalisation of the EPA with Japan – an EU-only agreement only covering matters of the EU's exclusive competence.[190]

In May 2018, the Council eventually espoused this new approach.[191] However, it also made clear that '[n]egotiating EU-only trade agreements should not lead to a loss of negotiation leverage for the EU to obtain ambitious standalone investment agreements [...] EU investment agreements, where deemed necessary, should in principle be negotiated in parallel to FTAs'.[192] With this warning, the Council sought to limit the loss in terms of the bargaining power of the Union, which constitutes, as noted above, one of the main reasons supporting the establishment of a comprehensive Union's competence over foreign investment.

This approach was adopted for the EU-Singapore and EU-Vietnam trade and investment agreements. The original comprehensive agreements were divided into an FTA and an investment protection agreement to speed up the ratification process.[193] The EUSFTA and the EUVIFTA feature respectively 16 and 17 chapters, containing rules on, inter alia, market access, trade remedies, government procurement, and sustainable development. After a swift ratification procedure, the FTAs entered into force respectively on 21 November 2019 and 1 August 2020. The EUVIPA and EUSIPA, on the other hand, contain provisions on investment promotion and protection and are still going through the Member States' ratification processes (see chapter five).

X. CONCLUSION

This chapter has recounted how foreign investment gradually gained more relevance both within the then EC/EU internal market and in the context of the EC/EU common commercial policy. The internal liberalisation of capital movements triggered the emergence of an incomplete and implicit external

[189] European Commission, 'A balanced and progressive trade policy to harness globalisation', COM (2017) 492 final, 7.

[190] European Commission, 'EU and Japan finalise Economic Partnership Agreement', Press release, 8 December 2017.

[191] Council of the European Union, Draft Council conclusions on the negotiation and conclusion of EU trade agreements – Adoption, 8622/18, para 3.

[192] ibid., para 4.

[193] European Commission, 'Commission presents EU-Vietnam trade and investment agreements for signature and conclusion', Press release, 17 October 2018; European Commission, 'Trade: European Commission proposes signature and conclusion of Japan and Singapore agreements', Press release, 18 April 2018.

competence of the then European Community over foreign investment. In the post-Maastricht Treaty period, the EC started to include pre-establishment commitments in a wide range of international agreements concluded with third states. But it also encouraged its Member States to enter post-establishment obligations with non-EC states, which joined the European Union a couple of years later.

At the same time, the Commission repeatedly pushed for amending the EC Treaty to include an express exclusive competence of the then Community over foreign investment, but with no success. It was not until the entry into force of the Treaty of Lisbon that foreign direct investment was introduced among the matters falling within the scope of the EU common commercial policy. It soon became clear, however, that the Lisbon Treaty amendment to the provision defining the scope of the EU common commercial policy did not confer on the Union a comprehensive and exclusive competence over foreign investment. In Opinion 2/15, the CJEU found that the 'new' Union's exclusive competence only encompassed foreign direct investment. Thus, it did not empower the Union to act alone when entering international obligations relating to foreign indirect investment or when establishing investor-state dispute settlement mechanisms.

It is with this account in mind that the twofold interaction of the EU with international investment law will be examined in the remainder of this book.

3

The Internal Dimension: The Relationship between EU Law and Intra-EU IIAs

LESS THAN TWO months after the Czech Republic joined the European Union,[1] a Dutch sugar producer operating in the Czech Republic initiated a case under an intra-EU IIA (the Czech Republic-Netherlands BIT).[2] This was the first of such cases, but soon many others followed.

The emergence of a series of intra-EU investment disputes brought to the fore the 'internal dimension' of the relationship between EU law and international investment law. In other words, this development raised the question of whether IIAs between EU Member States, ie, the intra-EU BITs and the Energy Charter Treaty (ECT), were compatible with EU law and vice versa.

When addressing these questions, one should bear in mind that the EU has a protean nature. As noted in chapter one, the Union is a *sui generis* entity that shares several features with municipal legal orders, but, at the same time, it ultimately rests upon an international treaty. As Professor Pellet aptly put it, international law, far from being alien to EU law, actually constitutes its fundamental underpinning.[3] It follows that, depending on the perspective one takes, the interaction between intra-EU IIAs and EU law may be regarded as that between two international treaties or as that between a constitutional legal order and an international treaty.

This chapter examines the internal dimension of the relationship between EU law and intra-EU IIAs from both perspectives. As a preliminary point, it starts by identifying the possible areas of conflict between EU law and intra-EU IIAs, and the instruments to deal with such potential conflicts. Bearing this in mind, it illustrates how EU institutions, namely the Commission and the

[1] On 1 May 2004, the Czech Republic, Cyprus, Estonia, Hungary, Latvia, Lithuania, Malta, Poland, Slovak Republic, and Slovenia joined the EU. In 2007, Romania and Bulgaria became EU members.

[2] *Eastern Sugar B.V. (Netherlands) v Czech Republic*, Partial Award (27 March 2007), SCC 088/2004.

[3] A Pellet, *Les fondements juridiques internationaux du droit communautaire* (Collected Courses of the Academy of European Law, 1997) 48: 'Il ne saurait faire de doute que, loin d'être étranger au droit communautaire, le droit international en est le fondement même'.

CJEU, dealt with these issues by adopting an 'EU law-centred approach'. This view will be contrasted with the 'international law-centred approach' taken by arbitral tribunals. After describing the irreducible cleavage between these two positions, it considers how EU Member States intervened in this debate. Finally, it discusses the shortcomings of the 'EU law-centred approach' and its possible implications on the external dimension of the EU law-international investment law relationship.

I. POSSIBLE AREAS OF TENSION BETWEEN EU LAW AND INTRA-EU IIAs

Intra-EU IIAs and the EU Treaties are both instruments promoting international economic integration. Yet, they pursue this common overall objective by adopting different approaches and using different instruments. On the one hand, the EU Treaties underlie a rather sophisticated model of economic integration, which balances market integration with other goals and interests.[4] On the other hand, IIAs are generally simpler instruments[5] whose primary purpose is to promote and protect foreign investments.

These fundamental differences may give rise to tensions between intra-EU IIAs and EU law.

A. Different Approaches to the Regulation of Cross-Border Investment

Intra-EU IIAs and EU law regulate cross-border capital flows in somewhat different manners. The former generally contain transfer clauses, under which investors have the right to repatriate to the state of origin profits and other sums relating to the investment. These clauses often provide for an unfettered or almost unfettered right to transfer.[6]

[4] EU internal market rules primarily focus on market access. See T Andersen and S Hindelang, 'The Day After: Alternatives to Intra-EU BITs' (2016) 17 *Journal of World Investment and Trade* 984, 993.

[5] It should be noted that more recent IIAs are generally longer and more complex instruments. See L Johnson and L Sachs, 'International Investment Agreements, 2011–2012: A Review of Trends and New Approaches' in A Bjorklund (ed), *Yearbook on International Investment Law and Policy* (Oxford University Press, 2014); L Johnson, L Sachs and J Coleman, 'International Investment Agreements, 2014: A Review of Trends and New Approaches' in A Bjorklund (ed), *Yearbook on International Investment Law and Policy* (Oxford University Press, 2016); UNCTAD, 'The changing landscape: new treaties and recent policy developments', IIA Issue Note, 2020.

[6] See, eg, Art 7 France-Slovenia BIT, Art 8 France-Slovak Republic, Art 7 Germany-Romania BIT, Art 6 Greece-Latvia BIT; *cf* Art 4 Romania-Poland BIT; Arts 9 and 11 Germany-Poland BIT. In recent IIAs, however, the right to transfer is subject to a variety of exceptions, including exceptions for the safeguard of balance of payments, the protection of the rights of creditors in the context of insolvency or bankruptcy proceedings and the application of criminal laws or of the laws governing the issuing and dealing of securities. See, eg, Art 11 Canada-Guinea BIT; Art 16 Japan-Ukraine BIT.

By contrast, under EU law, the free circulation of capital and payments between Member States is subject to more pervasive limitations. Under Article 65 TFEU, EU Member States have the power to limit circulation when it is necessary to ensure the application, inter alia, of tax laws, prudential supervision laws, and counter-terrorism measures.[7] Furthermore, the restrictions to the free movement of capital and payments, like those to the other fundamental freedoms, can be justified on the basis of 'mandatory requirements' of general interest,[8] namely unwritten exceptions which can be invoked to justify proportional and non-discriminatory domestic measures.[9]

Thus, a measure restricting cross-border capital flows between two Member States may be justified under EU law, while being plainly illegal under the applicable intra-EU IIA. In this respect, it is also worth recalling that the CJEU has ruled on the EU compatibility of transfer clauses included in IIAs between Member States and non-EU Members. In particular, it found that several BITs containing unconditional transfer clauses were inconsistent with the exceptions laid down in Articles 57, 59 and 60 of the EC Treaty (current Articles 64, 66 and 75 TFEU).[10]

B. Differences in the Content of Substantive Rules

Another source of tension lies in the fact that EU law and international investment law contain identically labelled legal concepts, which are not necessarily coextensive.

The principle of protection of legitimate expectations is a case in point. On the one hand, the CJEU's case law has traditionally considered the legitimate expectation doctrine as a general principle of EU law.[11] On the other hand,

[7] See S Hindelang, *The Free Movement of Capital and Foreign Direct Investment: The Scope of Protection in EU Law* (Oxford University Press, 2009) 214–236. M Kellerbauer, 'Article 75' in M Kellerbauer, M Klamert and J Tomkin (eds), *The EU Treaties and the Charter of Fundamental Rights: a Commentary* (Oxford University Press, 2019) 794–797; P Van Elsuwege, 'EU External Action after the Collapse of the Pillar Structure: In Search of a New Balance Between Delimitation and Consistency' (2010) 47 *Common Market Law Review* 987, 1012; C Eckes, 'EU Counter-Terrorist Sanctions against Individuals: Problems and Perils' (2012) 17 *European Foreign Affairs Review* 113, 120–122.

[8] *Commission v Portugal*, C-367/98, EU:C:2002:326, para 52. Hindelang (n 7) 255–266.

[9] C-367/98 (n 8) para 49.

[10] *Commission of the European Communities v Austria*, C-205/06, EU:C:2009:118, paras 35–37; *Commission of the European Communities v Finland*, C-118/07, EU:C:2009:715, paras 26–31; *Commission of the European Communities v Sweden*, Case C-249/06, EU:C:2009:119, para 38.

[11] This principle was first proclaimed in the *Lemmerz-Werke* judgment. See *Lemmerz-Werke GmbH v High Authority of the ECSC*, C-111/63, EU:C:1965:76. See also *SpA Eridania-Zuccherifici nazionali and SpA Società italiana per l'industria degli zuccheri v Minister of Agriculture and Forestry, Minister for Industry, Trade and Craft Trades, and SpA Zuccherifici Meridionali*, Case 230/78, EU:C:1979:216, para 22; *Dürbeck v Hauptzollamt Frankfurt a. M.*, Case 112/80, EU:C:1981:94, para 48. For an in-depth analysis of this concept see HCH Hofmann, GC Rowe and AH Turk, *Administrative Law and Policy of the European Union* (Oxford University Press, 2011) 178–190; P Craig, *EU Administrative Law* (Oxford University Press, 2012) 553–589.

arbitral case law has construed fair and equitable and expropriation clauses as including the protection of investors' legitimate expectations.[12] In sum, in both systems the legitimate expectations doctrine imposes on public authorities the duty to act in a coherent and reasonable fashion. However, divergences may arise when determining which acts generate such expectations, whether retroactive measures are admissible and so forth. After all, divergent views about these issues have also emerged within the international investment regime, with some tribunals requiring specific host state's commitments in order for legitimate expectations to arise and others considering general regulatory acts as a source of legitimate expectations.[13] It is worth noting that the interpretation of the legitimate expectations doctrine under EU law and its relationship with the homonymous concept under the ECT has been the subject of a recent request for a preliminary ruling by the Regional Administrative Tribunal of Latium (*Tribunale Amministrativo Regionale del Lazio*).[14] In particular, the referring Court asked the CJEU to assess whether the phasing out of financial support to photovoltaic energy producers[15] was consistent with the principle of protection of legitimate expectations under Article 17 CFREU and Article 10 ECT.[16]

[12] M Valenti, 'The Protection of General Interests of Host States in the Application of the Fair and Equitable Treatment Standards' in G Sacerdoti, P Acconci, M Valenti and A De Luca (eds), *General Interests of Host States in International Investment Law* (Cambridge University Press, 2014), 39–48; A De Luca, 'Indirect Expropriation and Regulatory Takings: What Role for the "Legitimate Expectations" of Foreign Investors?' in G Sacerdoti, P Acconci, M Valenti and A De Luca (eds), *General Interests of Host States in International Investment Law* (Cambridge University Press, 2014) 58–74; E Snodgrass, 'Protecting Investors' Legitimate Expectations: Recognising and Delimiting a General Principle' (2006) 21 *ICSID Review-Foreign Investment Law Journal* 1, 36; Y Nouvel, 'Les mesures équivalant à une expropriation dans la pratique récente des tribunaux arbitraux', (2002) 106 *Revue générale de droit international public* 79, 89; R Higgins, *The Taking of Property by the State: Recent Developments in International Law* (Collected Courses of the Hague Academy of International Law, 1982) 276–277.

[13] See, eg, *Masdar Solar & Wind Cooperatief U.A. v Spain*, Award (28 September 2018) ICSID Case No. ARB/14/1489-491; *Total S.A. v Argentina*, Decision on liability (27 December 2010), ICSID Case No. ARB/04/01, paras 119–123; *Gami Investments Inc. v Mexico*, Final award (15 November 2004), UNCITRAL, para 93; *Marvin Roy Feldman Karpa v Mexico*, Award (16 December 2002), ICSID Case No. ARB(AF)/99/1, para 128; *Noble Ventures Inc. v Romania*, Award (12 October 2005), ICSID Case No. ARB/01/11, para 182; *Bayindir Insaat Turizm Ticaret Ve Sanayi A.S. v Pakistan*, Award (27 August 2009), ICSID Case No. ARB/03/29, para 240; *Occidental Petroleum Corporation and Occidental Exploration and Production Company v Ecuador*, Award (1 July 2004), LCIA Case No. UN3467, para 191.

[14] *Federazione nazionale delle imprese elettrotecniche ed elettroniche (Anie) and Others v Ministero dello Sviluppo Economico, Gestore dei servizi energetici (GSE) SpA*, joined Cases C-798/19 and C-799/18, EU:C:2021:280.

[15] This measure was adopted to implement Directive 2009/28/EC of the European Parliament and of the Council of 23 April 2009 on the promotion of the use of energy from renewable sources and amending and subsequently repealing Directives 2001/77/EC and 2003/30/EC.

[16] The measure challenged was the Decree-Law 91/2014, adopted by the Italian Government and subsequently transposed into the Law 116/2014.

The Court, however, did not clarify whether the legitimate expectations doctrine under EU law and the ECT are coextensive, because it found that the ECT did not apply to that particular case.[17] It follows that the relationship between these two concepts remains unsettled.

C. Investment Protection Rules and EU Competition and State Aid Rules

A further possible source of tension lies in the interplay between intra-EU IIAs and EU competition rules. The enforcement of such rules[18] may have a negative impact on the economic value of businesses and thus may give rise to investment claims under the fair and equitable treatment clause or the expropriation clause.

Moreover, investment protection rules may also come into conflict with the EU state aid regime.[19] Typically, conflicts may arise when a Member State repeals and recovers a state aid measure, which is deemed illegal under Article 107 TFEU.[20]

Arbitral case law is fraught with examples of investment claims targeting host states' measures adopted to comply with EU state aid rules. For instance, the *Micula* case[21] originated from a measure repealing tax incentives. The majority of the tribunal held that this measure was inconsistent with the FET clause under the Romania-Sweden BIT, even though it aimed to adapt the law of the host state (Romania) to EU law requirements. This award opened a long and still ongoing judicial saga involving the Commission, the CJEU and several national courts (see section XIII).

Similarly, the *Electrabel*[22] case arose out of a measure adopted by Hungary to comply with a European Commission's state aid decision. More specifically, *Electrabel* contended that Hungary violated the ECT by terminating a power purchase agreement between the state-owned energy supply company and a foreign-owned power plant operator in which it held shares. In this case, however, the investor's claims were all dismissed.

[17] Joined Cases C-798/19 and C-799/18 (n 14) paras 69–70. Advocate General Saugmandsgaard, however, addressed this question by stating that Art 10 ECT 'is not intended [...] to give greater protection to investors opposing such a reform than is afforded by the guarantees already provided for by EU law, and more specifically by Articles 16 and 17 of the Charter'. See Opinion of Advocate General Saugmandsgaard Øe, in joined Cases C-798/19 and C-799/18, EU:C:2020:876, para 96.

[18] Under Regulation 1/2003, the European Commission and national competition authorities have the power to apply Arts 101 and 102 TFEU.

[19] T Eilmansberger, 'Bilateral Investment Treaties and EU Law' (2009) 46 *Common Market Law Review 383*, 414–415.

[20] Illegal state aid should be recovered pursuant to Art 108 TFEU. See also Council Regulation 2015/1589 of 13 July 2015 laying down detailed rules for the application of Art 108 of the Treaty on the Functioning of the European Union.

[21] *Ioan Micula, Viorel Micula, S.C. European Food S.A, S.C. Starmill S.R.L. and S.C. Multipack S.R.L. v Romania*, Final award (11 December 2013), ICSID Case No. ARB/05/20.

[22] *Electrabel S.A. v Hungary*, Award (25 November 2015), ICSID Case No. ARB/07/19. *AES Summit Generation Ldt.* See also *AES Summit Generation Ltd. and AES-Tisza Erömü Kft v Hungary*, Award (23 September 2010), ICSID Case No. ARB/07/22.

A further illustration of this tension may be found in the series of investment claims targeting EU Member States' measures repealing solar power support schemes. EU Member States discontinued them because of their excessive cost. However, these measures were also likely to be inconsistent with EU state aid rules.[23] Thus, Member States probably avoided EU infringement proceedings by revoking them.

D. Investment Protection and the EU's Climate Commitments

Intra-EU IIAs may also come into conflict with EU climate policy.[24]

For instance, intra-EU IIAs may not sit well with the EU's flagship initiative to fight climate change: the Emission Trading System (ETS).[25] The EU ETS is a cap-and-trade scheme that applies to the economic activities producing CO2 listed in Directive 2003/87/EC.[26] Under this scheme, a limited number of tradable emission allowances are issued for a specific validity period. The overall quantity of allowances progressively decreases to curb greenhouse gas emissions.[27] Seen from the perspective of international investment law, such a measure may be problematic in several respects. First, investors might claim that the ETS violates the non-discrimination principle under the fair and equitable treatment, because it does not apply to all businesses operating in the EU but only to those listed in the ETS Directive.[28]

[23] P Ortolani, 'Intra-EU Arbitral Awards vis-à-vis Article 107 TFEU: State Aid Law as a Limit to Compliance' (2015) 6 *Journal of International Dispute Settlement* 118, 126. See, eg, *Antaris Solar GmbH and Dr. Michael Göde v Czech Republic*, PCA Case No. 2014-01; *I.C.W. Europe Investments Limited v Czech Republic*, PCA Case No. 2014-22; *Blusun S.A., Jean-Pierre Lecorcier and Michael Stein v Italy*, ICSID Case No. ARB/14/3.

[24] The Union has been one of the trailblazers of climate legislation. A Jordan and T Rayner, 'The Evolution of Climate Policy in the European Union: An Historical Overview' in A Jordan, D Huitema, H van Asselt, T Rayner and F Berkhout (eds), *Climate Change Policy in the European Union* (Cambridge University Press, 2011) 53–68; S Bogojevic, 'Climate Change Law and Policy in the European Union' in KR Gray, R Tarasofsky and C Carlarne (eds), *The Oxford Handbook of International Climate Change Law* (Oxford University Press, 2016) 675–676.

[25] Directive 2003/87/EC of the European Parliament and of the Council of 13 October 2003 establishing a scheme for greenhouse gas emission allowance trading within the Community and amending Council Directive 96/61/EC. It should be noted that the Commission has recently put forward a proposal for the revision of the directive.

[26] See ibid.

[27] The ETS Directive has gone through three implementation phases, namely the first phase (2005–2007), the second phase (2008–2012) and the third phase (2013–2020). The revision of the ETS Directive aims to lay the ground for the fourth phase (2021–2030).

[28] It is worth recalling that a similar claim has been raised before the CJEU in the context of a preliminary reference procedure. *Société Arcelor Atlantique et Lorraine and others v Premier ministre, Ministre de l'écologie et du développement durable and Ministre de l'économie, des finances et de l'industrie* C-127/07, EU:C:2008:728. See J Viñuales, *Foreign Investment and the Environment in International Law* (Cambridge University Press, 2012) 261–262.

Second, emission allowances might qualify as protected investments.[29] Thus, investors might argue that host states' measures affecting the number, the validity or the value of such allowances amount to expropriation or a violation of the fair and equitable treatment clause.

More generally, it is likely that the emission reduction targets and the climate neutrality objective embedded in EU law may indirectly compound the tension between EU law and intra-EU IIAs.[30] To achieve these objectives, EU Member States may take measures, such as phasing out fossil fuel subsidies or refusing to authorise the construction of coal-fired power plants, which are potentially inconsistent with investment protection rules.

E. The Coexistence of Two Distinct Adjudicatory Bodies

A last cause of tension lies in the coexistence of two distinct adjudicatory bodies.[31] Intra-EU IIAs normally contain investor-state dispute settlement clauses,[32] which empower investors to start arbitral proceedings against the host state in case of alleged violation of the applicable IIA. In other words, an investor hailing from an EU Member State may sue another Member State (the host state) before an arbitral tribunal instead of going before its domestic courts.

The EU judicial system, on the other hand, is built around the CJEU, which is the ultimate guardian of the observance of EU law.[33] A corollary to this principle is that EU Member States cannot 'submit disputes concerning interpretation or application of the EU Treaties to any method of settlement other than those provided for therein'.[34] The EU Treaties provide the court with a wide array of instruments to carry out this duty. First, it has a preventive ex ante control power over the EU compatibility of 'envisaged' international agreements, namely international agreements not yet entered into force.[35] Second, it exercises an ex post control over the observance of EU law by Member States and EU institutions

[29] J Munro, *Emissions Trading Schemes Under International Economic Law* (Oxford University Press, 2018) 106–116.

[30] Reg 842/2018 of the European Parliament and of the Council of 30 May 2018 on binding annual greenhouse gas emission reductions by Member States from 2021 to 2030 contributing to climate action to meet commitments under the Paris Agreement and amending Regulation 525/2013; Reg 2021/1119 of the European Parliament and of the Council of 30 June 2021 establishing the framework for achieving climate neutrality and amending Regulations 401/2009 and 2018/1999 ('European climate law').

[31] T Fečak, *International Investment Agreements and EU Law* (Kluwer Law International, 2016) 372.

[32] See, eg, Art 9 BLEU-Latvia BIT; Art 6 BLEU-Romania BIT; Art 8 France-Latvia BIT; Art 11 Germany-Poland BIT.

[33] Art 19 TEU.

[34] Art 344 TFEU.

[35] Art 218 TFEU.

through the infringement procedure[36] and the action for annulment.[37] Last, the CJEU, upon request of Member States' courts, may issue preliminary rulings on the interpretation of EU law and the validity of acts of the Union.[38]

II. DEALING WITH THE TENSIONS BETWEEN EU LAW AND INTRA-EU IIAs: A MATTER OF PERSPECTIVE

The multiple areas of overlap and potential tension between EU law and intra-EU IIAs inevitably cast doubts about whether EU law and intra-EU IIAs can coexist. In other words, it is worth considering whether such areas of tension between the two systems translate into effective conflicts and how such possible conflicts should be resolved. As the reader may well imagine, there is no single and conclusive answer to these questions. The main reason being that, as noted in chapter one, the EU combines the characteristics of an international treaty with those of a constitutional legal order. Therefore, it is possible to construe the relationship between these two systems from two opposite perspectives.

A. Ensuring the Autonomy and the Primacy of EU Law: The 'EU Law-Centred' Approach

The first possible reading of the relationship between EU law and intra-EU IIAs is premised on the idea that the EU is not an ordinary international organisation, but a *sui generis* entity that resembles domestic legal systems in many respects. This assumption has one main implication: the possible tensions between EU law and intra-EU IIAs should be addressed by resorting to rules and principles laid down in the EU Treaties. At this point, however, a qualification needs to be made. The EU Treaties do not contain any provision directly governing their interaction with international agreements between EU Member States. They only feature a mechanism to deal with conflicts between EU law and international agreements between Member States and non-EU states.[39] Under Article 351 TFEU, the international agreements concluded before the Treaty of Rome of 1957 or, for non-founding states, before their accession to the Union and those concluded after these dates are subject to two different

[36] Art 258 TFEU.

[37] Art 263 TFEU.

[38] Art 267 TFEU.

[39] 'Article 307 [Article 351 TFEU] is the only article in the entire edifice of the EU relating to the status of treaties concluded by the EU's member states vis-à-vis EU law'. See J Klabbers, *Treaty Conflict and The European Union* (Cambridge University Press, 2009) 10. This provision constitutes a corollary to the general duty of cooperation under Art 4 TEU. See M Klamert, *The Principle of Loyalty in EU Law* (Oxford University Press, 2014) 16.

regimes. The former agreements remain unaffected by the provisions of the EU Treaties; while Member States are under the obligation to 'take all appropriate measures' to remove the incompatibilities with EU law from the latter agreements.[40] As this provision only applies to international agreements between EU Member States and non-EU states,[41] Member States inter se international agreements are subject to a different regime.[42] They are treated just as EU Member States' domestic laws: that is to say, if a conflict with EU law arises, the latter automatically prevails.[43] Key to assessing the EU compatibility of such agreements is the principle of autonomy of the EU legal order.[44] Like the principle of primacy, the principle of autonomy emerged in the context of the relationship between the EU legal order and domestic legal orders,[45] with the primary objective of ensuring the unity, the coherence and the proper functioning of the EU legal order.[46] This principle, however, soon acquired external relevance, namely, it became an instrument to keep in check the influence of international rules over the EU legal order.[47] The scope of this principle, which is essentially a judicial creation, has been repeatedly clarified and enlarged by the Court of Justice.

Opinion 1/76 is, to my knowledge, the first case where the Court applied the principle of (external) autonomy.[48] The Court relied on this principle when assessing whether the rules governing the decision-making procedure and the dispute settlement mechanism established by the draft agreement on a European laying-up fund for inland waterway vessels were consistent with EU law. Since then, the Court has shaped this principle to cover virtually all possible interactions between EU law and international agreements.[49]

[40] *The Queen v Secretary of State for Home Department, ex parte Evans Medical Ltd and Macfarlan Smith Ltd.*, C-324/93, EU:C:1995:84, para 32. *Commission of the European Communities v Portugal*, C-62/98, EU:C:2000:358, para 49.

[41] *Annunziata Matteucci v Communauté française de Belgique and Commissariat général aux relations internationales de la communauté française de Belgique*, Case 235/87, EU:C:1988:460, para 21.

[42] A Rosas, 'The Status in EU Law of International Agreements Concluded by EU Member States' (2011) 34 *Fordham International Law Journal* 1304, 1320.

[43] *Flaminio Costa v E.N.E.L.*, Case 6/64, EU:C:1964:66; *Internationale Handelsgesellschaft v Einfuhr- und Vorratstelle für Getreide und Futtermittel*, Case 11/70, EU:C:1970:114, para 3; *Amministrazione delle Finanze dello Stato v Simmenthal*, Case 106/77, EU:C:1978:49, paras 17–22.

[44] JW van Rossem, 'The Autonomy of EU Law: More is Less?' in R Wessel and S Blockmans (eds), *Between Autonomy and Dependence: The EU Legal Order Under the Influence of International Organisations* (Asser Press-Springer, 2013) 18; C Contartese, 'The Autonomy of the EU Legal Order in the ECJ's External Relations Case Law: From the "Essential" to the "Specific Characteristics" of the Union and Back Again' (2017) 54 *Common Market Law Review* 1627, 1632.

[45] The notion of the autonomy was already implicit in the seminal judgment in *Costa*, where the Court defined the EEC Treaty as an 'independent source of law'. See J Odermatt, *International Law and the European Union* (Cambridge University Press, 2021) 177.

[46] M Öberg, *The Boundaries of the EU Internal Market Law* (Cambridge University Press, 2020) 186; R Barents, *The Autonomy of Community Law* (Kluwer Law International, 2004) 171–172.

[47] Öberg (n 46) 261.

[48] Opinion 1/76, EU:C:1977:63.

[49] Contartese (n 44) 1629.

In Opinion 1/91,[50] the Court found that the dispute settlement mechanism established under the EEA draft agreement,[51] the EEA Court, was inconsistent with the principle of autonomy.

The first source of concern for the Court of Justice was that the EEA Court had the power to determine the meaning of the term 'Contracting party' under the EEA Agreement. In the Court of Justice's view, such power would allow the EEA Court to decide whether the provisions of the agreement apply to the Community, to the Community and the Member States or to the Member States alone.[52] Thus, the EEA Court could interfere with the division of competences between Member States and the Union under the EC Treaty.[53]

A further threat to the autonomy of the EU legal order stemmed from the fact the EEA Court could escape the Court of Justice's control when interpreting the EEA Agreement.[54] More specifically, the EEA Court was only under obligation to interpret the EEA Agreement in light of the rulings of the Court of Justice issued before the signature of the latter, but not in light of those issued after that date. In the Court of Justice's view, this was problematic because the provisions of the EEA Agreement were textually identical to those of the EC Treaty.[55] Therefore, the EEA Court could end up determining not only the interpretation of the EEA Agreement, but also that of the EC Treaty.[56]

Last, the Court of Justice found that the autonomy of the EU legal order was threatened by the fact that the courts of EEA Member States were under no obligation to comply with its preliminary rulings.[57]

The Court restated these findings in Opinion 1/92,[58] where it found that the amended EEA agreement addressed the concerns expressed in Opinion 1/91.

In Opinion 1/00,[59] the Court held that the Agreement establishing the European Common Aviation Area was consistent with EU law, because it did not affect the allocation of powers between the then Community and its Members States. Nor did it alter the essential character of the powers of the Community institutions.[60]

The Court then added a further tile to the autonomy mosaic in the *MOX Plant* case.[61] The Commission brought this case against Ireland, because the

[50] Opinion 1/91, EU:C:1991:490.

[51] This treaty sought to establish an economic area between, on the one hand, the European Community and its Member States and on the other hand, the members of the European Free Trade Area.

[52] Opinion 1/91 (n 50) para 34.

[53] ibid, para 35.

[54] ibid, para 44.

[55] ibid, paras 29–30.

[56] ibid, paras 46–47.

[57] ibid, para 61.

[58] Opinion 1/92, EU:C:1992:189.

[59] Opinion 1/00, EU:C:1992:189.

[60] ibid, paras 14–22.

[61] *Commission of the European Communities v Ireland*, C-459/03, EU:C:2006:345.

latter submitted a dispute with another Member State (the UK) to an arbitral tribunal established under the UNCLOS.[62] The Court's judgment in this case is particularly relevant because the Court construed the principle of autonomy together with Article 292 EC Treaty (currently Article 344 TFEU).[63] Indeed, in the Court of Justice's view, the violation of the obligation under Article 344 TFEU also implied a violation of the principle of autonomy, because Ireland 'presented those Community measures not only as relevant for the purpose of clarifying the meaning of the general provisions of the Convention in issue in the dispute but also as rules of international law to be applied by the Arbitral Tribunal'.[64] In other words, the Court held that allowing an international tribunal to interpret EU primary or secondary law[65] as 'ordinary' international law would undermine the autonomy of the EU legal order.

The principle of autonomy was also key to the reasoning of the Court in Opinion 1/09 concerning the compatibility of the draft agreement on the ECPC with the EU Treaties, which established a unified patent litigation system.[66] This case differed from the *MOX Plant* case in that it did not concern an inter-state dispute settlement mechanism but disputes between individuals and states. Nevertheless, the Court once again found that the ECPC could undermine the autonomy of the EU legal order for the following reasons. First, the draft agreement conferred on the ECPC the power 'to interpret and apply not only the provisions of that agreement but also the future regulation on the Community patent and other instruments of European Union law' and 'to determine a dispute pending before it in the light of the fundamental rights and general principles of European Union law, or even to examine the validity of an act of the European Union'.[67] Second, it established a preliminary reference procedure, which could hinder the functioning of the preliminary reference procedure provided for by the EU Treaties.[68]

In Opinion 2/13,[69] the CJEU also held that the Union's accession to the ECHR would jeopardise the autonomy of the EU legal order, for it would

[62] These included the Convention for the Protection of the Marine Environment of the North-East Atlantic (OSPAR Convention), the United Nations on the Law of the Sea (UNCLOS), and the Annex VII of the UNCLOS. See N Schrijver, 'Annotation to Case C-459/03, *Commission of the European Communities v. Ireland*, Judgment of the Court (Grand Chamber) of 30 May 2006' (2010) 47 *Common Market Law Review* 863, 863–866.

[63] See N Lavranos, 'The *MOX Plant* and *Ijzeren Rijn* Disputes: Which Court is the Supreme Arbiter?' (2006) 19 *Leiden Journal of International Law* 223, 234–235. See also for a critical reading of this passage of the decision, B De Witte, 'A Selfish Court? The Court of Justice and the Design of International Dispute Settlement Beyond the European Union' in M Cremona and A Thies (eds), *The European Court of Justice and External Relations Law* (Hart Publishing, 2014) 48.

[64] C-459/03 (n 61) paras 149–154.

[65] Contartese (n 44) 1639–1640.

[66] Opinion 1/09, EU:C:2011:123. See Draft Agreement on the European and Community Patents Court, 7928/09.

[67] ibid, para 78.

[68] ibid, paras 79–85.

[69] Opinion 2/13, EU:C:2014:2454.

subject EU institutions to the decisions of the European Court of Human Rights.[70] Moreover, in line with Opinion 1/09, the Court found that the advisory opinion procedure provided for by Protocol No. 16 to the ECHR would come into conflict with the preliminary reference procedure under Article 267 TFEU,[71] because both these mechanisms required the involvement of Member States' courts and tribunals.[72] The CJEU also found that the co-respondent mechanism, under which the ECtHR could invite a contracting party to act as co-respondent,[73] would also be problematic in terms of the autonomy of the EU legal order. In fact, by granting to the ECtHR the power to apportion the responsibility between Member States and the Union for a violation of the ECHR, this mechanism affected the division of powers laid down in the EU Treaties.[74]

In sum, the 'EU law-centred' approach views other international agreements as a potential threat, which should be assessed in light of the principle of autonomy of the EU legal order.[75] Moreover, it requires that conflicts between EU law and Member States inter se agreements should be invariably resolved in favour of EU law.

B. The 'International Law-Centred' Approach: The Role of the Vienna Convention on the Law of Treaties

The relationship between EU law and intra-EU IIAs might also be regarded through the lens of international law. Under the 'international law-centred' approach, the overlaps and the tensions between intra-EU IIAs and EU law are just a further manifestation of the phenomenon commonly referred to as fragmentation of international law,[76] namely the co-existence of a variety of

[70] ibid, paras 185–186. The CJEU here seemed to suggest that the principle of autonomy confers on the Court itself the final say on 'whether EU law, particularly the Charter of Fundamental Rights, applies and whether a particular case falls within the remit of the ECHR'. See A Łazowski and RA Wessel, 'When Caveats Turn into Locks: Opinion 2/13 on Accession of the European Union to the ECHR' (2015) 16 *German Law Journal* 179, 189.

[71] Opinion 2/13 (n 69) para 196.

[72] ibid. 'Why would a second European preliminary rulings system affect the autonomy and effectiveness of the EU one? Are preliminary rulings to be conceived of as some type of EU intellectual property, which may not be duplicated? Nor is it easy to see how this concern, even if it were justified, has anything to do with the Accession Agreement. Protocol 16 has been signed and will or will not enter into force, independently of EU accession to the Convention. If Member States' highest courts were to make use of the Protocol in a way which violates their EU law obligations, such a violation would be distinct from the EU's own accession. It could take place any way'. See P Eeckhout, 'Opinion 2/13 on EU Accession to the ECHR and Judicial Dialogue: Autonomy or Autarky' (2015) 38 *Fordham International Law Journal* 955, 971.

[73] Draft Agreement on the European and Community Patents Court (n 66) Art 3(5).

[74] Opinion, 2/13 (n 69) paras 224–231.

[75] For a critical reading of the CJEU's case law on autonomy see De Witte (n 63) 48.

[76] See Report of the Study Group of the International Law Commission, 13 April 2006, A/CN.4/L.682.

sub-systems of international law.[77] The fundamental assumption underlying this approach is that both EU Treaties and intra-EU IIAs are 'ordinary' treaties. Therefore, the potential conflicts between them should be avoided or resolved by using the VCLT's rules.

The most relevant conflict-avoidance instrument for our purposes is Article 31(3) VCLT.[78] Under such a provision, the interpreter shall construe a specific treaty rule by taking into account, together with the context, 'any subsequent agreement between the parties regarding the interpretation of the treaty or the application of its provisions' and 'any relevant rules of international law applicable in the relations between the parties'.[79] The former sentence refers to international agreements containing stipulations clarifying the provision of another treaty.[80] These agreements differ from those referred to in Article 31(2) VCLT, because they are not made 'in connection with' the treaty that they intend to clarify. They are indeed concluded after it.[81] The latter sentence covers in contrast all 'relevant' international norms, namely 'those touching on the same subject matter as the treaty provision or provisions being interpreted or which in any way affect that interpretation'.[82] This rule is thus an expression of the idea that all international treaties exist and operate as components of the international legal order.[83]

Avoiding treaty conflicts, however, is not always possible.[84] Therefore, when a potential conflict between two treaties cannot be reconciled by means of interpretation, one can resort to the conflict solution rules contained in the VCLT. The first conflict solution rule is Article 30(2) VCLT, under which '[w]hen a treaty specifies that it is subject to, or that it is not to be considered as incompatible with, an earlier or later treaty, the provisions of that other treaty prevail'. This provision clearly refers to the clauses often included in international treaties to govern the interplay with other international instruments. Intra-EU IIAs generally provide for 'non-derogation' or 'preservation' clauses.[85]

[77] See A Fischer-Lescano and G Teubner, 'Regime-Collisions: The Vain Search for Legal Unity in the Fragmentation of Global Law' (2004) 25 *Michigan Journal International Law* 999,1014–1017; I Bufffard, 'Une relecture de la théorie des sous-systèmes en droit international' in I Buffard, J Crawford, A Pellet and S Wittich (eds), *International Law Between Universalism and Fragmentation* (Brill, 2009) 19–23. The fragmentation of international law is arguably related to its expansion. See T Treves, *The Expansion of International Law* (Collected Courses of the Hague Academy of International Law, 2015).

[78] J Pauwelyn, *Conflict of Norms in Public International Law: How WTO Law Relates to Other Rules of International Law* (Cambridge University Press, 2003) 251.

[79] Art 31 (3) lett. a) and lett. c), VCLT.

[80] R Gardiner, *Treaty Interpretation* (Oxford University Press, 2015) 242–243.

[81] ibid.

[82] ibid, 300.

[83] C McLachlan, 'The Principle of Systemic Integration and Article 31(3)(c) of the Vienna Convention' (2005) 54 *International and Comparative Law Quarterly* 279, 280.

[84] Gardiner (n 80) 227, 299.

[85] For instance, Art 3 Netherlands-Romania BIT stipulates that: '[i]f the provisions of law of either Contracting Party or obligations under international agreements existing at present or established hereafter between the Contracting Parties in addition to the present Agreement contain a regulation,

These provisions have been generally interpreted as 'without prejudice' clauses,[86] namely clauses allowing another international treaty to derogate from the applicable IIA insofar as it affords a more favourable treatment to investors.[87]

It follows that 'non-derogation' clauses would in principle govern the relationship between EU law and intra-EU IIAs. Yet, these mechanisms might be difficult to apply in practice, because they require a comparison between the treatment afforded to investors under EU law and under the relevant IIA.[88] Thus, one might alternatively resort to Article 30(3) VCLT,[89] under which when the same states are parties to two subsequent treaties on the same subject matter that contain incompatible provisions, the provision laid down in the latter treaty prevails.[90]

A similar principle applies if a potential conflict is not circumscribed to specific treaty provisions but affects two treaties in their entirety.[91] Under Article 59 VCLT,[92] an international agreement may be terminated by means of a subsequent treaty provided that the following conditions are cumulatively met. First, the parties to the earlier treaty are the same as those to the later one. Second, both treaties govern the same subject-matter. Third, the text of the later treaty or other elements relevant to its interpretation – eg, the *travaux préparatoires* of the treaty[93] – show the intention of the parties to terminate the

whether general or specific, entitling investments by investors of the other Contracting Party to a treatment more favourable than is provided for by the present Agreement, such regulation shall to the extent that it is more favourable prevail over the present Agreement'. See also Art 7 Hungary-Poland BIT; Art 8 Austria-Croatia BIT; Art 9 BLEU-Croatia BIT; Art 16 ECT.

[86] *SGS Société Générale de Surveillance S.A. v Philippines*, Decision of the tribunal on objections to Jurisdiction (29 January 2004), ICSID Case No. ARB/02/6, para 114. A. Newcombe, L Paradell, *Law and Practice of Investment Treaties: Standards of Treatment* (Kluwer Law International, 2009) 478; W Ben Hamida, 'La clause relative au respect des engagements dans les traités d'investissement' in C Leben (ed), *Le contentieux arbitral transnational relative à l'investissement* (Anthemis, 2006) 96–98.

[87] ibid.

[88] Some authors have argued that IIAs ensure a greater degree of protection. R Happ and JA Bischoff, 'Role and Responsibility of the European Union under the Energy Charter Treaty' in G Coop (ed), *Energy Dispute Resolution: Investment Protection, Transit and the Energy Charter Treaty* (Juris Publishing, 2011) 162.

[89] It has been noted that the criterion embedded in Art 30(2) VCLT, takes precedence over that under Art 30(3) VCLT. G Eulalio Do Nascimento e Silva, *Le facteur temps et les traités*, (Collected Courses of the Hague Academy of International Law, 1977) 262.

[90] A Aust, *Modern Treaty Law* (Cambridge University Press, 2013) 293.

[91] Arts 30 and 59 VCLT underlie the *lex posterior derogat prior* principle. See Eulalio Do Nascimento e Silva (n 89) 243.

[92] T Giegerich, 'Article 59' in O Dörr and K Schmalenbach (eds), *Vienna Convention on the Law of Treaties – A Commentary* (Springer, 2012) 1019; F Dubuisson, 'Article 59' in O Corten and P Klein (eds), *The Vienna Convention on the Law of Treaties – A Commentary* (Oxford University Press, 2011) 1342; A Orakhelashvili, 'Article 30' in O Corten and P Klein (eds), *The Vienna Convention on the Law of Treaties – A Commentary* (Oxford University Press, 2011), 772.

[93] Giegerich (n 92) 1017.

earlier one.[94] Last, the provisions of the later treaty are inconsistent with the earlier one.

Moreover, antinomies between international treaties may also be solved by deploying the customary *lex specialis* principle, under which if two international treaty provisions apply to the same subject-matter, the more specific one should prevail over that connoted by a higher degree of generality.[95]

The application of such instruments, however, might be at times less than straightforward. For one thing, it may be difficult to distinguish between a 'treaty conflict' and 'an accumulation of norms', namely the situation where a rule can add rights or obligations that are compatible with pre-existing rights and obligations or confirm pre-existing rights and obligations.[96] This is primarily because the definition of 'treaty conflict' remains unclear. According to a restrictive view, a treaty conflict 'arises only where a party to the two treaties cannot simultaneously comply with its obligations under both treaties'.[97] Under a more extensive view, a conflict may not only materialise in a divergence between two obligations, but also in the contradiction between a permissive norm and an obligation.[98]

Furthermore, the definition of 'same subject-matter' also lends itself to several interpretations.[99] Therefore, in the absence of a pre-existing and commonly accepted taxonomy of subjects, the detection and the solution of a treaty conflict largely, albeit not exclusively, depends on how subject-matters are classified and how the concept of 'sameness' is construed.[100]

III. CLASH OF PARADIGMS: 'EU LAW-CENTRED' APPROACH vs 'INTERNATIONAL LAW-CENTRED' APPROACH IN PRACTICE

Having outlined the terms of the debate on the relationship between EU law and intra-EU IIAs, this chapter now turns to consider how this debate has

[94] ME Villiger, *Commentary on the 1969 Vienna Convention on the Law of Treaties* (Martinus Nijhoff, 2009) 726.

[95] ibid, 403.

[96] See Pauwelyn (n 78) 161. Germane to the concept of 'accumulation' is the principle of parallelism between treaties, according to which treaties should be presumed to be compatible with each other. See *Watkins Holdings S.à.r.l. and others v Spain*, Award (21 January 2020), ICSID Case No. ARB/15/44, paras 224–225; *Southern Bluefin Tuna case (Australia and New Zealand v Japan), Southern Bluefin Tuna case (Australia and New Zealand v Japan)*, Decision on jurisdiction and admissibility (4 August 2000), ITLOS, Rep. of International Awards XXIII, para 52; *Aegean Sea Continental Shelf (Greece v Turkey)*, Judgment (19 December 1978), ICJ Rep. 1978, para 91.

[97] W Jenks, 'The Conflict of Law-Making Treaties' (1953) 30 *British Yearbook of International Law*, 426. See also E Vranes, 'The Definition of 'Norm Conflict' in International Law and Legal Theory' (2006) 17 *European Journal of International Law* 395, 399–401.

[98] See also Pauwelyn (n 78) 176–179.

[99] Report of the Study Group of the International Law Commission (n 76) 62; C Borgen, 'Resolving Treaty Conflicts' (2005) 37 *George Washington International Law Review* 573, 580–581. *cf* B Conforti, 'Consistency Among Treaty Obligations' in E Cannizzaro (ed), *The Law of Treaties Beyond the Vienna Convention* (Oxford University Press, 2011) 188.

[100] Report of the Study Group of the International Law Commission (n 76) paras 17–18, 63.

played out in practice. These competing views have primarily confronted themselves in the context of intra-EU arbitral proceedings. The main ground of confrontation has been the relationship between intra-EU arbitral tribunals and the EU judicial system. In fact, this question typically arises at the jurisdictional phase of arbitral proceedings, namely when arbitral tribunals assess their own jurisdiction. This question (generally referred to as 'intra-EU jurisdictional objection') has become the epitome of the uneasy relationship between EU law and intra-EU IIAs. Additionally, divergent views have also emerged regarding the relationship between EU substantive law and investment protection rules.

The debate about these issues initially took place between the Commission and arbitral tribunals, which acted as standard-bearers respectively of the 'EU law-centred' and the 'international law-centred' approach. Of course, this does not mean that the Commission did not deploy arguments based on international law in its *amicus curiae* briefs or that arbitral tribunals did not refer to EU law in their awards. But it means that the bulk of their reasonings were respectively based on EU law and international law.

IV. THE 'EU LAW-CENTRED' APPROACH IN THE AMICUS CURIAE BRIEFS OF THE EUROPEAN COMMISSION IN THE PRE-*ACHMEA* ERA

The EU was not party to the disputes arising out of the alleged violation of intra-EU IIAs, because these disputes only involved investors and EU Member States. However, such disputes soon attracted the Commission's attention, which in a series of amicus curiae briefs clearly illustrated its position on the relationship between EU law and intra-EU IIAs.[101] Admittedly, these are not the only documents displaying the Commission's position on this issue,[102] but they are particularly relevant because they express the Commission's view outside the EU legal order.[103]

[101] Two clarifications are in order at this point. First, as *amici* briefs are not always publicly available, this section will also cite the relevant passages of arbitral decisions summarising the Commission's arguments. Second, arbitral tribunals often rejected the Commission's requests to intervene as *amicus* on procedural grounds. See, eg, *RREEF Infrastructure (G.P.) Limited and RREEF Pan-European Infrastructure Two Lux S.à r.l. v Spain*, Decision on jurisdiction (6 June 2016), ICSID Case No. ARB/13/30, para 20; *Eiser Infrastructure Limited and Energía Solar Luxembourg S.à r.l. v Spain*, Final award (4 May 2017), ICSID Case No. ARB/13/36, para 70.

[102] See 'Commission asks Member States to terminate their intra-EU bilateral investment treaties', Press release, 18 June 2015. For a specific analysis of the infringement procedure launched against Sweden see J Dahlquist, H Lenk and L Rönnelid, 'The infringement proceedings over intra-EU investment treaties – Aen analysis of the case against Sweden', Swedish Institute for European Policy Studies, European Policy Analysis No. 4 (2016).

[103] This issue remained unaddressed until 2006. R Yotova, 'The New EU Competence in Foreign Direct Investment and Intra-EU Investment Treaties: Does the Emperor Have New Clothes?' in F Baetens (ed), *Investment Law Within International Law – Integrationist Perspectives* (Cambridge University Press, 2013) 396.

A. The 'EU Law-Centred' Approach and the Intra-EU BITs

The Commission has generally considered the ISDS mechanisms contained in intra-EU BITs as a threat to the functioning of the EU judicial system. In its view, intra-EU investment arbitration cripples the functioning of the EU judicial system, because it encroaches upon the CJEU's competence to hear preliminary references under Article 267 TFEU and decide infringement proceedings under Article 263 TFEU.[104] As the Commission clearly stated in the observations filed with the *EURAM* tribunal,

> investor-State arbitration [...] is incompatible with the provisions of the European Union treaties. The arbitral tribunal is not a 'court or tribunal' of an EU Member State but a parallel dispute settlement mechanism entirely outside the institutional and judicial framework of the European Union. Such a mechanism deprives courts of the Member States of their powers in relation to the interpretation and application of EU rules imposing obligations on EU Member States, which are presumably relevant in the arbitral proceeding. Furthermore, arbitrators are not obliged either to respect EU law, and cannot refer to the Court of Justice where an issue relating to the interpretation or validity of EU rules is raised in their proceedings.[105]

The Commission also contended that investor-state arbitration was inconsistent with the principle of non-discrimination based on nationality under EU law, as not all EU investors could rely on the protection afforded by intra-EU BITs.[106] In this regard, the Commission added that this discrimination could not be redressed by granting access to investor-state arbitration to all EU investors.[107]

In addition, in the Commission's view, not only was investor-state arbitration inconsistent with EU law, but it was also unnecessary in the intra-EU context, as the EU judicial system already provides a variety of instruments for the protection of investors' rights and liberties.[108]

The Commission also held that intra-EU BITs were inconsistent with EU substantive law. In its view, they constituted an 'anomaly within the internal market' in view of their 'at least partial overlap' with EU internal market rules.[109] Starting from this assumption, it concluded that EU law prevails over intra-EU BITs as of the accession to the EU.[110] This means that the principle of primacy of EU law supersedes the *pacta sunt servanda* rule of customary international law.[111] Consequently, intra-EU BITs are treated as EU Member States'

[104] *Achmea B.V.v Slovak Republic*, Award on jurisdiction, arbitrability and suspension (26 October 2010), UNCITRAL, PCA Case No. 2008-13, para 178: European Commission, Observations – *European American Investment Bank AG (EURAM) v Slovak Republic*, UNCITRAL, 3.

[105] ibid, 5.

[106] *Achmea B.V. v Slovak Republic* (n 104) para 183; European Commission, Observations (n 104) 2.

[107] ibid.

[108] *Achmea B.V. v Slovak Republic* (n 104) paras 179, 186; European Commission, Observations (n 104) 3.

[109] *Achmea B.V. v Slovak Republic* (n 104) para 177; European Commission, Observations (n 104) 3.

[110] *Eastern Sugar B.V. v Czech Republic* (n 2) para 119.

[111] European Commission, Observations (n 104) 3.

domestic legislation. That is to say, they should be read in light of EU law;[112] and, in case of conflict with EU law, they become inapplicable.[113]

In sum, relying on the 'EU law-centred' approach, the Commission invariably concluded that the ISDS mechanisms and the substantive provisions contained in intra-EU BITs are inconsistent with EU law.[114]

B. The 'EU Law-Centred' Approach and the ECT

The Commission expressed similar views in several ECT-based arbitrations. However, in the ECT context, it did not argue for the termination of the ECT as a whole, but only for its 'non-applicability' to intra-EU cases.

Its main argument was that the intra-EU application of ISDS system under the ECT would inevitably result in the circumvention of EU internal market rules and the rules governing the EU judicial system.[115]

The Commission also argued for the 'non-applicability' of the rules on investor-State arbitration under Article 26 ECT to intra-EU cases by emphasising the similarities and the institutional links between EU law and the ECT.[116] Under this view, this provision should not apply to intra-EU cases because EU law provides for substantive and procedural guarantees equivalent to those contained in the ECT.[117] The relationship between these two systems should be thus construed as that between EU law and the ECHR.[118]

With respect to the ECT substantive rules, the Commission deployed similar arguments. In particular, it contended that the intra-EU application of the

[112] *Achmea B.V. v Slovak Republic* (n 104) para 180; *Ioan Micula, Viorel Micula, S.C. European Food S.A, S.C. Starmill S.R.L. and S.C. Multipack S.R.L. v Romania* (n 21) para 317.

[113] *Achmea B.V. v Slovak Republic* (n 104) para 180.

[114] See *Eastern Sugar B.V. v Czech Republic*, Partial Award (27 March 2007), SCC 088/2004, para 119; *European American Investment Bank AG (EURAM) v Slovak Republic*, Award on jurisdiction (22 October 2012), UNCITRAL, para 118.

[115] *Blusun S.A., Jean-Pierre Lecorcier and Michael Stein v Italy*, Award (27 December 2016) ICSID Case No. ARB/14/3, paras 206–208; 214–216.

[116] ibid. *Electrabel S.A. v Hungary* (n 22) paras 4–99–4.106; 5.12–5.14.

[117] ibid, para 5.13.

[118] This principle has been famously proclaimed in the ECtHR's judgment in the *Bosphorus* case. 'In the Court's view, State action taken in compliance with such legal obligations [i.e. under EU law] is justified as long as the relevant [international] organisation is considered to protect fundamental rights, as regards both the substantive guarantees offered and the mechanisms controlling their observance, in a manner which can be considered at least equivalent to that for which the Convention provides. *By 'equivalent' the Court means 'comparable'*; any requirement that the organisation's protection be 'identical' could run counter to the interest of international cooperation pursued [...] However, any such finding of equivalence could not be final and would be susceptible to review in the light of any relevant change in fundamental rights protection. If such equivalent protection is considered to be provided by the organisation, the presumption will be that a state has not departed from the requirements of the Convention when it does no more than implement legal obligations flowing from its membership of the organisation' (emphasis added). See *Bosphorus Hava Yolları Turizm ve Ticaret Anonim Sirketi v Ireland* (2006) 42 EHRR 1, paras 154–155. See also R Schütze and T Tridimas, *Oxford Principles of European Union Law: The European Union legal Order* (Oxford University Press, 2018) 405–406.

investment rules under the ECT was either inconsistent with EU law or unnecessary, as EU law afforded investors a level of protection equivalent to that of the ECT.[119]

To sum up, the Commission took the view that the ECT contains an implicit 'disconnection clause', namely a clause preventing the intra-EU application of this treaty.[120]

V. THE INTERNATIONAL INVESTMENT TRIBUNALS' VIEW ON THE RELATIONSHIP BETWEEN EU LAW AND INTRA-EU IIAs IN THE PRE-*ACHMEA* ERA

Diametrically opposed to the view of the Commission is the approach that has emerged in arbitral case law. Though with some oscillations and nuances, arbitral tribunals have consistently affirmed the compatibility between intra-EU IIAs and EU law.

A. The Relationship between the EU Judicial System and the ISDS Mechanisms Contained in Intra-EU BITs

Starting from the premise that EU Treaties and intra-EU IIAs are first and foremost international agreements, arbitral tribunals dealt with the potential conflicts between them by resorting to the 'international law-centred' approach.[121]

[119] *Electrabel S.A. v Hungary* (n 22) paras 4-99–4.106; *Blusun S.A., Jean-Pierre Lecorcier and Michael Stein v Italy* (n 115) paras 208; 214–216.

[120] Such clauses are commonplace in EU mixed international agreements, because they ensure the primacy of EU law in the relationship between Member States and the Union. Despite the Commission's attempt to introduce it during the negotiations of the ECT, the final text of the treaty does not contain a 'disconnection clause'. M Smrkolj, 'The use of the "disconnection clause" in international treaties: what does it tell us about the EC/EU as an actor in the sphere of public International law?', SSRN, 2008, 4–6; M Cremona, 'Disconnection Clauses in EU Law and Practice' in C Hillion and P Koutrakos (eds), *Mixed Agreements Revisited: The EU and its Member States in the World* (Hart Publishing, 2010) 164–170. See also *Vattenfall AB and others v Germany*, Decision on the *Achmea* issue (31 August 2018), ICSID Case No. ARB/12/12, para 205. See also GM Alvarez, 'Redefining the Relationship Between the Energy Charter Treaty and the Treaty of Functioning of the European Union: From a Normative Conflict to Policy Tension' (2018) 33 *ICSID Review-Foreign Investment Law Journal* 560, 562; T Roe and M Happold, *Settlement of Investment Disputes Under the Energy Charter Treaty* (Cambridge University Press, 2011) 91; A Reuter, 'Taking Investors' Rights Seriously: The *Achmea* and CETA Rulings of the European Court of Justice do not Bar Intra-EU Investment Arbitration' (2020) 80 *Zeitschrift für ausländisches öffentliches Recht und Völkerrecht* 379, 396–397; JR Basedow, 'The *Achmea* Judgment and the Applicability of the Energy Charter Treaty in Intra-EU Investment Arbitration' (2020) 23 *Journal of International Economic Law* 271, 287–290.

[121] A notable exception is the *Micula* case, where the tribunal held that the respondent was not bound by EU law at the time when the facts of the case occurred. See *Ioan Micula, Viorel Micula, S.C. European Food S.A, S.C. Starmill S.R.L. and S.C. Multipack S.R.L. v Romania* (n 21) paras 319, 328.

The first question addressed by arbitral tribunals was whether the accession to the EU entailed the termination of pre-existing intra-EU IIAs pursuant to Article 59 VCLT. In *Eastern Sugar*,[122] the tribunal took the view that EU law and the Czech Republic-Netherlands BIT did not cover the same subject matter, for they regulated different phases of the investment life cycle. EU law focuses on the pre-establishment phase,[123] while IIAs granted protection to foreign investment after the establishment in the host state's territory thanks to a combination of substantive and procedural guarantees that had no equivalent under EU law.[124] This finding had two main implications. First, it was not possible to establish a common intention of the parties to the EU Treaty to supersede the applicable BIT.[125] Second, EU law and the Netherlands-Czech Republic BIT could be regarded as two compatible and 'complementary things'.[126]

Moreover, in the arbitral tribunal's view, the compatibility between these two treaties could not be called into question by the principle of non-discrimination under EU law. In particular, it held that

> [i]f the BIT gives rights to the Netherlands and Dutch investors that it does not give other EU countries and investors, it will be for those other countries and investors to claim their equal rights. But the fact that these rights are unequal does not make them incompatible.[127]

Here the tribunal seems to suggest that, to ensure full compatibility with the principle of non-discrimination under EU law, the network of intra-EU BITs should be extended to all EU Member States.

The *Oostergetel* tribunal[128] also held that the Slovak Republic's accession to the EU did not result in the termination of the Netherlands-Slovak Republic BIT under Article 59 VCLT. Similar to the *Eastern Sugar* tribunal, it found that EU Treaties and the applicable BIT did not cover the same subject matter.[129] Notably, it held that 'it is at least questionable whether the substantive protection afforded to the foreign investor under the BIT is indeed comparable to the safeguards found under the EC Treaty'.[130] In addition, in its view, there was no clear evidence that the parties intended to terminate

[122] *Eastern Sugar B.V. v Czech Republic* (n 2).

[123] ibid, 159–163.

[124] *Eastern Sugar B.V. v Czech Republic* (n 2) paras 164–166. Contrary to the US, EU Member States generally did not include liberalisation commitments in their BITs. See P Strik, *Shaping the Single European Market in the Field of Foreign Direct Investment* (Hart Publishing, 2016) 140; G Sacerdoti, *Bilateral Treaties and Multilateral Instruments on Investment Protection* (Collected Courses of the Hague Academy, 1997) 328–331.

[125] *Eastern Sugar B.V. v Czech Republic* (n 2) para 167.

[126] ibid, paras 168–169.

[127] ibid, para 170.

[128] *Jan Oostergetel and Theodora Laurentius v Slovak Republic*, Decision on jurisdiction (30 April 2010), UNCITRAL.

[129] ibid, para 75.

[130] ibid, para 76.

the BIT. Nor was there a clear incompatibility between the latter and the EU Treaties.[131]

In a similar vein, the *Binder* tribunal[132] found that the

> Czech-German BIT is not superseded by EC law, as the BITs, despite the supremacy of EC law, do not come into conflict with EC law or are even addressed by EC law. Intra-EU investor-state arbitration is not inconsistent with the EC legal order. Investor-state arbitration is not addressed by EC law, and the EC legal order has not offered a substitute for investor-state arbitration.[133]

In *Achmea*,[134] the tribunal arrived at identical conclusions by thoroughly comparing the substantive and procedural provisions of the applicable BIT and EU law.[135] According to the tribunal, the provisions of the BIT complemented the EU legal framework applicable to cross-border investment within the EU.[136] Notably, it observed that the free transfer clause, the fair and equitable treatment, the full protection and security clause, and the expropriation clause had no equivalent under EU law.[137] Nor was there any mechanism comparable to the investor-state dispute settlement mechanism under EU law.[138]

Similarly, the *EURAM* tribunal[139] stated that EU law and the Austria-Slovak Republic BIT did not relate to the same subject matter as the former 'deals with the creation of an internal market', whilst the latter fosters 'international flows of investment by protecting the rights of the investors'.[140] The tribunal then went on to say that in any event there was no clear proof of the 'subjective' intention of the parties to terminate the BIT.[141] Nor was it possible to deny that EU law and the relevant BIT could be applied 'cumulatively'.[142]

Arbitral tribunals have also assessed the relationship between EU law and intra-EU BITs in light of Article 30 VCLT. In particular, they focused on whether ISDS clauses included in intra-EU BITs conflicted with EU law.

In the *Eastern Sugar* case,[143] the tribunal found that the requirements for applying Article 30 VCLT were not satisfied. In its view, the BIT applicable to that case was not inconsistent with EU law. Rather, it only provided an

[131] ibid, paras 80–87.

[132] *Rupert Joseph Binder v Czech Republic*, Award on jurisdiction (6 June 2007), UNCITRAL.

[133] ibid, paras 40–45.

[134] *Achmea B.V. v Slovak Republic* (n 104).

[135] ibid, para 244.

[136] ibid, paras 262–263.

[137] As the tribunal put it, 'EU law does not provide substantive rights for investors that extend as far as those provided by the BIT. There are rights that may be asserted under the BIT that are not secured by EU law.' ibid, paras 255–263.

[138] ibid, para 264.

[139] *European American Investment Bank AG (EURAM) v Slovak Republic* (n 114).

[140] ibid, paras 178.

[141] ibid, paras 187–201.

[142] ibid, paras 211–212.

[143] *Eastern Sugar B.V. v Czech Republic* (n 2).

additional possibility for investors to commence arbitral proceedings against the host state.[144]

Along the same lines, the *Achmea* tribunal observed that

> [t]here is no rule [...] of EU law that prohibits investor-State arbitration. Far from it: transnational arbitration is a commonplace throughout the EU, including arbitrations between legal persons and States; and the European Court of Justice has given several indications of how questions of EU law should be handled in the course of arbitrations, including important questions of public policy. It cannot be asserted that all arbitrations that involve any question of EU law are conducted in violation of EU law.[145]

This finding seems to rest upon a full equation between commercial and investment arbitration, which arguably downplays the differences between the two.[146]

Be that as it may, the tribunal also found that the incompatibility of ISDS clauses with EU law could not be inferred from the fact that the EU legal order ensured monetary compensation for damages resulting from Member States' violations of EU law. In the tribunal's view, this instrument was not a substitute for investment arbitration, because the latter precisely aims to 'provide the disputing parties, by their consent, with an alternative to proceedings in national courts'.[147] Moreover, it also found that the ISDS clause contained in the applicable BIT did not violate Article 344 TFEU, because the latter only covers inter-state disputes.[148]

Last, the tribunal held that the fact that EU law might be relevant at the merits stage did not undermine its jurisdiction over the dispute, because the latter should be determined only on the basis of the applicable BIT.[149]

In *EURAM*,[150] the tribunal assessed whether Article 344 TFEU and Article 12 TEU superseded the ISDS clause contained in the Austria-Slovak Republic BIT by virtue of Article 30 VCLT. In other words, the arbitral tribunal determined

[144] ibid, para 180.

[145] *Achmea B.V. v Slovak Republic* (n 104) para 274.

[146] A great deal of ink has been spilled on the nature of investor-state arbitration and on its evolution. See generally E De Brabandere, *Investment Treaty Arbitration as Public International Law Procedural Aspects and Implications* (Cambridge University Press, 2014); G van Harten, *Investment Treaty Arbitration and Public Law* (Cambridge University Press, 2008) 46–68; A Mills, 'The Public-Private Dualities of International Investment Law and Arbitration' in K Miles and C Brown (eds), *Evolution in Investment Treaty and Arbtiration* (Cambridge University Press, 2011) 102–104; P Mayer, 'Investissements internationaux – Contract claims et clauses juridictionnelles des traités relatifs à la protection des investissements' (2009) 71 *Journal du Droit International* 71–75.

[147] *Achmea B.V. v Slovak Republic* (n 106) para 275.

[148] ibid, para 276. The tribunal expressly referred to the CJEU's judgment in the *MOX Plant* case in its reasoning. See C-459/03 (n 62). C Söderlund, 'Intra-EU BIT Investment Protection and the EC Treaty' (2007) 24(5) *Journal of International Arbitration* 455, 459; M Burgstaller, 'European Law and Investment Treaties' (2009) 26 *Journal of International Arbitration* 181, 190–191.

[149] *Achmea B.V. v Slovak Republic* (n 104) paras 280–281.

[150] *European American Investment Bank AG (EURAM) v Slovak Republic* (n 114).

whether intra-EU arbitration violated the obligation not to submit disputes relating to EU law to extra-EU dispute settlement mechanisms and the principle of non-discrimination under EU law.

As for the former question, the tribunal noted that the fact that arbitral tribunals often interpreted and applied EU law did not per se constitute a violation of Article 344 TFEU. In fact, in its view, such a provision does not establish a CJEU's monopoly over the interpretation of EU law.[151] Extra-EU courts and arbitral tribunals can interpret EU law, even if they do not have the power to submit preliminary questions to the CJEU.[152]

The tribunal then went on to say that Article 344 TFEU did not cover investor-state dispute settlement mechanisms, but only inter-state ones[153] Otherwise this provision would also preclude intra-EU commercial arbitration, which is on the contrary allowed under EU law.[154] Once again, the availability of international commercial arbitration within the EU was used to support the compatibility of intra-EU investment arbitration with EU law.

Moreover, in the tribunal's view, this finding could not be called into question by Opinion 1/09 of the CJEU[155] on the compatibility of the ECPC with the EU Treaties (see section II). The reason being that arbitral tribunals, unlike the ECPC, did not have the power to determine the validity of European Union's acts and were subject to the CJEU's control at the enforcement stage.[156]

The tribunal also pointed out that, in the post-award phase, the CJEU might be called upon to answer preliminary questions that are relevant to deciding enforcement or set-aside proceedings. This is certainly true for awards recognised and enforced in accordance with the New York Convention of 1958.[157] Such an ex post control, however, does not seem possible vis-à-vis ICSID awards, which are automatically recognised and enforced[158] and are only subject to the review mechanism outlined in the ICSID Convention (see section VII).[159]

Turning to the non-discrimination issue, the tribunal found that 'EU law does not exclude the existence of bilateral treaties giving some advantages to the nationals of the States Parties, if these advantages are reciprocal.'[160] In reaching

[151] ibid, para 249.
[152] ibid, paras 250–251.
[153] ibid, para 255.
[154] ibid, para 256.
[155] Opinion 1/09 (n 66).
[156] *European American Investment Bank AG (EURAM) v Slovak Republic* (n 112) paras 264–265.
[157] Convention on the Recognition and Enforcement of Foreign Arbitral Awards.
[158] Art 54(1) ICSID Convention. Interestingly, the drafters of the ICSID Convention borrowed this idea from the Treaty establishing the European Economic Community. See C Schreuer, L Malintoppi, A Reinisch and A Sinclair, *The ICSID Convention: a Commentary* (Cambridge University Press, 2009) 1118–1120.
[159] See Arts 52 and 53 ICSID Convention. *cf* Art V Convention on the Recognition and Enforcement of Foreign Arbitral Awards (n 157).
[160] *European American Investment Bank AG (EURAM) v Slovak Republic* (n 114) para 274.

this finding, the tribunal relied on the CJEU's judgment in the *D.* case,[161] where the Court found that a bilateral tax treaty granting specific advantages to the nationals of the contracting states was not inconsistent with EU law.[162] In short, the tribunal held that just as the absence of harmonisation in the tax domain did not prevent EU Member States from concluding bilateral tax treaties,[163] so the absence of a multilateral investment agreement on intra-EU cross-border investment allowed them to enter into BITs.[164]

In sum, arbitral tribunals consistently denied that the ISDS system contained in intra-EU BITs is inconsistent with EU law.[165]

B. The Relationship between Investment Protection Rules under Intra-EU BITs and EU Substantive Law

Arbitral case law also often addressed the question of whether EU substantive rules conflicted with investment protection rules under the intra-EU BITs.

In a first string of cases, EU law was considered irrelevant for the resolution of the disputes. The *Eastern Sugar* tribunal discussed the relevance of the law of the host state and its relationship with international law.[166] However, it did not explicitly refer to EU law.[167] In *Achmea*, the tribunal held that EU law would not come into play in the decision of the dispute. In particular, it found that

> [n]either Party in the present case argued that any specific provision of EU law bore upon the case in a manner that would affect the decision or reasoning of the Tribunal under this particular BIT. Having considered the position, the Tribunal is satisfied that no such question of EU law arises, and that it may apply the terms of the Treaty without exceeding its jurisdiction and without misapplying the applicable law.[168]

By contrast, the *Micula* tribunal gave a more relevant role to EU law. In its view, EU law constituted the 'factual matrix of the case'.[169] More specifically, the tribunal held '[t]he overall context of EU accession in general and the

161 *D. v Inspecteur van de Belastingdienst/Particulieren/Ondernemingen buitenland te Heerlen*, C-376/03, EU:C:2005:424. See M Cortez Pimentel, 'Distortion of the Common Market? Analysis and Perspective of the MFN Clause Within EC Law' (2005) 34 *Intertax* 485, 490; IM de Groot, 'Member States Must Apply Most Favoured Nation Treatment Under EU Law' (2014) 42 *Intertax* 405, 414. *cf* KE Sørensen, 'The Most-Favoured Nation Principle in EU Law' (2007) 34 *Legal Issues of Economic Integration* 315, 327.

162 ibid, paras 60–63.

163 C-376/03 (n 161) paras 51–52.

164 *European American Investment Bank AG (EURAM) v Slovak Republic* (n 114), para 277.

165 C Binder, 'A Treaty Law Perspective on Intra-EU BITs' (2016) 17 *Journal of World Investment and Trade* 964, 967–973.

166 *Eastern Sugar B.V. v Czech Republic* (n 2) paras 191–197.

167 ibid.

168 *Achmea B.V. v Slovak Republic* (n 104) para 275.

169 *Ioan Micula, Viorel Micula, S.C. European Food S.A, S.C. Starmill S.R.L. and S.C. Multipack S.R.L. v Romania* (n 21) para 328.

pertinent provisions of EU law in particular may be relevant to the determination of whether, *inter alia*, Romania's actions were reasonable in light of all the circumstances, or whether Claimants' expectations were legitimate'.[170]

C. The Relationship between the EU Judicial System and the ISDS Mechanism Contained in the ECT

Despite the differences between intra-EU BITs and the ECT, arbitral tribunals also consistently took side in favour of the intra-EU application of the ECT.

In *Charanne*,[171] the tribunal rejected the contention that Article 344 TFEU precluded investor-state arbitration under Article 26 ECT.[172] Moreover, the tribunal found that the contracting parties did not agree to derogate from the ECT in their inter se relations.[173] Nor could the existence of an implicit disconnection clause be inferred from the fact that the EU is a customs union.[174] Quite the contrary, the absence of an express disconnection clause proved, if anything, that there were no inconsistencies between the ECT and EU law.[175]

The *RREEF* tribunal[176] followed a rather similar line of reasoning. It first rejected the view that Article 344 TFEU established an 'interpretative monopoly' of the CJEU over EU law, which precluded intra-EU investment arbitration under the ECT.[177] It then found that the 'implicit disconnection clause' argument was inconsistent with the *pacta sunt servanda* principle, which requires the parties to a treaty that 'wish to exclude the application of that treaty in certain respect or circumstance' to make a reservation or include an unequivocal disconnection clause in the treaty itself.[178] Finally, like the *Charanne* tribunal, it held that the lack of a disconnection clause in the text of ECT indicated that the ECT was compatible with EU law.[179]

Similarly, the *Blusun* tribunal[180] noted that the ECT does not contain an explicit disconnection clause.[181] Nor can the existence of such a clause be implicitly deduced from the text of the ECT. In particular, the fact that both the Union and its Member States are parties to the ECT does not prevent the application of the ECT rules on foreign investment at the intra-EU level. Indeed,

[170] ibid.

[171] *Charanne and Construction Investments v Spain*, Award (21 January 2016), SCC 062/2012.

[172] ibid, para 434.

[173] ibid, para 435.

[174] ibid, para 437.

[175] ibid, para 438.

[176] *RREEF Infrastructure (G.P.) Limited and RREEF Pan-European Infrastructure Two Lux S.à.r.l. v Spain* (n 101).

[177] ibid, para 80.

[178] ibid, para 85.

[179] ibid, para 86.

[180] *Blusun S.A., Jean-Pierre Lecorcier and Michael Stein v Italy* (n 115).

[181] ibid, para 280.

in the tribunal's view, the EU did not fall within the definition of 'Regional Economic International Organisation' (REIO) under Article 1(3) ECT,[182] because EU Member States retained their own competence in the field of investment and investment dispute resolution.[183] Moreover, according to the tribunal, if Member States had wished to prevent the inter se application of the ECT, they would have appended to the ECT a 'declaration of competence' to clarify that the competence over all matters covered by the ECT lay with the Union.[184]

Similarly, the *Eiser* tribunal[185] found that the ordinary meaning of Article 26 ECT does not preclude the tribunal's jurisdiction over disputes between an investor hailing from a EU Member State and another Member State.[186] Moreover, neither the object nor the context of the ECT support the view that the ECT contains an implicit disconnection clause.[187] Finally, in line with the conclusions reached by the *Blusun* tribunal, it found that the EU does not constitute a REIO under Article 1(3) ECT.[188]

D. The Relationship between the EU Substantive Law and the Investment Protection Rules under the ECT

Arbitral tribunals also addressed the overlap and the potential tension between EU substantive law and the investment rules under the ECT.[189]

The *Electrabel* tribunal devoted a rather lengthy section of its decision to explaining its view on the relation between these two sets of rules. The starting point of its reasoning was that EU law is first and foremost part of the international legal order, as it is ultimately based on an international treaty.[190] As a commentator put it, the tribunal quoted the famous *Van gend en Loos* formula ('The Community constitutes a new legal order of international law')[191] only to emphasise the second part of that sentence ('legal order of international law').[192] In taking this view, the tribunal thus included EU law among the 'applicable rules and principles of international law', which, along with the ECT, constitute the law applicable by ECT tribunals pursuant to Article 26(6) ECT.[193]

[182] ibid, para 281.
[183] ibid.
[184] ibid, para 282.
[185] *Eiser Infrastructure Limited and Energía Solar Luxembourg S.à.r.l. v of Spain* (n 101).
[186] ibid, paras 179–182.
[187] ibid, paras 185–207.
[188] ibid, para 190.
[189] Some tribunals paid little or no heed to this question. See, eg, *AES Summit Generation Limited and AES-Tisza Erömü Kft v Hungary* (n 22); *Eiser Infrastructure Limited and Energía Solar Luxembourg S.à.r.l. v Spain* (n 101); *Charanne and Construction Investments v Spain* (n 171).
[190] *Electrabel S.A. v Hungary* (n 22) paras 4.119–4.123.
[191] *NV Algemene Transport en Expeditie Onderneming van Gend & Loos v Netherlands*, Case 26-62, EU:C:1963:1.
[192] A Kulick, 'Case Comment – *Electrabel S.A. v Hungary*' (2014) 15 *Journal of World Investment and Trade* 273, 276.
[193] *Electrabel S.A. v Hungary* (n 22) para 4.112.

Having clarified that EU law qualifies as public international law,[194] the tribunal then noted that several reasons militated in favour of a harmonious interpretation of the ECT and EU law.[195] First, given the crucial role played by the EU in the genesis of the ECT, it was reasonable to presume that the investment protection rules under the ECT are consistent with EU law.[196] Second, the two sets of rules share the same pro-competitive and pro-market objectives.[197] Third, the ECT implicitly recognises that the Commission's decisions are legally binding on all EU Member States.[198] The tribunal thus concluded that the investment rules under the ECT are generally consistent with EU law[199] and that, in the unlikely case of conflict between such sets of rules, EU law should prevail.[200]

Similarly, the *RREEF* tribunal also held that the ECT and EU law should be interpreted harmoniously.[201] Yet, contrary to the view of the *Electrabel* tribunal, it found that, in case of conflict between an ECT provision and an EU provision, the former should supersede the latter.[202]

In conclusion, arbitral tribunals generally stated that investment protection rules under the ECT are consistent with EU law.

VI. THE CJEU AND THE 'EU LAW-CENTRED' APPROACH: THE *ACHMEA* JUDGMENT

After more than a decade of debate about the relationship between the EU law and intra-EU IIAs, the long-awaited intervention of the CJEU arrived with a preliminary ruling requested by the German Federal Court of Justice (*Bundesgerichtshof*). The preliminary questions were raised in the context of an enforcement judgment concerning the abovementioned *Achmea* award, an arbitral decision rendered on the basis of the Netherlands-Slovak Republic BIT.[203] In particular, the Court was asked to establish whether the arbitration clause contained in that BIT was consistent with the obligation under Article 344 TFEU, the preliminary reference mechanism under Article 267 TFEU, and the prohibition against discrimination based on nationality under Article 18 TFEU. These questions thus exclusively concerned the compatibility

[194] ibid, paras 4.124–4.125.
[195] ibid, para 4.133.
[196] ibid, paras 4.134–4.136.
[197] ibid, paras 4.137–4.141.
[198] ibid, para 4.142.
[199] ibid, paras 4.143–4.172.
[200] ibid, para 4.191.
[201] *RREEF Infrastructure (G.P.) Limited and RREEF Pan-European Infrastructure Two Lux S.à r.l. v Spain* (n 101) para 76.
[202] ibid, para 75.
[203] *Slovak Republic v Achmea*, C-284/16, EU:C:2018:158.

of the investor-state dispute settlement mechanism with EU law. No question about the compatibility of investment protection rules with EU law was raised.

The Court only addressed the first two questions based on a plain 'EU law-centred' approach. Indeed, in its view, such preliminary questions entailed the assessment of the ISDS system in light of the principle of autonomy of the EU legal order.[204] Therefore, after recapitulating its case law on the principle of autonomy, most notably Opinion 1/09 and Opinion 2/13, the Court framed a three-pronged test to carry out such an assessment.[205]

A. Arbitral Tribunals and the Interpretation of EU Law

The first step of the Court's reasoning was to determine whether the arbitral tribunals established under the Netherlands-Slovak Republic BIT could interfere with the functioning of the EU judicial system. The key question here was whether such tribunals have the power to interpret and apply EU law.[206] In applying this prong of the test, the Court did not limit itself to analysing the treaty provision delimiting the jurisdiction of the tribunals established under the Slovak Republic-Netherlands BIT.[207] However, it read such provision jointly with the clause governing the law applicable to investment disputes, under which

> [t]he arbitral tribunal shall decide on the basis of the law, taking into account in particular though not exclusively: the law in force of the Contracting Party concerned; the provisions of this Agreement, and other relevant Agreements between the Contracting parties; the provisions of special agreements relating to the investment; the general principles of international law.[208]

This provision, in the Court's view, was problematic in terms of the principle of autonomy of the EU legal order, because it empowered arbitral tribunals to interpret and apply EU law. Due to its dual nature of domestic and international law, the latter qualified as 'law in force of the Contracting Party concerned'.[209] This is the main fault line between the CJEU and the *Achmea* tribunal (and, ultimately, between the 'EU law-centred' approach and the 'international law-centred' approach). The former considers the prospect that arbitral tribunals would interpret EU law as a threat to the autonomy of the EU legal order.[210]

[204] ibid, para 32.
[205] ibid.
[206] ibid, para 40.
[207] Art 8 Netherlands-Slovak Republic BIT reads as follows: '[a]ll disputes between one Contracting Party and an investor of the other Contracting Party concerning an investment of the latter shall if possible, be settled amicably.'
[208] ibid. C-284/16 (n 203) para 43.
[209] ibid, para 41.
[210] C Contartese and M Andenas, 'EU Autonomy and Investor-State Dispute Settlement Under *Inter Se* Agreements Between EU Member States: *Achmea*' (2019) 56 *Common Market Law Review* 157, 170.

By contrast, the latter emphasises that the jurisdiction of the arbitral tribunals established under the BIT in question only encompasses investment disputes.[211]

The Court's position has undoubtedly the merit of clarity, but it arguably lacks some subtlety. Indeed, in stark contrast to its Advocate General,[212] the Court seems to conflate two different things: taking into account EU law and assessing whether a given host state's measure is consistent with EU law. In so doing, it clearly went beyond its findings in Opinion 1/09, where, as noted above (see section II), it held that autonomy of the EU legal order was threatened by the ECPC's power to 'determine a dispute pending before it in the light of the fundamental rights and general principles of European Union law, or even to examine the validity of an act of the European Union'.[213]

In taking this view, the Court de facto enlarged the scope of the jurisdiction of the arbitral tribunals established under the Slovak Republic-Netherlands BIT.[214] In this respect, it is worth recalling that Article 8(1) circumscribes the jurisdiction of such tribunals to disputes 'concerning an investment',[215] while Article 8(6) of the BIT stipulates that the law of the contracting parties shall be 'taken into account'. Thus, neither the wording of Article 8(1) nor that of Article 8(6) of the BIT seems to support the idea that the arbitral tribunals established thereunder have the power to adjudicate EU law disputes.

It should also be noted that international courts and tribunals often 'take into account' municipal law.[216] As a matter of fact, they have often considered the law of the contracting parties as an element of the factual context of the case.[217] In other words, the law of the contracting parties acts as a 'buffer' or a 'hybrid between international law and facts' that makes 'the connection between facts and international law more understandable and constructive in investment arbitration'.[218] Suffice it to recall that domestic law comes into play with respect to the interpretation of key investment protection rules such as the fair and equitable treatment standard and the expropriation clause. For instance, domestic law acts as a contributory but not determinative element when assessing whether the host state violated the fair and equitable treatment

[211] *Achmea B.V. v Slovak Republic* (n 104) para 290.

[212] Advocate General Wathelet opined that 'the fact that EU law is part of the law applicable to disputes between investors and States in accordance with Article 8(6) of the BIT does not mean that those disputes concern the interpretation and application of the EU and FEU Treaties, for two reasons: in the first place, the jurisdiction of the arbitral tribunal is .confined to ruling on breaches of the BIT and, in the second place, the scope of that BIT and the legal rules which it introduces are not the same as those of the EU and FEU Treaties'. Opinion of Advocate General Wathelet in C-284/16, EU:C:2017:699, para 173; see also Contartese and Andenas (n 210) 169–170.

[213] Opinion 1/09 (n 66) para 78.

[214] Y Nouvel, 'Affaire *Achmea* – Commentaire' (2018) *Journal du Droit International* 23.

[215] Art 8 Netherlands-Slovak Republic BIT.

[216] Nouvel (n 214) 24.

[217] *Certain German Interests in Polish Upper Silesia (Germany v Poland)* [1926] PCIJ Rep Series A No. 7, 19, para 52; *Compañiá de Aguas del Aconquija S.A. and Vivendi Universal S.A. v Argentina*, Decision on annulment (3 July 2002), ICSID Case No. ARB/97/3, para 101.

[218] H Diaz-Candia, 'The Role of Municipal Laws in Investment Arbitration' in A Bjorklund (ed), *Yearbook on International Investment Law and Policy* (Oxford University Press, 2014) 531.

clause.[219] That is to say, it is one among the many elements to be taken into account in the interpretation and application of this investment protection rule. Similarly, in the context of the interpretation of the expropriation clause, domestic law is relevant to assess whether the host state may avail itself of the police powers defence or whether it fulfilled the due process requirement.[220]

Finally, the Court's approach also seems to disregard the fact that arbitral tribunals do not have the power to impose their own interpretation of EU law on EU institutions as they can only award damages in case of violation of the applicable BIT.[221]

B. Ex Ante Control Over the EU Consistency of Arbitral Awards

If 'taking into account' EU law constitutes a potential threat to the autonomy of the EU legal order,[222] then the only way to tame this threat is to bring arbitral tribunals under the control of the CJEU.[223] Therefore, the Court went on to assess whether arbitral tribunals are entitled to submit requests for preliminary rulings to the Court.[224] In other words, the Court sought to establish whether the *Achmea* tribunal qualified as a 'Court or tribunal' under Article 267 TFEU. As correctly pointed out by Advocate General Wathelet,[225] the CJEU has traditionally construed Article 267 TFEU as implying the following requirements:

(i) the referring court or tribunal must be established by the law, either primary or subordinate legislation;[226]
(ii) it must be independent, ie, it must be free from external influences and exercises its function in an impartial manner;[227]
(iii) it must have compulsory jurisdiction;[228]

[219] J Hepburn, *Domestic Law in International Investment Arbitration* (Oxford University Press, 2017) 34–40.
[220] ibid, 42–47.
[221] JH Pohl, 'Intra-EU Investment Arbitration after the *Achmea* Case: Legal Autonomy Bounded by Mutual Trust?' (2018) 14 *European Constitutional Law Review* 767, 778.
[222] V Korom, 'Jurisprudence *Achmea*: la fin de l'arbitrage d'investissement au sein de l'Union européenne?' (2018) 36 *Recueil Dalloz* 2005, 2007; Nouvel (n 214) 12. E Gaillard, 'The Myth of Harmony in International Arbitration' (2019) 34 *ICSID-Review-Foreign Investment Law Journal* 553, 556; P Koutrakos, 'The Autonomy of EU Law and International Investment Arbitration' (2020) 88 *Nordic Journal of International Law* 41, 50.
[223] De Witte (n 63) 51.
[224] C-284/16 (n 203) para 43.
[225] Opinion of Advocate General Wathelet, C-284/16, *Slovak Republic v Achmea BV* (n 212) paras 84–131.
[226] M Broberg and N Fenger, *Broberg and Fenger on Preliminary References to the European Court of Justice* (Oxford University Press, 2021) 44.
[227] ibid, 45–46.
[228] ibid, 49.

(iv) it must use an adversary procedure ('a procedure *inter partes*') and issue decisions based on the application of rules of law, namely not *ex bono et aequo* decisions;
(v) it must have a permanent nature.[229]

However, in the *Achmea* judgment, the Court only focused on the establishment by law requirement. Relying on the authority of the judgment in the case *Tribunal Arbitral Tributário*,[230] it found that such arbitral tribunals were extraneous to the EU judicial system, because they were not established by the laws of the Netherlands and the Slovak Republic.[231] In fact, they constituted an exception to the jurisdiction of the courts of such Member States. The Court thus did not buy into the Advocate General Wathelet's argument that investment tribunals' ultimate legal underpinning lies in the Slovak and Dutch legal orders, because a Slovak and a Dutch law authorised the ratification of the BIT.[232] Nor did it uphold the view that arbitral tribunals under the Netherlands-Slovak Republic BIT could be likened to the Benelux Court and were therefore an integral part of the EU judicial system.[233] In particular, the Court noted that

> [w]hereas the Benelux Court has the task of ensuring that the legal rules common to the three Benelux States are applied uniformly, and the procedure before it is a step in the proceedings before the national courts leading to definitive interpretations of common Benelux legal rules, the arbitral tribunal at issue in the main proceedings does not have any such links with the judicial systems of the Member States.[234]

Here the Court rightly emphasised the strong ties between the Benelux Court and the legal orders of Belgium, Luxembourg and the Netherlands, whose special status is expressly acknowledged by Article 350 TFEU.[235]

In light of the above, it thus concluded that the *Achmea* tribunal did not qualify as a 'court or tribunal' under Article 267 TFEU.[236]

C. Ex Post Control Over the EU Consistency of Arbitral Awards

Having found that arbitral tribunals do not have the power to submit preliminary questions, the Court turned to consider whether the autonomy of the EU legal order could be preserved ex post, namely at the enforcement stage. As noted above (see section V), at least for awards enforced in accordance with the

[229] ibid, 45.
[230] *Ascendi Beiras Litoral e Alta, Auto Estradas das Beiras Litoral e Alta* v *Autoridade Tributária e Aduaneira*, C-377/13, EU:C:2014:1754.
[231] C-284/16 (n 203) paras 44–45; Contartese and Andenas (n 210) 171.
[232] Opinion of Advocate General Wathelet in C-284/16 (n 212) para 96. See also A Briguglio, '*Achmea* and the Day After *Achmea*' (2018) *Rivista dell'Arbitrato* 504, 512.
[233] Opinion of Advocate General Wathelet in C-284/16 (n 212) paras 127–129.
[234] C-284/16 (n 203) para 48.
[235] Contartese and Andenas (n 210) 176.
[236] C-284/16 (n 203) para 45.

New York Convention of 1958, Member States' domestic courts may request the CJEU's intervention by triggering a preliminary reference procedure in the context of enforcement proceedings.

This solution, at least in principle, might be capable of protecting the autonomy of the EU legal order without sacrificing its 'openness'. However, the Court did not find it satisfactory, because it might allow arbitral awards to escape domestic courts' scrutiny.[237] In particular, the Court was concerned that the intensity of review would vary according to the place of arbitration,[238] which the disputing parties can freely choose.[239] In taking this view, the Court distanced itself from the approach adopted with respect to commercial arbitration.[240] It is indeed a well-established principle of the CJEU's case law that domestic courts exercise a narrow review of awards issued by international commercial tribunals.[241] This 'minimalist approach',[242] which is also common to many other courts around the world, evidences a fundamental trust in international arbitration and assumes that the advantages of arbitration exceed the possible threats posed by the latter to the EU legal order.[243] The Court, however, despite its similarities with commercial arbitration, did not apply this minimalist approach to investment arbitration.[244] It highlighted that investment arbitration differs from commercial arbitration in that it is not based on a 'freely expressed' consent, but rather, it is premised on 'a treaty by which Member States agree to remove from the jurisdiction of their own courts'.[245] The Court was thus particularly worried about how investment arbitral tribunals remove disputes from the jurisdiction of national courts.[246] Commercial arbitration is ultimately the expression of two private parties' freedom of contract, while investment arbitration rests upon an international treaty concluded between two Member States. In the Court's view, the fact that two Member States bestow on a virtually unlimited number of private parties[247] the power to sue them before undermined the mutual trust

[237] ibid, paras 52–53.

[238] ibid.

[239] B Hess, 'The fate of investment dispute resolution after the *Achmea* decision of the European Court of Justice', MPILux Research Paper 2018, 11. In this regard, it has been noted that the *lex loci arbitri* in the context of enforcement proceedings, such as that initiated before the German courts in *Achmea*, is not as relevant as in set-aside proceedings. See Pohl (n 221) 784.

[240] C-284/16 (n 203) para 54.

[241] *Eco Swiss China Time Ltd v Benetton International NV*, C-126/97, EU:C:1999:269, paras 35, 36, 40; *Elisa María Mostaza Claro v Centro Móvil Milenium SL*, C-168/05, EU:C:2006:675, paras 34–39.

[242] LG Radicati di Brozolo, 'Controllo del lodo internazionale e ordine pubblico' (2006) *Rivista dell'arbitrato* 629, 635.

[243] ibid.

[244] Contartese and Andenas (n 210) 180; Pohl (n 221) 788.

[245] C-284/16 (n 203) para 55.

[246] Contartese and Andenas (n 210) 788.

[247] H Ciurtini, 'Paradoxes of (sovereign) Consent: on the Uses and Abuses of a Notion in International Investment Law' in C Baltag (ed), *ICSID Convention after 50 Years: Unsettled Issues* (Kluwer Law International, 2016) 46.

between Member States.[248] In other words, investment arbitration is irreconcilable with the principle under which 'each Member State shares with all the other Member States, and recognises that they share with it, a set of common values on which the EU is founded, as stated in Article 2 TEU'.[249] The specificity of the EU emerged here again[250] and inevitably led the Court to conclude that a dispute settlement clause such as that included in the BIT applied in the *Achmea* case was inconsistent with Articles 344 and 267 TFEU.

VII. THE AFTERMATH: THE DEBATE ON THE IMPACT OF THE *ACHMEA* JUDGMENT

The bold version of the principle of autonomy and the extensive reading of Article 344 TFEU adopted in the *Achmea* judgment unsurprisingly sent shockwaves through the EU legal order and the arbitration community.[251] The Netherlands immediately announced that it would take steps to terminate the BIT with the Slovak Republic.[252] Moreover, the *Bundersgerichtshof* (German Federal Court of Justice) complied with the CJEU's judgment by setting aside the *Achmea* award.[253]

What remained unclear, however, was whether the *Achmea* judgment dealt a fatal blow to intra-EU investment arbitration as a whole or limited itself to making investment arbitration under the Netherlands-Slovak Republic BIT unavailable. Normally, the Court's judgments interpreting EU law are only binding on the referring courts, but not on other Member States' courts.[254] The latter are nonetheless required to 'take into account' the CJEU's interpretation of the relevant EU provisions.[255] Hence in principle the judgment of the Court in *Achmea* could influence the decisions of other Member States courts on similar issues. However, such judgment undoubtedly left some open questions.

A first question stemmed from the Court's finding that 'a provision in an international agreement concluded between Member States, such as Article 8 of the BIT'.[256] The phrase 'such as Article 8 of the BIT' could arguably be

[248] C-284/16 (n 203) para 58. M Fanou, 'Intra-European Union Investor-State Arbitration Post-*Achmea*: RIP?' (2019) 26 *Maastricht Journal of European and Comparative Law* 316, 329.

[249] Opinion 2/13, EU:C:2014:2454, para 168.

[250] E Regan, 'The Role of the Principles of Mutual Trust and Mutual Recognition in EU Law' (2018) 2 *Diritto dell'Unione Europea* 231, 235–246.

[251] Koutrakos (n 222) 50.

[252] M Davoise and M Burgstaller, 'Another one BIT the Dust: is the Netherlands' termination of intra-EU Treaties the latest symptom of a backlash against investor-State arbitration?', 11 August 2020, Kluwer arbitration blog.

[253] *Slovak Republic v Achmea*, I ZB 2/15.

[254] The preliminary rulings declaring the invalidity of an EU measure is binding for all the courts and authorities in the European Union. See Case 66/80 *International Chemical Corporation* v *Amministrazione Finanze*, EU:C:1981:102, para 13.

[255] *Kühne & Heitz v Productschap voor Pluimvee en Eieren*, C-453/00, EU:C:2004:17, para 27; *Adeneler and others* v *ELOG (Ellinikos Organismos Galaktos)*, Case C-212/04, EU:C:2006:443, para 48.

[256] C-284/16 (n 203) para 60.

understood as circumscribing the dictum of the judgment to intra-EU BITs having the same characteristics as the Netherlands-Slovak Republic BIT. Indeed, one could argue that such dictum would only apply to intra-EU BITs that, like the Netherlands-Slovak Republic BIT, included the law of the contracting parties among the sources of applicable law.[257]

However, it is possible to arrive at the opposite conclusion, if the phrase 'such as Article 8 of the BIT' is read together with the subsequent sentence ('under which an investor from one of those Member States may, in the event of a dispute concerning investments in the other Member State, bring proceedings against the latter Member State before an arbitral tribunal whose jurisdiction that Member State has undertaken to accept').[258] According to this reading, the *Achmea* dictum would apply to all intra-EU IIAs.

An additional element of uncertainty lay in the fact that the Court in *Achmea* specifically assessed whether an intra-EU tribunal established under a BIT was consistent with EU law. Indeed, the dictum of the judgment did not encompass 'stand-alone' arbitration agreements between the investor and the host state. Although it may look rather theoretical, this specific question arose in the context of an enforcement judgment of an arbitral award rendered on the basis of an intra-EU BIT.[259] More specifically, the investor contended that the arbitral award was valid and enforceable because the respondent did not raise the EU law-based jurisdictional objection. Under this view, the respondent's acquiescence to the jurisdiction of the tribunal amounted to an expression of consent to arbitration. The Swedish Court seised with the case (the *Svea Hovrätt* – Svea Court of Appeal) refused to apply the *Achmea* judgment on the grounds that it did not preclude the disputing parties from 'entering into an arbitration agreement and participating in arbitral proceedings regarding an investment-related dispute'.[260] The Court of Appeal then went on to say that the TFEU only precluded agreements between Member States stipulating

> that one Member State is obligated to accept subsequent arbitral proceeding with an investor and that the Member States thereby establish a system where they have excluded disputes from the possibility of requesting a preliminary ruling, even though the disputes may involve interpretation and application of EU law.[261]

[257] See Nouvel (n 214) 23.
[258] ibid. See B Cappiello, 'Il mantenimento in vigore dei BITs intra europei e la legittimità della clausola compromissoria negli accordi bilaterali e multilaterali di investimento alla luce della sentenza Achmea' (2019) *Giurisprudenza Commerciale* 258, 271.
[259] *PL Holdings S.à.r.l. v Poland*, SCC 2014/163.
[260] *Poland v PL Holdings S.à.r.l.*, Case T-8538–17, para 5.2.3.
[261] ibid, para 5.2.7.see also GA Guarin Duque, 'The Termination Agreement of Intra-EU Bilateral Investment Treaties: A Spaghetti-Bowl With Fewer Ingredients and More Questions' (2020) 37 *Journal of International Arbitration* 798, 804–805; J Hope and T Åkerlund 'All Eyes on Sweden: Swedish Challenge Cases Post-Achmea' in A Stanič and C Baltag (eds), *The Future of Investment Treaty Arbitration in the EU: Intra-EU BITs, the Energy Charter Treaty, and the Multilateral Investment Court* (Kluwer Law International, 2020) 110.

Consequently, it concluded that the award was valid and enforceable. The Court of Appeal's judgment was later challenged before the Swedish Supreme Court (*Högsta domstolen*), which in turn referred a preliminary question to the CJEU to clarify whether *Achmea* applied to stand-alone arbitration agreements, even if the respondent state refrained from raising a jurisdictional objection (see section XIV).[262]

A further lingering question was whether the findings of the CJEU in the *Achmea* case – which originated from an UNCITRAL award – also applied to ICSID awards. Undoubtedly, several factors militated in favour of extending the *Achmea* dictum to ICSID awards.[263] First, Article 42 of the ICSID Convention might raise the same concerns as Article 8 of the Netherlands-Slovak Republic BIT,[264] because it provides that the law of the contracting parties is applicable when they have not reached a specific agreement on this matter.

Second, the rules on enforcement and annulment set out in the ICISD Convention are probably even more problematic from the CJEU's perspective.[265] It is worth recalling that Article 54 stipulates that ICSID awards shall be 'recognized as binding' and the pecuniary obligations contained therein shall be enforced as if they were final judgments of 'a court in that State'. Moreover, such awards are only subject to the review mechanisms laid down in the ICSID Convention.[266] This means that such arbitral decisions are not subject to specific domestic recognition procedures (*exequatur*).[267] Nor can they be annulled or reviewed by national courts.[268] In fact, national authorities can only assess the authenticity of the award.[269]

That said, some degree of uncertainty remained because, under a strictly literal reading, the *Achmea* judgment did not expressly cover ICSID arbitration.

Last, but not least, the *Achmea* judgment did not specifically address the question of whether EU law also precluded intra-EU arbitration under the ECT.[270]

[262] *Poland v PL Holdings Sàrl*, C-109/20, EU:C:2021:875.

[263] C Istvan Nagy, 'Intra-EU Bilateral Investment Treaties and EU Law after Achmea: Know Well What Leads You Forward and What Holds You Back' (2018) 19 *German Law Journal* 981, 994.

[264] Schreuer, Malintoppi, Reinisch and Sinclair (n 158) 573–575. On the drafting history of Article 42 of the ICSID Convention see M Sasson, 'The Applicable Law and the ICSID Convention' in A Stanič and C Baltag (eds), *The Future of Investment Treaty Arbitration in the EU: Iintra-EU BITs, the Energy Charter Treaty, and the Multilateral Investment Court* (Kluwer Law International, 2020) 277–288; WM Reisman and MH Arsanjani, 'Applicable Law under the ICSID Convention: The Tortured History of the Interpretation of Article 42' in MN Kinnear, GR Fischer, J Minguez Almeida, LF Torres Arias and MU Bidegain (eds), *Building International Investment Law – The First 50 Years of ICSID* 3 (Kluwer Law International, 2015) 9–11.

[265] Pohl (n 214) 784; Contartese and Andenas (n 210) 181. See for a comparison between the setting-aside procedures and ICSID annulment K Bondar, 'Annulment of ICSID and non-ICSID Investment Awards: Differences in the Extent of Review' (2015) 32 *Journal of International Arbitration* 621, 624–634.

[266] Art 53, ICSID Convention.

[267] Schreuer, Malintoppi, Reinisch and Sinclair (n 158) 1128.

[268] ibid, 1103–1104.

[269] ibid, 1139.

[270] *cf* Opinion of Advocate General Saugmandsgaard Øe, in Joined Cases C-798/19 and C-799/18 (n 17) fn 55. See also Cappiello (n 258) 273.

As is well known, the ECT differs from intra-EU BITs in terms of content and membership. Most notably, the ECT is a multilateral international agreement to which both the Union and its Member States are parties. However, the ECT substantive and procedural rules for the protection of foreign investment are akin to those included in intra-EU BITs. Moreover, just like the Netherlands-Slovak Republic BIT, Article 26 ECT may confer on arbitral tribunals the power to interpret and apply EU law, because the latter may qualify as 'other applicable rules of international law' under Article 26 ECT.

To sum up, there was no conclusive argument for considering the *Achmea* judgment as an indictment of all types of intra-EU investment arbitration. Therefore, this judgment, far from settling the matter once and for all, elicited divergent responses from the Commission and arbitral tribunals.

VIII. DOUBLING-DOWN ON THE 'EU LAW-CENTRED' APPROACH: THE COMMISSION'S COMMUNICATION OF 19 JULY 2018

A few months after the delivery of the *Achmea* judgment, the Commission expressed its views on the matter in the Communication 'The protection of intra-EU investment.'[271] All too predictably, the Commission sought to stretch the scope of the *Achmea* judgment. In one stroke, it overcame all doubts about the possibility to infer from its dictum implications for all types of intra-EU investment arbitration. It bluntly stated that arbitration clauses included in intra-EU IIAs are inconsistent with the principle of autonomy of the EU legal order[272] and are thus inapplicable.[273] Inapplicability in turn implies that arbitral tribunals established pursuant to these treaties lack jurisdiction over the investment disputes submitted to them. Consequently, Member States 'must also draw all necessary consequences from the *Achmea* judgment'.[274]

Besides, the Commission held that the Court's findings about the incompatibility between EU law and Article 8 of the Netherlands-Slovak Republic BIT also made the ECT inapplicable to intra-EU cases.

Underlying this view was once again the idea that EU law granted a level of protection that was equivalent to that of IIAs. Indeed, in the Commission's view, the combination of EU primary and secondary law protected intra-EU investment throughout their investment 'life cycle',[275] namely both in the pre-establishment and the post-establishment phases. This rather rosy account, however, did not factor in the shortcomings affecting many EU Member States' judicial systems, which are regularly denounced by the Commission in its annual

[271] European Commission, Protection of intra-EU investment, COM (2018) 547 final.
[272] ibid, 3.
[273] ibid.
[274] ibid.
[275] ibid, 5.

'EU justice scoreboard'.[276] This Communication can be seen as a further reassertion of the 'EU law-centred' approach, which aimed to induce all other actors involved in the intra-EU IIAs predicament to cave in. However, it was not hard to predict that arbitral tribunals established both under the intra-EU BITs and under the ECT would not hail this solution with enthusiasm. In fact, the wholesale acceptance of the 'EU law-centred' was never an option for them.

IX. INTRA-EU INVESTMENT ARBITRATION AFTER *ACHMEA*: THE ARBITRAL CASE LAW'S PERSPECTIVE

The ball was now in the arbitral tribunals' court. Despite the *Achmea* judgment, intra-EU investment arbitration was far from being over. Investors were not dissuaded from initiating arbitral proceedings on the basis of intra-EU BITs,[277] while host states regularly raised intra-EU jurisdictional objections based on the *Achmea* judgment. The latter thus inevitably became the elephant in the room for arbitral tribunals dealing with such disputes. Except for a handful of arbitral awards, which dismissed this objection on purely procedural grounds or did not even address it,[278] the vast majority of arbitral tribunals dealt with the effects of the *Achmea* judgment on their jurisdiction.

In the ICSID context, arbitral tribunals generally refused to comply with the CJEU's judgment and thus rejected the objections based on the CJEU's decision.[279]

In *Marfin*,[280] the arbitral tribunal found that 'the *Achmea* judgment [was] not strictly binding upon this Tribunal',[281] because the applicable BIT (Greece-Cyprus BIT) differed from the BIT applicable to the *Achmea* case. In the tribunal's view, the main difference between the two treaties lay in the fact that the Greece-Cyprus BIT did not include domestic law among the applicable sources of law.[282] Thus, under such BIT, the arbitral tribunal was primarily 'called upon to apply the provisions of the Treaty and customary international law'.[283] In fact, the law of the contracting states, including EU law, could serve

[276] See European Commission, The 2020 EU Justice Scoreboard. For a similar remark see N Lavranos and T Singla, 'Achmea: Groundbreaking or Overrated?' (2018) 6 *SchiedsVZ – German Arbitration Journal* 348, 351.

[277] There were however some exceptions. See, eg, L Yong, *Airbus Withdraws Treaty Claim Against Poland*, Global Arbitration Review, 22 May 2018.

[278] See, eg, *Antaris Solar GmbH and Dr. Michael Göde v Czech Republic*, Award (2 May 2018) PCA Case No. 2014-01, para 73; *Infrastructure Services Luxembourg S.à.r.l. and Energia Termosolar B.V. (formerly Antin Infrastructure Services Luxembourg S.à.r.l. and Antin Energia Termosolar B.V.) v Spain*, Award (15 June 2018) ICSID Case No. ARB/13/31, paras 56–58; *Georg Gavrilovic and Gavrilovic d.o.o. v Croatia*, Award (25 July 2018), ICSID Case No. ARB/12/39, para 79.

[279] *Kühne & Heitz v Productschap voor Pluimvee en Eieren* (n 255) paras 21–25.

[280] *Marfin Investment Group v Cyprus*, Award (26 July 2018), ICSID Case No. ARB/13/27.

[281] ibid, para 580.

[282] Art 8 Cyprus-Greece BIT.

[283] *Marfin Investment Group v Cyprus* (n 280) para 580.

at best a subsidiary source of law pursuant to Article 42 ICSID Convention.[284] Moreover, the tribunal stated that its jurisdiction was based on an offer to arbitrate pursuant to Article 25 ICSID Convention, under which the parties cannot unilaterally withdraw their consent to arbitrate once they express it.[285]

In *UP*,[286] the tribunal took a similar stance by emphasising once again the specific features of ICSID arbitration.[287] In the tribunal's view, the irrelevance of the *Achmea* judgment vis-à-vis ICSID awards was also evidenced by the fact that the CJEU in *Achmea* did not make any reference to ICSID arbitration, but only dealt with UNCITRAL arbitration.[288] Consequently, given the differences between ICSID and UNCITRAL arbitration, the *UP* tribunal concluded that the CJEU's findings in *Achmea* did not apply to non-ICSID arbitration.[289]

In the ECT context, arbitral tribunals had even less difficulty in dismissing the objections to their jurisdiction based on the *Achmea* judgment.

The *Masdar* tribunal[290] squarely rejected the view that the *Achmea* judgment had a bearing on ECT-based arbitration, on the grounds that that judgment only addressed investment arbitration based on intra-EU BITs.[291] To buttress this conclusion, the tribunal extensively quoted Advocate General Wathelet's opinion in *Achmea*, where he made clear that the question referred to the Court did not concern the ECT, but only intra-EU BITs.[292] It also stated that the CJEU implicitly upheld this passage of the Advocate General's opinion, because it did not specifically confute it.[293]

The *Vattenfall* tribunal[294] handed down a decision entirely devoted to determining whether EU law and the *Achmea* judgment could affect its jurisdiction. The tribunal conceded that the *Achmea* judgment was a 'new development' in the field of intra-EU arbitration.[295] Yet, it noted that it remained to be seen whether it could be of any relevance outside the boundaries of the specific case submitted to the CJEU.[296] In particular, it was unclear whether EU law and the

[284] ibid.

[285] ibid, para 592. See also *Magyar Farming Company Ltd, Kintyre Kft and Inicia Zrt v Hungary*, Award (13 November 2019), ICSID Case No. ARB/17/27, para 208.

[286] *UP (formerly Le Chèque Déjeuner) and C.D Holding Internationale v Hungary*, Award (9 October 2008), ICSID Case No. ARB/13/35.

[287] ibid, para 256.

[288] ibid, para 258.

[289] ibid, paras 260–266.

[290] *Masdar Solar & Wind Cooperatief U.A. v Spain*, Award (16 May 2018), ICSID Case No. ARB/14/1.

[291] ibid, para 679.

[292] ibid, para 681.

[293] ibid. See also *Foresight Luxembourg Solar 1 S.Á.R1., et al. v Spain*, Final award (14 November 2018), SCC 2015/150, para 220; *CEF Energia BV v Italy*, Award (16 January 2019), SCC 158/2015, para 96.

[294] *Vattenfall AB and others v Germany* (n 120).

[295] ibid, para. 139.

[296] ibid.

CJEU's judgment could come into play in the determination of the tribunal's jurisdiction. The tribunal started by noting that EU law, despite its peculiarities, qualified as international law.[297] Then, it went on to say that EU law could be relevant in the interpretation of the ECT pursuant to Article 31(3) lett. c) VCLT.[298] In this respect, the tribunal also made clear that taking EU law into account in accordance with Article 31(3) lett. c) VCLT did not mean rewriting 'the treaty being interpreted' or substituting 'a plain reading of a treaty provision with other rules of international law, external to the treaty being interpreted, which would contradict the ordinary meaning of its terms'.[299] Finally, it found that in any case neither the EU Treaties nor the *Achmea* judgment affected its jurisdiction or were relevant for the solution of the case at issue.[300] In fact, the latter did not even address investor-state arbitration pursuant to the ECT, but only BIT-based arbitration.[301]

Likewise, the *Greentech* tribunal[302] held that the *Achmea* judgment only applied to awards rendered on the basis of intra-EU BITs.[303] Interestingly, the tribunal also found that the European Commission's Communication of 19 July 2018 could not affect this conclusion as the latter was not a binding legal document and, even if it were so, it would not produce binding effects outside of the EU legal system.[304]

What emerges with outright clarity from the arbitral decisions issued after the *Achmea* judgment is that arbitral tribunals were not willing to yield to the CJEU. They still regarded themselves as possessing jurisdiction over intra-EU investment disputes. In reaching this conclusion, they did not openly contest the CJEU's judgment. Rather, they circumvented it by stating that it did not apply to ICSID arbitral proceedings and ECT-based arbitrations. They justified this approach either by emphasising the structural differences between the ECT and intra-EU BITs or the peculiarities of the ICSID system.

It remains to be seen, however, how non-ICSID tribunals reacted to the *Achmea* judgment. The *Antaris Solar* tribunal was the first of such arbitral tribunals to be called upon to deal with the '*Achmea* objection' (ie, EU law-based jurisdictional objection). Its decision, however, does not say much about this issue. The tribunal, in fact, rejected the *Achmea* objection on procedural grounds.[305]

[297] ibid, paras 140–145.
[298] ibid, para 154.
[299] ibid.
[300] ibid, paras 160–161.
[301] *Vattenfall AB and others v Germany* (n 120), para 163.
[302] *Greentech Energy Systems A/S, et al v Italy*, Final award (23 December 2018) SCC 2015/095.
[303] ibid, para 398.
[304] ibid, para 402.
[305] See *Antaris Solar GmbH and Dr. Michael Göde v Czech Republic* (n 278) para 73.

The *GPF GP* tribunal[306] also dealt with the relationship between the ISDS mechanism under the Poland-BLEU BIT and EU law.[307] In this respect, it is worth highlighting that the Poland-BLEU BIT, like the BIT applicable to the *Achmea* case, empowers arbitral tribunals to apply, inter alia, the domestic law of the contracting parties when deciding investment disputes.[308] Given the importance placed on this element by the CJEU in its judgment, one would have expected a thorough analysis of the CJEU's reasoning in *Achmea*. But the *GPP* tribunal handled this issue as if no CJEU's judgment on this matter had already been delivered. It affirmed that the ISDS system was compatible with the EU legal system. Neither Article 344 TFEU, nor Article 267 TFEU, nor Article 19 TEU could be construed as precluding it.[309] In its view, these provisions could 'at most be understood as a carve-out – as opposed to a complete preclusion – from the subject-matter scope of Article 9 of the BIT in respect of disputes that relate to the interpretation of EU Treaties, or the validity and interpretation of acts of the EU institutions'.[310]

This decision dealt a further blow to the prospect of getting arbitral tribunals to accept the CJEU and the Commission's view. From the arbitral case law's perspective, there was no difference between before and after *Achmea*. EU law and international investment law could coexist. They were not bound to conflict with each other. Nor was the primacy of EU law over intra-EU BITs and the ECT ineluctable. Thus, the *Achmea* judgment, far from solving once and for all the questions stemming from the interplay between EU law and intra-EU IIAs, ushered in a new phase of transition and uncertainty.[311]

X. THE MEMBER STATES' DECLARATIONS ON THE LEGAL EFFECTS OF THE *ACHMEA* JUDGMENT

Against this background, it became apparent that the dialogue between the two legal systems was extremely difficult, if not impossible. The CJEU and investment tribunals were two fat birds sitting on two different branches: one claiming the ownership of the whole tree; and the other replying that there was enough space for everyone. Neither of them was willing to back down. Thus, the only option available was to cut one of the branches.

It is with this objective in mind that 22 Member States concocted a declaration on the legal consequences of the *Achmea* judgment.[312] The statement

[306] *GPF GP S.à.r.l v Poland*, Award (29 April 2020), SCC 2014/168.

[307] Art 9, BLEU-Poland BIT.

[308] ibid.

[309] *GPF GP S.à.r.l v Poland* (n 306) paras 378–380.

[310] ibid, para 381.

[311] This had been already predicted two years before the *Achmea* decision. Andersen and Hindelang (n 4) 987.

[312] Declaration of the Member States of 15 January 2019 on the legal consequences of the *Achmea* judgment and on investment protection.

was published on 15 January 2019. The day after the remaining Member States issued two further declarations on the same issue. One expressed the views of Finland, Luxembourg, Malta, Slovenia, and Sweden.[313] The third declaration outlined Hungary's position on the matter.[314]

All the declarations reaffirmed the CJEU's view that, in case of conflict between EU law and IIAs between Member States, the former prevails. However, they reached different conclusions as to the implications and the scope of application of such a principle. According to the 22-Member State declaration[315] and Hungary's declaration,[316] all investor-state arbitration clauses concluded between Member States are incompatible with EU law and 'thus inapplicable'.[317] By contrast, the five-Member State Declaration of 16 January 2019 only proclaimed the inapplicability of bilateral agreements containing clauses 'such as the one described in *Achmea*'.[318] The signatories of such a declaration thus seemed to circumscribe the relevance of the *Achmea* judgment to intra-EU BITs, which, like the Netherlands-Slovak Republic BIT, included the law of the contracting states among the sources of law applicable to investment disputes.

It should be noted that all the declarations specified that intra-EU BITs were inapplicable in their entirety. Therefore, they also targeted the sunset clauses, under which investors enjoy the procedural and substantive guarantees laid down in BITs even after their termination.[319]

The declaration of 15 January 2019 also took a bold stance with respect to intra-EU arbitration under the ECT. In line with the Commission's Communication of 19 July 2018, it found that interpreting Article 26 ECT as applicable to intra-EU investment disputes, as several arbitral tribunals did, would result in a violation of the EU Treaties. Conversely, the five-Member State declaration stated that the CJEU's decision did not allow them to conclude that the ECT and EU law were incompatible with each other.[320] Likewise, Hungary's declaration noted that, as *Achmea* did not provide any guidance as to the intra-EU application of the ECT, it was 'inappropriate' for a Member State to express

[313] Declaration of the Representatives of the Member States of 16 January 2019 on the enforcement of the judgment of the Court of Justice in *Achmea* and on investment protection in the European Union.

[314] Declaration of the Representative of the Government of Hungary of 16 January 2019 on the legal consequences of the judgment of the Court of Justice in *Achmea* and on investment protection in the European Union.

[315] Declaration of the Member States of 15 January 2019 (n 312).

[316] Declaration of the Representative of the Government of Hungary of 16 January 2019 (n 314).

[317] Declaration of the Member States of 15 January 2019 (n 312) 1; Declaration of the Representative of the Government of Hungary of 16 January 2019 (n 314) 1.

[318] Declaration of the Representatives of the Member States of 16 January 2019 (n 313) 1.

[319] Declaration of the Representative of the Government of Hungary of 16 January 2019 (n 314) 1. Declaration of the Member States of 15 January 2019 (n 312) 2; Declaration of the Representatives of the Member States of 16 January 2019 (n 313) 1. See K Nowrot, 'Termination and Renegotiation of International Investment Agreements' in S Hindelang and M Krajewski (eds), *Shifting Paradigms in International Investment Law* (Oxford University Press, 2016) 242.

[320] Declaration of the Member States of 16 January 2019 (n 313) 3.

its views on that matter.[321] Such an approach may be at least partially explained as an attempt to defend the specific national interests of the signatories. Sweden arguably sought to preserve the arbitration industry thriving in one of the world's leading arbitration centres for energy disputes, the Arbitration Institute of the Stockholm Chamber of Commerce. Similarly, Luxembourg's stance may probably be explained in light of the great importance of foreign direct investment for its national economy.[322]

Despite the partially different approaches underlying the declarations, they served a similar purpose: apprising the main actors of intra-EU investment arbitration of the implications deriving from *Achmea*.[323] They were first and foremost addressed to arbitral tribunals before which investment disputes were pending. Second, they urged investors to refrain from bringing new investment claims based on intra-EU BITs. Last, they requested both their own and third-states' courts not to enforce arbitral awards rendered on the basis of intra-EU BITs.

Moreover, the declarations also contained very similar commitments. The signatories envisaged the termination of all intra-EU bilateral investment treaties either by means of a plurilateral or a bilateral treaty to be concluded or ratified by 6 December 2019.[324] Furthermore, they also committed to ensure effective legal protection for the investors involved in arbitral proceedings at the time of the termination.

When it comes to the intra-EU application of the ECT, however, the commitments laid down in the declarations reflect their different views on the relationship between the ECT and EU law.[325] The five-Member State declaration, in a rather vague fashion, stated that the Member States stood 'ready to discuss with other Member States and the Commission whether additional steps are necessary to draw all the consequences from the CJEU's judgment'.[326] Hungary also refused to take a clear position on the issue, which in its view required further discussion.[327] On the contrary, the signatories of the declaration of 15 January

[321] Declaration of the Representative of the Government of Hungary of 16 January 2019 (n 314) 3.

[322] According to World Bank data, the net inflow of FDI has been 84.7% of the country's GDP. See data.worldbank.org/indicator/BX.KLT.DINV.WD.GD.ZS?end=2020&locations=EU-LU&start=1970&view=chart.

[323] Declaration of the Representative of the Government of Hungary of 16 January 2019 (n 314) 2; Declaration of the Member States of 15 January 2019 (n 312) 3; Declaration of the Representatives of the Member States of 16 January 2019 (n 313) 3.

[324] Declaration of the Member States of 15 January 2019 (n 312) 5; Declaration of the Representative of the Government of Hungary of 16 January 2019 (n 314) 3; Declaration of the Representatives of the Member States of 16 January 2019 (n 313) 4.

[325] C Baltag and S Dudas, 'Achmea, Arbitral Tribunals and the ECT: Modernisation or Regression?' in A Stanič and C Baltag (eds), *The Future of Investment Treaty Arbitration in the EU: Intra- EU BITs, the Energy Charter Treaty, and the Multilateral Investment Court* (Kluwer Law International, 2020) 29.

[326] Declaration of the Member States of 15 January 2019 (n 312) 5.

[327] Declaration of the Representative of the Government of Hungary of 16 January 2019 (n 314) 3.

2019 explicitly agreed to engage in further discussion regarding the consequences of *Achmea* vis-à-vis the intra-EU application of the ECT.[328]

XI. ARE THE 'MASTERS OF THE TREATIES' STILL IN CHARGE? THE ROLE OF MEMBER STATES' DECLARATIONS IN INTRA-EU INVESTMENT ARBITRATION

The Member States' declarations did not have a remarkable impact on arbitral jurisprudence. When arbitral tribunals did not simply ignore them,[329] they held that the declarations had no relevance in interpreting intra-EU BITs and the ECT.

In *United Utilities*,[330] the tribunal found that the declaration of 15 January 2019 proved, if anything, that the Estonia-Netherlands BIT still incorporated a valid offer to arbitrate.[331] The reason being that the signatories to the declaration did not terminate such a BIT, but they only committed to do so by 6 December 2019.

In a similar vein, the *Magyar Farming* tribunal[332] denied that the declarations of 15 and 16 January 2019[333] could undermine its jurisdiction, for they could not be regarded as denunciations of the UK-Hungary BIT.[334] The tribunal added that, even assuming that they did terminate the BIT, this would not affect its jurisdiction, because the '[c]laimants accepted the BIT's offer to arbitrate prior to its purported termination'.[335] The tribunal then excluded that the declarations could qualify as 'subsequent agreements' pursuant to Article 31(3) lett. a), VCLT, because they did not clarify the meaning of the provisions contained in intra-EU BITs.[336] Rather, they 'seek to explain the legal consequences of the Achmea Decision, rather than to give an interpretation of the meaning of intra-EU investment treaties'.[337] It then went on to say that, even if one regarded them

[328] Declaration of the Representatives of the Member States of 16 January 2019 (n 313) 4.

[329] See, eg, *Voltaic Network GmbH v Czech Republic*, Award (15 May 2019), PCA Case No. 2014-20, paras 348–370; *ICW Investments v Czech Republic*, Award (15 May 2019), PCA Case No. 2014-22, paras 396–418; *WA Investments Europa Nova Ltd. v Czech Republic*, Award (15 May 2019), PCA Case No. 2014-19, 438–460; *9REN Holding S.a.r.l. v Spain*, Award (31 May 2019), ICSID Case No. ARB/15/15, paras 168–173; *CEF Energia BV v Italy* (n 293) paras 96–100. See *Cube Infrastructure Fund SICAV and others v Spain*, Decision on jurisdiction, liability and partial decision on quantum (19 February 2019), ICSID Case No. ARB/15/20, paras 118–160; *Watkins Holdings S.à.r.l. and others v Spain*, Award (21 January 2020), ICSID Case No. ARB/15/44, paras 180–226.

[330] *United Utilities (Tallinn) B.V. and Aktsiaselts Tallinna Vesi v Estonia*, Award (21 June 2019) ICSID Case No. ARB/14/24.

[331] ibid, 557–559.

[332] *Magyar Farming Company Ltd, Kintyre Kft and Inicia Zrt v Hungary* (n 285).

[333] Declaration of the Member States of 15 January 2019 (n 312); Declaration of the Representative of the Government of Hungary of 16 January 2019 (n 314).

[334] *Magyar Farming Company Ltd, Kintyre Kft and Inicia Zrt v Hungary* (n 285) para 213.

[335] ibid.

[336] ibid, para 216.

[337] ibid.

as 'subsequent agreements' to be 'taken into account' in the interpretation of the dispute settlement clause of the applicable BIT, they could not override the unequivocal offer to arbitrate set out therein.[338]

Similarly, in *Addiko Bank*,[339] the tribunal also found that the declaration of 15 January 2019 addressed the perceived '"legal consequences" of a 2018 CJEU judgment',[340] but it did not clarify the interpretation of the applicable BIT.[341] The tribunal also added that in any case the declaration could be 'at best [...] seen as offering a new shared intention with respect to the BIT's arbitration clause, rather than confirming a previously shared Understanding'.[342]

Turning to the ECT case law, it is possible to discern a wider range of approaches. This can be partly explained by the fact that the *Achmea* judgment did not specifically address the issue of the incompatibility between EU law and ECT-based arbitration. Moreover, the Member States' declarations lacked stringent commitments on the non-application of the ECT at the intra-EU level.

Some tribunals ignored or denied the relevance of the declarations. The *Soles Badajoz* tribunal[343] swiftly concluded that the declarations did 'not affect the reasoning that the Tribunal has used in addressing the objection to its jurisdiction'.[344] In *Opera Fund*,[345] although the respondent argued at length that the declaration of 15 January 2019 precluded investment arbitration pursuant to the ECT,[346] the tribunal affirmed its jurisdiction over the case without mentioning it.[347]

According to a second school of thought, the language of the declarations and the fact that none of them encapsulated the views common to all Member States deprived them of any legal effect.

The *Rockhopper* tribunal[348] held that the inconsistencies between the declarations clearly indicated that none of them incorporated the common view of the Member States[349] nor could they be considered as EU legal instruments.[350]

[338] ibid, paras 218–220.

[339] *Addiko Bank AG and Addiko Bank d.d. v Croatia*, Decision on Croatia's jurisdictional objection related to the alleged incompatibility of the BIT with the EU *acquis* (12 June 2020), ICSID Case No. ARB/17/37.

[340] ibid.

[341] ibid, para 288.

[342] ibid, para 289.

[343] *SolEs Badajoz GmbH v Spain*, Award (31 July 2019), ICSID Case No. ARB/15/38.

[344] ibid, para 253; see also *NextEra Energy Global Holdings B.V. and NextEra Energy Spain Holdings B.V. v Spain*, Final award (31 May 2019), ICSID Case No. ARB/14/11, para 334.

[345] *OperaFund Eco-Invest SICAV PLC and Schwab Holding AG v Spain*, Award (6 September 2019), Case No. ARB/15/20.

[346] ibid, para. 349.

[347] ibid, paras 378–388. In *RWE Innogy*, the tribunal only said that it had 'studied' the position of the Member States set out in the Declarations. See *RWE Innogy GmbH and RWE Innogy Aersa S.A.U. v Spain*, Decision on jurisdiction, liability and certain issues of quantum (30 December 2019), ICSID Case No. ARB/14/34, para 309.

[348] *Rockhopper Italia S.p.A., Rockhopper Mediterranean Ltd, and Rockhopper Exploration Plc v Italy*, Decision on the intra-EU jurisdictional objection (29 June 2019), ICSID Case No. ARB/17/14.

[349] ibid, para 179.

[350] ibid, para 180.

After a careful analysis of each component of the declarations, the tribunal then concluded that it was 'difficult to ascertain any collective declaration of interpretation'.[351]

In *Belenergia*,[352] the respondent (Italy) invoked the declaration that it had signed on 15 January 2019 and the declaration that Luxembourg (the state of nationality of the investor) had signed on 16 January 2019.[353] The tribunal, however, held that they had limited relevance because they contained rather vague and divergent stipulations on the intra-EU application of the ECT.[354]

A third group of arbitral tribunals explicitly referred to Articles 31 and 32 VCLT when analysing such declarations. The *Sun Reserve* tribunal[355] rejected the view that the declarations of 15 January and 16 January 2019 produced binding effects and stated that they could be considered at best as interpretative instruments under Articles 31 and 32 VCLT.[356] Such statements could be thus 'taken into account in the interpretative process',[357] even if their interpretative value was greatly diminished by the fact that the content of the declarations was divergent in many respects.[358]

In *EFSP*,[359] the tribunal held that the declaration of 15 January 2019[360] was not an agreement relating to the interpretation of another treaty under Article 31(2) lett. a) VCLT because it was not made 'in connection with' the ECT.[361] In addition, the tribunal also found that declarations did not meet the requirements under Article 31(3) lett. a), as only some of the ECT contracting states had signed it.[362] Interestingly, the tribunal added that interpreting the declaration as an exception to Article 26 ECT, that is to say as a retroactive and explicit 'disconnection clause' would amount to a surreptitious modification of the treaty.[363] In other words, this approach would lead the tribunal to

> interpret a clear granting of rights to all Investors to international arbitration as having been void *ab initio*, ignoring all of the established international law provisions for modification of treaties, without any notice to the Contracting States to the ECT

[351] ibid, paras 185–194.
[352] *Belenergia S.A. v Italy*, Award (28 August 2019), ICSID Case No. ARB/15/40.
[353] ibid, paras 204–205.
[354] ibid, paras. 326–329; see also *The PV Investors v Spain*, Final award (28 February 2020), PCA Case No. 2012-14, paras 544–548; *Rockhopper Italia S.p.A., Rockhopper Mediterranean Ltd, and Rockhopper Exploration Plc v Italy* (n 348) paras 179.
[355] *Sun Reserve Luxco Holdings SRL v Italy*, Award (25 March 2020), SCC 132/2016.
[356] ibid, para 435.
[357] ibid.
[358] ibid, para 436.
[359] *ESPF Beteiligungs GmbH, ESPF Nr. 2 Austria Beteiligungs GmbH, and InfraClass Energie 5 GmbH & Co. KG v Italy*, Award (14 September 2020), ICSID Case No. ARB/16/5.
[360] Declaration of the Member States of 15 January 2019 (n 314).
[361] *ESPF Beteiligungs GmbH, ESPF Nr. 2 Austria Beteiligungs GmbH, and InfraClass Energie 5 GmbH & Co. KG v Italy* (n 359) para 323.
[362] ibid, para 324.
[363] ibid.

> and without any regard for the rights of the Investors whose rights have crystallised and who have commenced arbitrations accepting the 'unconditional consent' offered by those States.[364]

It thus concluded that it was not possible to read the declaration as a tacit disconnection clause preventing the application of the ECT to intra-EU cases, for this would bring about unsustainably unfair consequences for the investors.[365]

Last, the *Eskosol* tribunal[366] devoted an extensive passage of its award to the declaration of 15 January 2019,[367] where it borrowed many of the arguments referred to above. First, it observed that the declaration went far beyond the position expressed by the CJEU in *Achmea*.[368] Second, due to its wording – notably the use of the future tense for its salient stipulations – the declaration was incapable of having an immediate impact on ongoing ECT arbitral proceedings.[369] Then, it found that the declaration did not qualify as an interpretative agreement under Article 31(2) VCLT, because it had not been adopted at the time of the conclusion of the treaty.[370] Neither did it constitute a subsequent agreement on interpretation under Article 31(3) lett. a) VCLT, for it had not been adopted by all the parties to the ECT.[371] Additionally, it found that the declaration did 'not actually purport to "interpret" any particular term of the underlying treaty [...] To the contrary, while denominated as "interpretation," [it was] more a statement of current political will'.[372] In light of such considerations, the tribunal thus concluded that the declaration was at best 'a means of information of the position of the EU Member States' that had signed it.[373]

In sum, according to arbitral case law, the declarations did not qualify as interpretative agreements or subsequent practice under Article 31 VCLT,[374] and did not affect in any case their jurisdiction over intra-EU investment disputes.

[364] ibid, para 326.
[365] ibid, para 325.
[366] *Eskosol S.p.A. in liquidazione v Italy*, Decision on termination request and intra-EU objection (7 May 2019), ICSID Case No. ARB/15/50.
[367] Declaration of the Member States of 15 January 2019 (n 312).
[368] *Eskosol S.p.A. in liquidazione v Italy* (n 366) paras 213–216.
[369] ibid, para 228.
[370] ibid, para 219.
[371] ibid, paras 220–221.
[372] ibid, para 222.
[373] ibid, para 227.
[374] Interestingly, had these declarations been regarded as 'subsequent practice', they would have de facto brought about the termination of intra-EU BITs. They would thus constitute an example of abrogative practice, whose admissibility is still very controversial. See M Kohen, 'Keeping Subsequent Agreements and Practice in Their Right Limits' in G Nolte (ed), *Treaties and Subsequent Practice* (Oxford University Press, 2013) 35–36.

XII. THE RETURN OF THE 'MASTERS OF THE TREATIES': THE TERMINATION AGREEMENT

If the legal value of the Member States' declarations was dubious, at least for arbitral tribunals, their political importance was incontestable. Such declarations undoubtedly paved the way to the conclusion of the Agreement for the termination of Bilateral Investment Treaties between Member States of the EU (hereinafter referred to as 'TA'). The majority of the contracting parties to the TA had indeed signed the declaration of 15 January 2019 – except for Ireland, which was party to no intra-EU BIT – while the remaining contracting states, namely Luxembourg, Malta, and Hungary, had signed the declarations of 16 January.[375] The TA largely reflects the views expressed in the 22-Member State declaration of 15 January 2019.[376] It stipulates that all intra-EU BITs listed in Annex A will be terminated upon its ratification.[377] Therefore, contrary to what the five-Member State declaration of 16 January 2019 stated,[378] the TA does not only target the agreements like the one interpreted in *Achmea*.[379] For instance, Annex A to the TA features the BLEU-Hungary BIT, which, like the Netherlands-Slovak Republic BIT, lists the law of the contracting parties among the applicable sources of law;[380] but it also includes the Netherlands-Slovenia BIT, which does not specifically address this matter.[381]

The TA also terminates the sunset clauses generally contained in intra-EU IIAs. More specifically, it neutralises the effects of sunset clauses included in BITs that were still effective at the time of conclusion of the TA as well as those included in BITs that had been terminated before that time.[382]

[375] Declaration of the Representatives of the Member States of 16 January 2019 (above n 313). The signatories of the TA are: Belgium, Bulgaria, Czech Republic, Denmark, Germany, Estonia, Greece, Spain, France, Croatia, Italy, Cyprus, Latvia, Lithuania, Luxembourg, Hungary, Malta, Netherlands, Poland, Portugal, Romania, Slovenia, Slovak Republic. Portugal is the only contracting State that has yet ratified it. Four contracting States also appended a declaration or a reservation to the treaty. Lithuania, Portugal and Luxembourg appended a declaration urging the establishment of an intra-EU investment protection mechanism to fill the vacuum of protection left by the termination of the intra-EU BITs. The Netherlands instead stated that the *Achmea* judgment only applied to its European territory, but not to its overseas territories. Declaration/Reservation appended by Lithuania to the Termination Agreement; Declaration/Reservation appended by Luxembourg to the Termination Agreement, Declaration/Reservation appended by Portugal to the Termination Agreement; Declaration/Reservation appended by the Netherlands to the Termination Agreement.

[376] Declaration of the Member States of 15 January 2019 (n 312).

[377] Arts 2, 4 and Annex A TA. *Fynerdale Holdings BV v Czech Republic*, Award (29 April 2021) PCA Case No. 2018-18, para 294.

[378] Declaration of the Representatives of the Member States of 16 January 2019 (n 313).

[379] J Tropper and A Reinisch, 'The 2020 Termination Agreement of Intra-EU Bits and its Effect on Investment Arbitration in the EU – A Public International Law Analysis of the Termination Agreement' (2022) 16 *Austrian Yearbook on International Arbitration* 301, 305.

[380] Art 9 BLEU-Hungary; Art 7 Lithuania-Poland BIT, Art 8 Romania-Spain BIT.

[381] Art 9 Netherlands-Slovenia BIT. Some other BITs only refer to 'international law' or 'principles of international law'. See Art 8 France-Bulgaria BIT; Art 9 France-Hungary BIT.

[382] See Arts 2, 3 and 16 TA.

The TA then distinguishes between new, pending and concluded arbitration proceedings by using as a watershed the date of delivery of the *Achmea* judgment, ie, 6 March 2018.[383] 'Pending arbitration proceedings' are those initiated before 6 March 2018, while 'new arbitration proceedings' are those initiated after this date. 'Concluded arbitration proceedings' are those that ended prior to 6 March 2018 with a final award, which has been executed before the same date or annulled or set aside before the entry into force of the TA.

The TA provides that arbitration clauses are inconsistent and thus inapplicable as between Member States.[384] Hence, they do not constitute a valid legal basis for starting new arbitration proceedings.[385] This latter provision, however, does not apply to 'pending proceedings'[386] and does not affect concluded proceedings, which 'shall not be reopened'.[387].

When involved in 'new' or 'pending' arbitrations, contracting states shall inform arbitral tribunals about the incompatibility with EU law and inapplicability of intra-EU arbitration clauses.[388] Additionally, they shall request the competent domestic courts 'to set the arbitral award aside, annul it or to refrain from recognising and enforcing it'.[389] Interestingly, the contracting states may address this request to their own courts or also to the courts of third states. The investors involved in 'pending' arbitral proceedings are not left without legal protection. Indeed, they may resort to the 'structured dialogue' under Article 9 TA or seek redress before Member States' courts pursuant to Article 10 TA, unless they agree on an appropriate and EU-consistent resolution of the dispute.[390]

The structured dialogue is a rather complex settlement procedure overseen by a 'facilitator', who satisfies the independence and impartiality requirements under Article 9(8) TA. The parties to a 'pending' investment dispute appoint the facilitator by common agreement.[391] If they do not reach an agreement within one month from the start of the settlement procedure, the Director General of the Legal Service of the European Commission appoints, after consulting the parties to the dispute, a former member of the CJEU.[392]

The parties to an investment dispute may enter such a settlement procedure within six months from the termination of the applicable intra-EU BIT provided that two alternative conditions are met.[393] If the final award has

383 Art 1 TA.
384 Art 4 TA.
385 Art 5 TA.
386 Tropper and Reinisch (n 379) 306.
387 Art 6 TA.
388 Art 7 TA.
389 ibid.
390 Art 8 TA.
391 Art 9 TA.
392 ibid.
393 ibid.

not been issued yet, the arbitral proceedings must have been suspended upon request of the investor. Alternatively, if the award has been issued already, the investor must commit to refrain from executing the award. Moreover, Article 9(3) TA stipulates that the disputing parties 'shall' start a settlement procedure if a final decision of the CJEU or a Member State's court has ruled that the measure challenged in a pending arbitration is inconsistent with EU law. This provision seems to imply that under the circumstances referred therein (ie, an ascertained violation of EU law) the disputing parties are not free to choose between the 'structured dialogue' and access to national courts. Conversely, Article 9(4) establishes a prohibition to start a settlement procedure if the CJEU, a national court or the Commission found that the measure contested in the arbitral proceedings under paragraph 1 is consistent with EU law.

Ideally, the procedure ends with an amicable settlement.[394] However, if no such settlement is reached, the parties express their respective views on the possible terms for the solution of the dispute. Based on the parties' views, the facilitator formulates a final written proposal, which will constitute the final agreement if accepted by the disputing parties.[395] If one of the disputing parties rejects the final written proposal, it shall provide a written explanation to justify its decision.[396]

Member States' courts are the alternative to the structured dialogue procedure. Investors involved in 'pending' arbitral proceedings may bring their claims before the competent national court even if the time limits under the applicable domestic law have already expired.[397] The TA clarifies that investors can resort to national courts when the settlement procedure was not used or was unsuccessful.[398] When investors opt for this solution, they shall commit: (i) to renounce its claims under the applicable BIT; (ii) to refrain from executing awards rendered on the basis of that BIT; and (iii) to abstain from starting 'new' arbitral proceedings.[399]

XIII. THE END OF INTRA-EU BITs? APPRAISING THE POSSIBLE EFFECTS OF THE TERMINATION AGREEMENT

The importance of the TA can hardly be overstated. Twenty-three Member States stepped up to plate and terminated the BITs concluded between them. In so doing, most of the EU Member States decidedly gravitated toward the

[394] ibid.
[395] Art 9 TA.
[396] Art 9 TA.
[397] Art 10 TA.
[398] ibid.
[399] ibid.

position of the CJEU and the Commission. The entry into force of the TA, however, might not mark the end of intra-EU investment arbitration, because several factors might dilute its impact.

A. The Material Scope of Application of the TA

The first factor is the material scope of application of the TA. Due to the lack of consensus between Member States as to the implications of the *Achmea* judgment in the ECT context,[400] the TA expressly keeps the intra-EU application of the ECT out of its purview. In other words, the TA does not preclude intra-EU investment arbitration under the ECT. As we shall see (see section XV), however, this issue has been addressed in the context of the ECT modernisation process.

B. The Effects Ratione Temporis of the TA

A further limitation to the impact of the TA may stem from its temporal effects. The TA is in principle suitable to discontinue the pre-existing intra-EU BITs. Indeed, it is a well-established principle of customary law that the parties to an international treaty may dissolve the treaty bond by common agreement.[401] However, in the case of intra-EU IIAs, things are more complicated, because such agreements normally contain sunset clauses. It is thus worth wondering how such clauses interact with the TA. Does the latter supersede and neutralise such provisions? Or, on the contrary, do these provisions continue to produce their effects despite the TA?

Unfortunately, providing a straightforward answer to these questions is not possible. For one thing, the category 'sunset clauses' includes rather different objects, namely those operating in the event of natural expiry of the agreement[402] and those applying in case of unilateral termination.[403]

Besides, the response to the above questions depends on how one conceptualises international investment law. Some construe IIAs as conferring procedural and substantive rights directly on investors ('direct rights theory').[404] A more nuanced version of this theory affirms that IIAs would only bestow procedural

[400] Baltag and Dudas (n 325) 29.

[401] This principle is embedded in Art 54 VCLT. T Giegerich, 'Article 54' in O Dörr and K Schmalenbach (eds), *Vienna Convention on the Law of Treaties-A commentary* (Springer, 2012) 948.

[402] See, eg, Art 12 France-Romania BIT; Art 12 France-Hungary BIT.

[403] See for instance Art 12 Croatia-Spain BIT; Art 13 Greece-Slovenia BIT.

[404] A Roberts, 'Power and Persuasion in Investment Treaty Interpretation: The Dual Role of States' (2010) 104 *American Journal of International Law* 179, 184.

rights on investors, whereas contracting states remain the sole holders of substantive rights. Both views depart from the traditional state-centric approach, whereby IIAs confer rights only on the contracting states.[405]

If one starts from the assumption that IIAs confer procedural or substantive rights on investors,[406] it is possible to argue that the sunset clauses produce their effects despite the TA. This reading seems to be more consistent with the overall objective of political stability underlying international investment law.[407] Indeed, investment treaties would be hollowed out if the contracting states had the power to terminate them with immediate and retroactive effect, particularly because foreign investments generally have a rather long-time span.

Furthermore, Articles 70 and 37 VCLT may also provide arguments in support of the 'ultra-activity' of sunset clauses.[408] The former provides that the termination of a treaty does not affect any right, obligation or legal situation of the parties created through the execution of the treaty before its termination. The latter stipulates that a right conferred by a treaty, when intended to be irrevocable, cannot be revoked or modified by the parties. Although Article 70 and 37 VCLT have been generally construed as applying to states, not individuals,[409] it cannot be ruled out that some arbitral tribunals might extend their scope of application to include investors.[410] It is thus possible to argue that the TA might fall short of terminating with immediate effect at least some of the intra-EU IIAs.

C. The TA and the Enforcement of Intra-EU Arbitral Decisions

The TA might also not ensure that no intra-EU arbitral award will be enforced. There is no guarantee that non-EU courts will comply with the request not to recognise and enforce the award under Article 7 TA.[411]

[405] ibid; T Voon, A Mitchell and J Munro, 'Parting Ways: The Impact of Mutual Termination of Investment Treaties on Investor Rights' (2014) 29 *ICSID Review – Foreign Investment Law Journal* 451, 454.

[406] The reasons underlying the emergence of investor arbitration seems to support the direct rights theory. See Z Douglas, 'The Hybrid Foundations of Investment Treaty Arbitration' (2003) 74 *British Yearbook of International Law* 151, 182.

[407] J Harrison, 'The Life and Death of BITs: Legal Issues Concerning Survival Clauses and the Termination of Investment Treaties' (2012) 13 *Journal of World Investment and Trade* 928, 933.

[408] For a more critical take on the application of such provisions to the case under consideration see Tropper and Reinisch (n 379) 315–320.

[409] Voon, Mitchell and Munro (n 405) 469; Nowrot (n 319) 250.

[410] Harrison (n 407) 948–949.

[411] See A Stanič, 'Enforcement of Awards and Other Implications of *Achmea*' in A Stanič and C Baltag (eds), *The Future of Investment Treaty Arbitration in the EU: Intra- EU BITs, the Energy Charter Treaty, and the Multilateral Investment Court* (Kluwer Law International, 2020) 161–162.

The non-enforcement and non-recognition of awards within the EU should not be taken for granted either. In this respect, it is worth recalling that, although the ICSID enforcement regime leaves virtually no room for national courts to refuse the execution of arbitral awards,[412] the UK Supreme Court enforced an arbitral award rendered by an ICSID tribunal even after the delivery of the *Achmea* judgment.[413]

XIV. BEYOND *ACHMEA*: THE CJEU'S BID FOR THE ERADICATION OF INTRA-EU INVESTMENT ARBITRATION

The conclusion of the TA is a political fact of primary importance in that it signals the emergence of some degree of consensus among EU Member States about the incompatibility with EU law of intra-EU investment arbitration. By terminating the BITs applicable to inter se relations, the 23 contracting states narrowed the space for intra-EU investment arbitration. The TA went even beyond the *Achmea* dictum, because it terminated a considerable number of intra-EU BITs containing both ICSID and non-ICSID arbitration clauses. And yet, this agreement might not bar the access to intra-EU arbitration once and for all for the reasons illustrated above (see section XIII).

This state of things, however, was especially unpalatable for the CJEU, which soon came back on this issue. In a string of subsequent decisions, the Court not only expanded the *Achmea* dictum to include all the other types of intra-EU investment arbitration, but also addressed the interplay between EU substantive law and investment protection rules.

A. The Enlargement of the *Achmea* Dictum

Without any doubt, intra-EU arbitration under the ECT was the elephant in the room. The structural differences between the ECT and the intra-EU BITs raised serious doubts about the possibility of extending the *Achmea* doctrine to investment arbitration proceedings based on the ECT (see section VII).[414] However, both the ECT and intra-EU BITs contain an ISDS mechanism. Therefore, if one starts from the assumption that ISDS mechanisms under intra-EU BITs

[412] See Art 53 ICSID Convention.

[413] UK Supreme Court, *Micula and others v Romania*, 19 February 2020 [2020] UKSC 5, paras 86–117. The Commission has launched infringement proceedings against the UK over this judgment. See European Commission, 'Sincere cooperation and primacy of EU law: Commission refers UK to EU Court of Justice over a UK Judgment allowing enforcement of an arbitral award granting illegal State aid', Press release, 9 February 2022.

[414] To be sure, the *Achmea* judgment did not automatically lead Member States' courts to stop the enforcement of intra-EU awards issued by ECT Tribunals. See, eg, *CEF Energia BV v Italy*, Case T-4236-19; *Greentech Energy System A/S et al. v Italy*, Case T-3239-19.

jeopardise the autonomy of the EU legal order, then also investment arbitration under the ECT should be illegal under EU law.[415]

The CJEU had the chance to address this thorny issue three years and a half after *Achmea*. The occasion came about in the context of another preliminary reference procedure, which originated from an action of annulment of an arbitral award pending before the Court of Appeal of Paris (*Cour d'appel de Paris*).[416] Interestingly, however, such an award was rendered at the end of an arbitration involving a non-EU investor (*Komstroy*) and a non-EU state (Moldova). Despite the tenuous links with the EU legal order, the Court asserted its jurisdiction over the case.[417] Then, it indulged in an obiter dictum that was not strictly relevant to solve the preliminary questions submitted by the referring court. In particular, relying on the *Achmea* judgment, the Court explained in this rather long digression that intra-EU arbitration under the ECT was inconsistent with EU law. The main concern of the Court was once again that arbitral tribunals would interpret and apply EU law.[418] In the Court's view, granting this power to arbitral tribunals, namely dispute settlement bodies that cannot refer preliminary questions to the CJEU, would undermine the effectiveness of EU law and the autonomy of the EU legal order.[419] The Court then went on to consider whether the multilateral nature of the ECT would preclude the extension of those findings to the case at hand. It reached a negative conclusion on the grounds that 'Article 26 ECT is intended, in reality, to govern bilateral relations between two of the Contracting Parties, in an analogous way to the provision of the bilateral investment treaty at issue in the case giving rise to the judgment of 6 March 2018, *Achmea*'.[420] Thus, instead of engaging with the interpretation of Article 26 ECT, the Court focused on how ECT-based and BIT-based investment arbitration work. From the Court's perspective, both instruments are problematic for the autonomy of the EU legal order, because they impinge on the jurisdiction of Member State's courts and the role of the

[415] Relying on this simple premise, the Netherlands sought from two German courts a declaration of inadmissibility of arbitral proceedings under Section 1032 of the German Code of Civil Procedure. See *RWE AG and RWE Eemshaven Holding II BV v Kingdom of the Netherlands*, ICSID Case No. ARB/21/4. Croatia also filed an application for a declaration of inadmissibility. See *Raiffeisen Bank International AG and Raiffeisenbank Austria d.d. v Croatia*, ICSID Case No. ARB/17/34. See *Croatia v Raiffeisen Bank International AG*, 26 SchH 2/20.

[416] *Moldova v Komstroy LLC*, C-741/19, EU:C:2021:655. Subsequently, the Court also issued an Opinion pursuant to Art 218 TFEU on the compatibility of the draft modernised ECT with EU law. The request for such an Opinion was rejected as inadmissible, because the Court did not have sufficient information on the content of the draft text. Opinion 1/20, not yet published, paras 40–46.

[417] In particular, it found that 'where a provision of an international agreement can apply both to situations falling within the scope of EU law and to situations not covered by that law, it is clearly in the interest of the European Union that, in order to forestall future differences of interpretation, that provision should be interpreted uniformly, whatever the circumstances in which it is to apply'. C-741/19 (n 416) para 29.

[418] ibid, paras 60–61.

[419] ibid.

[420] ibid, para 64.

CJEU. Based on this 'substantialist' approach, the Court thus concluded that intra-EU arbitration under the ECT is inconsistent with EU law and, consequently, is inapplicable at the intra-EU level.[421]

Having extended the *Achmea* doctrine to intra-EU arbitration under the ECT, the Court subsequently dealt with another question left open by the *Achmea* judgment and the TA – namely whether 'stand-alone' arbitration agreements are consistent with EU law (see section VII). Unlike the ECT and the BITs, these instruments embed the consent to arbitrate one or several specific disputes rather than an indefinite number of disputes.[422] Thus, they may appear, at least theoretically, less dangerous for the autonomy of the EU legal order. It is probably with this hope in mind that the investor contended that the *Achmea* dictum did not cover arbitral proceedings initiated on the basis of a 'stand-alone' arbitration agreement. More specifically, it shrewdly argued that the respondent had accepted to arbitrate that specific dispute by not raising the intra-EU objection to the jurisdiction of the arbitral tribunal. For all its ingeniousness, this argument did not persuade the CJEU, which remained faithful to its 'substantivist' approach. In particular, it held that:

> [t]o allow a Member State, which is a party to a dispute which may concern the application and interpretation of EU law, to submit that dispute to an arbitral body with the same characteristics as the body referred to in an invalid arbitration clause contained in an international agreement [...] by concluding an ad hoc arbitration agreement with the same content as that clause, would in fact entail a circumvention of the obligations arising for that Member State under the Treaties and, specifically, under Article 4(3) TEU and Articles 267 and 344 TFEU, as interpreted in the judgment of 6 March 2018, *Achmea*.[423]

Furthermore, the Court also found that allowing arbitral proceedings based on a 'stand-alone' agreement to continue would also run afoul of the obligation to challenge the validity and not to enforce or recognise intra-EU awards under Article 7 TA.[424] Last, it rejected the investor's request to limit the temporal effects of its judgment, because this would limit 'the effects of the interpretation of those provisions provided by the Court in the judgment of 6 March 2018, *Achmea*'.[425]

Like *Komstroy*, this judgment closely follows in *Achmea*'s footsteps. These judgments demonstrate that, in the Court's view, the persistent availability of intra-EU investment arbitration was no longer tolerable. Arguably, the decision to hand down an otherwise unnecessary obiter dictum in *Komstroy* and to give immediate effect to its decision in *PL Holdings* clearly illustrates the sense of urgency pervading the Court.

[421] ibid, paras 65–66.
[422] *Poland v PL Holdings Sàrl* (n 262).
[423] ibid, para 47.
[424] ibid, para 53.
[425] ibid, para 66.

None of these judgments, however, contained an explicit statement on the compatibility with EU law of intra-EU ICSID arbitration. The vacuum initially left by the Court has been viewed as indicative of a different attitude of the Court towards intra-EU ICSID arbitration.[426] However, the CJEU's silence on this issue can be arguably explained by the fact that ICSID awards, as noted above (see section VII), are automatically recognised and enforced and can only be challenged in accordance with rules of the ICSID Convention. Therefore, national courts do not have the opportunity to raise preliminary questions in the context of annulment or execution proceedings. That is why the Court eventually ruled on the EU compatibility of intra-EU ICSID arbitration in the course of an annulment procedure under Article 263 TFEU. It was the last episode of the notorious *Micula* saga, a long legal battle that originated from an ICSID arbitral decision awarding compensation to the investor on the basis of the Sweden-Romania BIT (see section V).[427] Romania (the host state) paid part of the compensation,[428] despite the Commission's warning not to do so.[429] The question was thus whether Romania granted illegal state aid under EU law by executing such an award.[430] The Court answered this question in the positive: the sums paid to the investor constituted illegal state aid. It thus went on to address the investor's contention that Romania could not escape compliance with the award, because it had consented to submit that dispute to arbitration in the first place.[431] Relying on *Achmea*, the Court found that, because of the accession to the EU, the consent to intra-EU ICSID arbitration was no longer effective.[432] Therefore, it eventually extended the *Achmea* dictum to intra-EU ICSID arbitration. This further expansion of the *Achmea* doctrine was clearly at odds with Article 25(1) ICSID Convention,

[426] It has been argued that neither *Achmea* nor *Komstroy* imply the unavailability of intra-EU ICSID arbitration. Underpinning this view is an 'analogic' interpretation of Art 351 TFEU. In particular, it has been suggested that Art 351 TFEU would also apply when the Union has acquired a competence as a result of an amendment of the EU founding Treaties. Thus, since the EU Member States, which are parties to the ICSID Convention, entered into the latter before the establishment of the Union's competence over foreign direct investment, the ICSID Convention would take precedence over EU law. See C Tjetje, D Ruff and M Schmitt, 'Final Countdown in EU Investment Protection Law: Does the ECJ's Komstroy Ruling also Apply in Intra-EU ICSID Proceedings?' (2022) *Institut für Wirtschaftsrecht* 7.

[427] The saga started with an arbitral decision awarding compensation for a violation of the Romania-Sweden BIT, which was voluntarily executed by Romania. Subsequently, the European Commission adopted a decision declaring that the sums paid as compensation constituted illegal state aid under EU law. The investors challenged this decision before the General Court, which partially reversed the Commission's decision. The Commission in turn appealed the General Court's decision before the CJEU. T-624/15, T-694/15 and T-704/15. See *S.C. European Food S.A, S.C. Starmill S.R.L., S.C. Multipack S.R.L and others v European Commission*, ECLI:EU:T:2019:423; *European Commission v European Food SA and others*, C-638/19, EU:C:2022:50.

[428] ibid, 30.

[429] European Commission, Letter to Romania, C(2014) 6848 final.

[430] C-638/19 (n 427) para 138. Matters were further complicated by the fact that it was controversial whether the violations of the applicable BIT occurred after the accession of Romania to the EU.

[431] ibid, para 143.

[432] ibid, para 144.

which expressly stipulates that consent to ICSID arbitration is irrevocable. But the CJEU once again found that the principle of autonomy of the EU legal order superseded the customary rule *pacta sunt servanda* of which Article 25(1) ICSID is a clear manifestation.[433]

B. The CJEU's View on the Interplay between EU Substantive Law and Investment Protection Rules

The CJEU's judgment in *Micula* is also relevant because it provides an illustration of how the Court construes the relationship between EU substantive law and investment protection rules. As mentioned in the previous paragraph, the Court had little difficulty in stating that the spontaneous payment of an arbitral award constituted a violation of EU state aid law.[434] In fact, the Court did not even discuss whether EU state aid law should prevail over the applicable BIT. Rather, it straightforwardly concluded that EU state aid law precludes the enforcement of the pecuniary obligations set forth in the award. Once again, it solved the tension between EU law and intra-EU BITs by resorting to the 'EU law-centred' approach. EU law should thus prevail over allegedly conflicting international norms by virtue of the principle of primacy, even if this implies a violation of the applicable BIT and the ICSID Convention.

XV. WHAT'S NEXT? INTRA-EU INVESTMENT ARBITRATION UNDER THE ECT AFTER *KOMSTROY*

With its judgments in *Komstroy*, *PL Holdings* and *Achmea*, the Court left no doubt as to whether the EU legal order could allow purely internal cases to be submitted to arbitral tribunals. Relying on the 'EU law-centred' approach, the Court made it clear that intra-EU arbitral proceedings have no place within the EU legal order – no matter how they are established. Additionally, it also stated that EU substantive law prevailed over investment protection rules. This predictable, though crucial, extension of the *Achmea* doctrine provided EU Member States with a powerful argument to challenge the jurisdiction of ECT arbitral tribunals. They did so in newly instituted proceedings or even sought the annulment or the reconsideration of pre-existing arbitral decisions. In their annulment and reconsideration applications, EU Member States framed their intra-EU objections by emphasising the novel and ineludible character of the *Komstroy* judgment. Stripped to its essence, their main contention was that,

[433] Schreuer, Malintoppi and Reinisch (n 158) 254.

[434] The position of the CJEU in this respect does not differ from those expressed in the General Court's judgment and in the Commission's decision.

if prior to *Komstroy*, ECT arbitral tribunals could still turn a blind eye to the CJEU's position on the intra-EU application of the ECT, this was no longer possible.

However compelling this argument may sound, it failed to persuade arbitral tribunals and annulment or reconsideration committees, which regarded *Komstroy* just as a restatement of *Achmea*. As the *Cavalum* Committee put it, '*Komstroy* added nothing material to *Achmea* apart from its express application to the ECT'.[435] Moreover, in the view of the *Sevilla Beheer* tribunal, the fact that the Court came to address the issue of the compatibility with EU law of intra-EU arbitration under the ECT in an obiter dictum further weakened the relevance of *Komstroy* for ECT tribunals.[436] In reaching this finding, however, the *Sevilla Beheer* tribunal seems to disregard that the CJEU, unlike common law courts, does not distinguish between ratio decidendi and obiter dictum.[437] According to the CJEU's case law, the operative part of the preliminary rulings should be read in light of the grounds of the judgment.[438] It follows that the Court 'may, in principle, draw on any legal statement in any of its previous decisions not merely those that are necessary to resolving the case before it'.[439] In any event, even admitting that obiter dicta do not produce binding effects, it is incontestable that that specific passage of the *Komstroy* judgment fully encapsulates the current position of the Court on that matter. Therefore, should another court request a preliminary ruling of the CJEU on that specific issue, the answer would probably be the same.

The ECT arbitral tribunals also took issue with the way in which the *Komstroy* judgment conceived the role of EU law and, consequently, of the CJEU in determining the jurisdiction of intra-EU arbitral tribunals. They rejected the notion that the jurisdiction of arbitral tribunals should be determined in accordance with the ECT *and* EU law.[440] In their view, admitting the relevance of EU law in the jurisdictional phase would de facto transfer to the CJEU their *Kompetenz-Kompetenz*, namely the power to decide about their own jurisdiction.[441] In sum, ECT tribunals generally did not budge from their strict adherence to the 'international law-centred' approach. Yet, the support for such an approach is no longer unanimous in arbitral case law. In fact, the

[435] *Cavalum SGPS, S.A. v Spain*, Reconsideration decision (10 January 2022), ICSID Case No. ARB/15/34, para 96; *Infracapital F1 S.à.r.l. and Infracapital Solar B.V. v Spain*, Decision on respondent's request for reconsideration regarding the intra-EU objection and the merits (1 February 2022), ICSID Case No. ARB/16/18, para 102.

[436] *Sevilla Beheer B.V. and others v Spain*, Decision on jurisdiction, liability and principles of quantum (11 February 2022), ICSID Case No. ARB/16/27, para 667.

[437] G Beck, *The Legal Reasoning of the Court of Justice* (Hart Publishing, 2021) 249.

[438] *Robert Bosch GmbH v Hauptzollamt Hildesheim*, Case 135/77, ECLI:EU:C:1978:75.

[439] Beck n 437) 250. *cf* A Reuter 'Taking Investors' Rights Seriously: The *Achmea* and *CETA* Rulings of the European Court of Justice do not Bar Intra-EU Investment Arbitration' (2020) 80 *Zeitschrift für ausländisches öffentliches Recht und Völkerrecht* 379, 410–413.

[440] *Sevilla Beheer B.V. and others v Spain* (n 436) para 668.

[441] *Infracapital F1 S.à r.l. and Infracapital Solar B.V. v Spain* (n 435) paras 106–107.

Green Power tribunal[442] distanced itself from previous arbitral decisions. The tribunal justified its departure from the 'international law-centred' approach with a well-articulated motivation. It indeed refused to base its decision only on a literal interpretation of Article 26 ECT, because this solution overlooked the 'complexities of the case'.[443] Therefore, it analysed Article 26 ECT in light of the context[444] and the purpose of the ECT, as required by Article 31 VCLT. After conducting this two-pronged inquiry, the tribunal concluded that 'interpreting Article 26 ECT without resorting to EU law was inconclusive in the circumstances of the case'.[445] It thus turned to consider whether and how EU law affected the assessment of its own jurisdiction. The answer was of course in the positive. The tribunal held that the *Achmea* judgment applied to ECT arbitral proceedings. It found that Articles 267 and 344 TFEU, as interpreted in *Achmea*, rendered invalid the unilateral offer to arbitrate intra-EU disputes under Article 26 ECT.[446] Key to the tribunal's decision was the fact that the dispute arose out of the abrogation of a solar power subsidy, namely a matter falling within the competence of the EU. Thus, in the tribunal's view, the EU, as a REIO, had the power to adopt binding decisions on this matter, as provided for by Article 1(3) ECT.[447]

Moreover, the tribunal added that, even if it were to affirm its jurisdiction over the case, it could not decide the merits of the case, because this would exceed its powers under the ECT read in light of EU law.[448] In other words, the *Green power* tribunal found not only that EU law was relevant in the interpretation of the ECT, but also that the former should prevail in case of conflict with the latter. As the tribunal put it, 'the primacy of EU law in the relations between Member States […] is not a matter of *lex specialis* or of *lex posterior*, but one of *lex superior*'.[449] In this respect, the approach taken by the *Green Power* tribunal did not differ from that adopted by *Electrabel* tribunal. Both tribunals held that, in case of conflict with the ECT, EU law should prevail. What distinguishes one from the other is that the *Electrabel* found no incompatibility

[442] *Green Power Partners K/S Sce Solar Don Benito Aps v Spain*, Award (16 June 2022), SCC 2016/135.

[443] ibid, para 343.

[444] The tribunal made clear that the context includes not only the text of the other relevant provisions of the ECT, but also the instruments referred to in Arts 31(2) lett. b) VCLT, subsequent agreements and subsequent practice between the host state and the state of nationality of the investor under Art 31(3) lett. a) and lett. b) VCLT, and any other relevant rule of international law pursuant to Art 31(3) lett. c) VCLT. This clarification was somewhat redundant, because Art 31(2) expressly stipulates that the context of a treaty includes instruments referred therein. Moreover, the means of interpretation mentioned in Art 31(3) VCLT can also be considered as part of the context. See Villiger (n 94) 427.

[445] *Green Power Partners K/S Sce Solar Don Benito Aps v Spain* (n 442) para 412.

[446] ibid, para 426.

[447] ibid.

[448] ibid.

[449] ibid, para 469.

between the ECT and EU law, because it still adopted the 'international law-centred' approach. Hence, this finding had no practical relevance in that case. By contrast, it was crucial in the *Green Power* decision, because the tribunal did identify several collision points between the ECT and EU law.

In conclusion, the *Green Power* tribunal has been the first one to ditch the 'international law-centred' approach, even though it is not the only dissenting voice coming from the investment arbitration community.[450] At first glance, this decision might appear as an outlier, which is unlikely to reverse well-established interpretative trends.

However, looking at the broader picture, what looked like a fringe view in the arbitral case law landscape might soon become a precursor of a new phase in the relations between the ECT and EU law. Indeed, the *Green Power* decision was issued only a couple of days before the end of the negotiations on the modernisation of the ECT.[451] The agreement in principle reached by the contracting parties of the ECT contains a provision excluding the application of Article 26 ECT between Members of the same REIO.[452] It is worth highlighting that this is not an *inter se* agreement between EU Member States, but an agreement between all the contracting parties of the ECT. This is not a negligible difference, because only *inter se* agreements are subject to the conditions under Article 41 VCLT. This provision stipulates that the parties to a multilateral treaty may enter into an *inter se* agreement if the latter expressly allows them to do so. Alternatively, some of the parties to a multilateral agreement may amend it provided that such an amendment: (i) is not expressly prohibited thereunder; (ii) does not 'affect the enjoyment by the other parties of their rights under the treaty or the performance of their obligations'; and (iii) does 'not relate to a provision, derogation from which is incompatible with the effective execution of the object and purpose of the treaty as a whole'. An agreement between some of the members of the ECT excluding the intra-EU application of the treaty would

[450] In his dissenting opinion to the majority's decision in *Portigon*, Professor Giorgio Sacerdoti held that: 'arbitral tribunals have not properly considered the effect that the Court's determination of the incompatibility with EU law of ECT intra-EU arbitration (and the reasons thereof) has on EU Member States participation to the ECT. By holding that EU law *prevents* Member States to agree on intra-EU arbitration under the ECT, the EUCJ has implicitly stated that they lacked or have lost the competence, under their own constitutional law, to agree on such arbitration'. Dissenting Opinion by Giorgio Sacerdoti, *Portigon AG v Spain*, ICSID Case No. ARB/17/15, (on file with the author) para 9.

[451] Energy Charter Secretariat, Public Communication explaining the main changes contained in the agreement in principle, 24 June 2022, para 6.

[452] The negotiating directives adopted by the Council made clear that the EU did not 'support the amendment of the REIO provision in ECT modernisation process'. The REIO issue should be discussed only if the negotiation with the other contracting states were to cover it. In that case, however, the Commission's mandate would consist in ensuring 'that the aim of the provision in the Modernised ECT remains that of providing that none of the ECT provisions should be construed so as to oblige any Party to the ECT which is a party to an Economic Integration Agreement ('EIA') to extend to another Party of the ECT which is not a party to that EIA any preferential treatment applicable between the parties of the EIA'. Council of the European Union, Negotiating Directives for the Modernisation of the Energy Charter Treaty, 2 July 2019, 10745/19 ADD 1.

probably fail to fulfil the first condition. In fact, such an *inter se* agreement may come into conflict with Article 16 ECT, under which other international agreements may derogate from the ECT rules on investment protection and investment dispute settlement to the extent that they are more favourable to the investor.[453] An *inter se* agreement excluding the intra-EU application of the ECT would probably leave investors worse off, because the EU legal order does not confer on EU investors a direct power of action before an international dispute settlement mechanism.[454]

Furthermore, such an amendment could also collide with the object and the purpose of the ECT.[455] Indeed, it may be argued that the investment protection standards and the ISDS system are an integral part of the object and purpose of the ECT.

These conditions, however, do not apply to a treaty amendment, such as that under consideration, which was agreed upon by all the contracting parties of the ECT. In addition, unlike the TA, such an amendment of the ECT does not seem subject to the umbrella clause under Article 47 ECT, as this provision operates only in the case of 'withdrawal' of a contracting state.

Therefore, this amendment might constitute the endgame of intra-EU arbitration under the ECT unless the ratification process fails. The failure of the ratification process cannot be ruled out, because the modernised ECT will enter into force if three-fourths of the contracting parties complete their domestic ratification procedures.

XVI. CONCLUSION

The partial overlap between intra-EU IIAs and EU law may create tensions between these two sets of rules. In particular, the ISDS mechanisms and the substantive provisions contained in intra-EU IIAs may not always be reconciled with EU law. The Commission and the CJEU have dealt with this issue by adopting the 'EU law-centred' approach, whose primary objective is to ensure the correct functioning of the EU judicial system and the prevalence of EU substantive law.[456] According to this view, all types of intra-EU investment arbitration, including investment arbitration under the ECT, threaten the autonomy of the EU legal order.

[453] G Lampo, 'The Relationship Between Intra-EU Investment Arbitration Under the Energy Charter Treaty and the Lisbon Treaty in Light of Article 41 of the Vienna Convention on the Law of Treaties' in G Pascale and S Tonolo (eds), *The Vienna Convention on the Law of Treaties-The Role of the Treaty on Treaties in Contemporary International Law* (Edizioni Scientifiche Italiane, 2022) 330–332.

[454] ibid.

[455] K Odendahl, 'Article 41' in O Dörr and K Schmalenbach (eds) *Vienna Convention on the Law of Treaties – A Commentary* (Springer, 2012) 725.

[456] This approach is no stranger to the EU Institutions. KS Ziegler, 'Beyond Pluralism and Autonomy: Systemic Harmonisation as a Paradigm for the Interaction of EU Law and International Law' (2016) 35 *Yearbook of European Law* 667, 681; see also De Witte (n 63) 52–53.

This approach, however, failed to win the hearts and minds of arbitral tribunals, which construed the relationship between EU law and intra-EU IIAs in accordance with the 'international law-centred' approach. This view is predicated upon the assumption that EU Treaties and intra-EU IIAs are first and foremost international agreements. Therefore, potential conflicts between them should be resolved by resorting to the VCLT. Relying on such instruments, arbitral tribunals have generally concluded that there is no conflict between, on the one hand, the ISDS system and the substantive rules contained in intra-EU IIAs and, on the other hand, EU law. In fact, they invariably held that IIAs, far from being a threat to the functioning of the EU legal order, afford complementary protection to intra-EU cross-border investment.

EU Member States, with some hesitation, have eventually embraced the 'EU law-centred' approach and agreed on the termination of intra-EU BITs. Similarly, the agreement in principle reached in the context of the ECT modernisation process specifically addresses the intra-EU investment arbitration issue. It thus seems that the 'EU law-centred' approach has gradually gained significant traction. Yet, at present it has not achieved its primary objective, namely making the Union an IIA-free area and making EU law the only body of transnational law applicable to intra-EU cross-border investment. As a matter of fact, investment arbitration is still available to investors and the execution of intra-EU awards, particularly outside the EU, is still possible. Furthermore, the ratification of the agreement in principle on the modernisation of the ECT is far from being completed.

Besides all this, the 'EU law-centred' approach gives rise to several concerns. First, in the medium-long term, it may lead investors to restructure their investments in a manner that allows them to benefit from the protection of IIAs.[457] Thus, the complete or partial eradication of intra-EU IIAs may eventually result in capital flights to third countries.[458] Second, it may end up creating a vacuum of protection, particularly in EU Member States where the observance of rule of law is not always ensured.[459] Finally, the 'EU law-centred' approach is problematic, because it casts doubts about the coherence of the Union's action in this field. Indeed, the broad and bold version of the principle of autonomy, underlying the 'EU law-centred' approach, may not be congenial to the development of the EU external investment policy or even impinge on the EU's credibility as a negotiator of IIAs.

[457] Lavranos and Singla (n 276) 356–357.

[458] ibid.

[459] D Kochenov and N Lavranos, '*Achmea* Versus the Rule of Law: CJEU's Dogmatic Dismissal of Investors' Rights in Backsliding Member States of the European Union' (2021) *Hague Journal on the Rule of Law* 19.

4

The External Dimension: The EU as a Player in the Investment Treaty-Making Arena

THE EUROPEAN UNION entered the investment treaty-making arena at a time when the international investment regime was suffering a widespread backlash. This discontent triggered 'destructive' responses, such as the termination of BITs and the denunciation of the ICSID Convention by some individual members. But it also prompted a lively debate about the reform of the international investment regime. A look at investment treaty practice shows that three main reform strategies have emerged so far.[1] First, the incrementalist strategy only supports limited modifications to the design of IIAs.[2] Implicit to this strategy is the idea that IIAs still constitute the best solution for regulating cross-border investment. Second, the systemic reform strategy calls for a deeper change of the international investment regime, particularly of the investor-state dispute settlement mechanism.[3] Third, the paradigm shift strategy rests upon the idea that the investment protection system is distorted by design.[4] It thus seeks to impose environmental and labour-related obligations on investors and replace the ISDS mechanism with alternative dispute resolution mechanisms.

The EU has presented itself from the very launch of its post-Lisbon investment policy as a reformer of the international investment regime. This chapter shows that its reform strategy has changed over time. It suggests that the combination of the constitutional and political constraints affecting the development of its international investment policy led the Union to shift from an incrementalist reform strategy to a systemic reform strategy. The first part of the chapter analyses the initial Union's approach to investment treaty-making. To this end, it analyses the main substantive and procedural provisions of EU IIAs and investment chapters by setting them against the general investment treaty practice

[1] A Roberts, 'Incremental, Systemic, and Paradigmatic Reform of Investor-State Arbitration' (2018) 112 *American Journal of International Law* 410, 410–411.

[2] ibid.

[3] ibid.

[4] ibid.

background. Then, it illustrates why the Union came to espouse a systemic reform strategy by proposing the establishment of the Investment Court System (ICS) and envisaging the creation of a Multilateral Investment Court (MIC). After examining the main features of the ICS, it explores the relationship between the ICS and the principle of autonomy of the EU legal order. Finally, it attempts to identify the political obstacles preventing the 'multilateralisation' of the ICS.

I. THE INITIAL EU'S APPROACH TO INVESTMENT TREATY-MAKING: SEEKING INCREMENTAL REFORM

The EU is a newcomer in the investment treaty-making arena. In fact, as repeatedly noted in this book, the EU did not even have the competence to conclude IIAs and investment chapters before the entry into force of the Lisbon Treaty. Notwithstanding that, the Union did not start from scratch when designing its international investment policy. Indeed, three main factors shaped this new policy. First, the content of such agreements should comply with the EU constitutional requirements. Most notably, EU IIAs and investment chapters should be informed by the goals laid down in Article 21 TEU, namely fostering 'the sustainable economic, social and environmental development of developing countries' and developing 'international measures to preserve and improve the quality of the environment and the sustainable management of global natural resources, in order to ensure sustainable development'.[5] Moreover, in designing such agreements, the Union shall ensure consistency with its external action and its internal policies.[6]

A further element influencing the design of these new agreements is the pre-Lisbon trade and investment treaty practice.[7] The trade and investment agreements concluded by the Union in this period contain a variety of instruments for the protection of its own regulatory power and that of EU Member States.[8] These include, inter alia, Article XX GATT-fashioned exception clauses, provisions discouraging the lowering of labour and environmental standards

[5] Art 21 TEU.

[6] ibid.

[7] J Waleson, 'Corporate Social Responsibility in EU Comprehensive Free Trade Agreements: Towards Sustainable Trade and Investment' (2015) 40 *Legal Issues of Economic Integration* 143, 155. European Commission, Global Europe-Competing in the world COM (2006) 567, 12. See also European Commission, Shared Vision, Common Action: A Stronger Europe – A Global Strategy for the European Union's Foreign and Security Policy, 2017, 8.

[8] C Titi, 'International Investment Law and the European Union: Towards a New Generation of International Investment Agreements' (2015) 26 *European Journal of International Law* 639, 643; W Shan and S Zhang 'The Treaty of Lisbon: Half Way Toward a Common Investment Policy' (2011) 21 *European Journal of International Law* 1049, 1051; D Horng, 'Reshaping the EU's FTA Policy in a Globalized Economy: the Case of the EU-Korea FTA' (2012) 46 *Journal of World Trade* 301, 310–312.

(also referred to as 'non-lowering standard clauses'),[9] and specific chapters governing the interplay between trade and non-trade issues.[10]

Last, when negotiating its post-Lisbon IIAs and investment chapters, the EU could not ignore the process of reform of the international investment regime that started in the mid-2000s.[11]

The Commission's Communication 'Towards a comprehensive EU international investment policy' highlights the relevance of the above elements. In fact, the Commission not only stressed the need for a high and homogenous level of investment protection[12] embedding Member States' 'best practices';[13] but it also made clear that '[i]nvestment agreements should be consistent with the other policies of the Union and its Member States, including policies on the protection of the environment, decent work, health and safety at work, consumer protection, cultural diversity, development policy, and competition policy'.[14]

That said, to proclaim broad policy objectives is one thing, but to translate them into specific treaty provisions is quite another. It is thus necessary to appraise how far the reformist effort of the Union went in EU IIAs and investment chapters. The following paragraphs analyse their main components, namely the: (i) fair and equitable treatment clause; (ii) the expropriation clause; (iii) the provisions governing the interaction between general interest objectives and investment protection rules; and (iv) the rules on investor-state dispute settlement.

A. The Fair and Equitable Treatment Clause

i. Content and Evolution of the Fair and Equitable Treatment Clause

The substantive content of the FET clause is mainly a jurisprudential creation. As a commentator put it, arbitral tribunals, through purposive and contextual interpretation, turned a 'bulwark against flagrant mistreatment of foreign nationals into an all-encompassing guarantee of highly flexible notions of fairness, equity

[9] Arts 73 and 224 EU-CARIFORUM EPA; Arts 1.1 and 2.15 EU-Korea FTA.

[10] Chapter 12, EU-Korea FTA (above n 9); chs IV and V, EU-CARIFORUM EPA (above n 9).

[11] ME Footer, 'BITs and Pieces: Social and Environmental Protection in the Regulation of Foreign Investment' (2009) 18 *Michigan State Journal of International Law* 33, 46; P Acconci, 'The Integration of Non-Investment Concerns as an Opportunity for the Modernisation of International Investment Law: Is a Multilateral Approach Desirable?' in G Sacerdoti, P Acconci, M Valenti and A De Luca (eds), *General Interests of Host States in International Investment Law* (Cambridge University Press, 2014) 173, JE Alvarez, 'The Return of the State' (2011) 20 *Minnesota Journal of International Law* 223, 235–237.

[12] European Commission, Towards a comprehensive European international investment policy, COM (2010) 343 final, 5; European Parliament, Resolution of 6 April 2011 on the future European international investment policy, P7_TA(2011)0141, 15.

[13] European Commission (n 12) 11; European Parliament (n 12) para 19.

[14] European Commission (n 12) 9. See also European Parliament (n 12) paras 23–26.

and due process'.[15] As noted in chapter one, the FET clause has rich substantive content, including protection against discrimination, due process, transparency obligations, and the protection of investor's legitimate expectations.[16] Key to the astounding development of the content of the FET clause was its rather broad and vague formulation.[17] 'Old generation' IIAs, including EU Member States' ones, have generally featured FET provisions laconically stipulating that investors should be granted fair and equitable treatment.[18] Moreover, FET clauses often refer to international law or the principles of international law.[19] In the NAFTA context, the Free Trade Commission construed the reference to international law contained in Article 1105 NAFTA as implying that the content of the FET clause is equivalent to that of the customary international minimum standard of treatment.[20]

Recent treaty practice has shown a tendency to better define and 'codify' the substantive content of the FET clause.[21] For example, Article 5 of the 2004 US Model BIT provides that 'fair and equitable treatment' includes the 'obligation to not deny justice in criminal, civil, or administrative adjudicatory proceedings in accordance with the principle of due process embodied in the principal legal

[15] G Van Harten, *Investment Treaty Arbitration and Public Law* (Oxford University Press, 2008) 89.

[16] L Voisot, 'La norme du traitement juste et équitable de l'investisseur étranger et ses développements' (2011) 56 *Revue de la Faculté de Droit de l'Université de Liège* 326 331–333; M Valenti, *Gli standard di trattamento nell'interpretazione dei trattati in materia di investimenti stranieri* (Giappichelli, 2009) 190; M Valenti, 'The Protection of General Interests of Host States in the Application of the Fair and Equitable Treatment Standard', in G Sacerdoti, P Acconci, M Valenti and A De Luca (eds), *General Interests of Host States in International Investment Law* (Cambridge University Press, 2014) 34.

[17] M Paparinskis, *The International Minimum Standard and Fair and Equitable Treatment* (Oxford University Press, 2013) 112–114. The inherent vagueness of such clauses ensured their adaptability and avoid their obsolescence. See C Tietje and K Crow, 'The Reform of Investment Protection Rules in CETA, TTIP, and Other Recent EU FTAs: Convincing?' in S Griller, W Obwexer and E Vranes (eds), *Mega-Regional Trade Agreements: CETA, TTIP, and TiSA: New Orientations for EU External Economic Relations* (Oxford University Press, 2017) 91.

[18] These clauses typically read as follows: '[e]ach contracting party shall in its territory [...] in any case accord such investments fair and equitable treatment'. See Art 3 Finland-Romania BIT; Art 3 Austria-Croatia BIT. In some treaties, this standard is combined with other clauses, such as the prohibition against arbitrary and discriminatory measures, the full protection and security of the investment, the national treatment and/or the most favoured nation clauses. See Art 2 Bangladesh-Italy BIT, Art 3 Egypt-France BIT.

[19] See also Art 3 France-Uganda BIT; Art 3 France-Russia BIT; Art 4 France-Kuwait BIT. A Roberts, 'Clash of Paradigms: Actors and Analogies Shaping the Investment Treaty System' (2013) 107 *American Journal of International Law* 45, 80. P Juillard, 'The Law of International Investment – Can the Balance be Redressed?' in KP Sauvant (ed), *Yearbook of International Investment Law and Policy* (Oxford University Press, 2009) 278; Alvarez (n 11) 236.

[20] NAFTA Free Trade Commission, Notes of Interpretation of Certain Chapter Eleven Provisions, 31 July 2001. See P Dumberry, *The Fair and Equitable Treatment Standard – A Guide to NAFTA Case Law on Article 1105* (Kluwer Law International, 2013) 65–83.

[21] See generally, KW Abbott, RO Keohane, A Moravcsik, A Slaughter and D Snidal, 'The Concept of Legalisation' (2000) 54 *International Organisation* 401.

systems of the world'.[22] Similarly worded FET clauses have been subsequently included in investment chapters of 'macroregional' economic agreements, such as the CUSMA and the TPP (currently CPTPP).[23] Recent investment treaties and model investment treaties have also narrowed the substantive content of the FET clause. For instance, Article 3 of the India Model BIT stipulates that a violation of the FET standard arises only in case of denial of justice, serious violation of due process or blatantly abusive conduct, such as coercion and harassment.[24]

One of the most relevant aspects of the process of reformulation of the FET concerns the protection of investors' expectations, which, as noted in chapter three, constitutes an important, yet very controversial, component of the FET clause. Under this doctrine, the host state is subject to the obligation to act in a coherent manner. Arbitral tribunals have taken divergent views as to when and how such expectations may arise. Some tribunals adopted a restrictive reading of this doctrine.[25] For instance, the *Electrabel* tribunal[26] held that

> [w]hile the investor is promised protection against unfair changes, it is well-established that the host State is entitled to maintain a reasonable degree of regulatory flexibility to respond to changing circumstances in the public interest. Consequently, the requirement of fairness must not be understood as the immutability of the legal framework, but as implying that subsequent changes should be made fairly, consistently and predictably, considering the circumstances of the investment.[27]

However, according to another school of thought, legitimate expectations could even stem from the laws and regulations of the host state.[28] Therefore, the host state might frustrate investors' legitimate expectations by repealing previously enacted laws or regulations.

In response to the high volatility of arbitral case law on this matter, some recent IIAs have introduced provisions embracing a restrictive reading of investors' legitimate expectations. For instance, CUSMA stipulates that '[f]or greater certainty, the mere fact that a Party takes or fails to take an action that may be

[22] Art 5 2012 US Model BIT; see also Art 11.5 Canada-Korea IIA; Art 5, ASEAN-Hong Kong China SAR Investment Agreement.

[23] Art 9.6 CPTPP; Art 14.6 CUSMA; Art 10.5 RCEP.

[24] Art 5, ASEAN – Hong Kong, China SAR Investment Agreement; Art 9, PACER Plus.

[25] *Total v Argentina*, Decision on liability (27 December 2010), ICSID Case No ARB/04/01, para 119.

[26] *Electrabel S.A. v Hungary*, Decision on Jurisdiction (30 November 2012), ICSID Case No ARB/07/19.

[27] ibid, para 7.77. See also *Charanne and Construction Investments v Spain*, Award (21 January 2016), SCC 062/2012, para 493.

[28] *Bayindir v Pakistan*, Award (27 August 2009), ICSID Case No ARB/03/29, para 240; *Occidental Petroleum Corporation and Occidental Exploration and Production Company v Ecuador*, Award (1 July 2004), LCIA Case No UN3467, para 191; *Saluka v Czech Republic*, Partial Award (17 March 2006), UNCITRAL, para 307. In a similar vein, some tribunal found that the host state was under obligation to maintain a stable regulatory framework. See *CMS v Argentina*, Award (12 May 2005), ICSID Case No ARB/01/8, para 277; *Técnicas Medioambientales Tecmed S.A. v Mexico, Award* (29 May 2003), ICSID Case No ARB (AF)/00/2, para 154; *PSEG Global et al. v Turkey*, Award (19 January 2007), ICSID Case No ARB/02/5, paras 252–253.

inconsistent with an investor's expectations does not constitute a breach of this Article, even if there is loss or damage to the covered investment as a result'.[29] A similar goal is pursued by the provision, under which 'the mere fact that a subsidy or grant has not been issued, renewed or maintained, or has been modified or reduced, by a Party, does not constitute a breach of this Article, even if there is loss or damage to the covered investment as a result'.[30]

ii. The FET Clause in EU IIAs and Investment Chapters

The fair and equitable treatment clauses set forth in EU IIAs and investment chapters reflect many of the trends that emerged in recent treaty practice. To begin with, they contain a rather lengthy definition of the substantive content of the FET clause,[31] which includes: (i) the denial of justice in criminal, civil and administrative proceedings; (ii) a fundamental breach of due process; (iii) a manifestly arbitrary conduct (or manifest arbitrariness); and (iv) harassment, coercion, abuse of power or similar bad faith conduct.[32] In addition to these elements, CETA and the EUVIPA prohibit discrimination based on gender, race and religious belief, which complements the protection against discrimination afforded by the MFN and NT clauses.[33] The language of these clauses seems to suggest that the lists of FET constitutive elements are exhaustive, for they use the word 'constitute' rather than expressions like 'such as' or 'including' before listing them.[34] The negotiating history of CETA also supports this reading. In an earlier version of the agreement, the list of FET constitutive elements also included 'any other treatment of covered investments or investors which is contrary to the fair and equitable treatment obligation recognized in the general practice of States accepted as law'.[35] This formulation left an open door for future expansion of the substantive content of the FET clause. Yet, this provision was eventually expunged from the text of the treaty.[36] Additionally, an open-ended list would be difficult to reconcile with the review and amendment procedures laid down in EU IIAs and investment chapters, under which the contracting states have the power to modify the content of the FET clause.[37]

It should also be noted that the FET clauses included in EU IIAs and investment chapters do not contain any reference to the customary international law

[29] Art 14.6 CUSMA; Art 9.6 CPTPP.

[30] Art 9.6 CPTPP.

[31] F Jadeau and F Gélinas, 'CETA's Definition of the Fair and Equitable Treatment Standard: Toward a Guided and Constrained Interpretation' (2016) *Transnational Dispute Management* 7–9.

[32] Art 8.10 CETA; Art 2.4 EUSIPA; Art 2.5 EUVIPA; Art 15 EU-Mexico FTA.

[33] U Kriebaum, 'FET and Expropriation in the (Invisible) EU Model BIT' (2014) 15 *Journal of World Investment and Trade* 454, 476.

[34] Art 2.4 EUSIPA; Art 2.5 EUVIPA; Art 8.10 CETA; Art 15, ch 17, EU-Mexico FTA.

[35] Art X.9 CETA Draft (2013).

[36] Art X.9, CETA Draft (2014).

[37] Art 2.4 EUSIPA, Art 8.10, CETA, Art 2.5; Art 15, ch 17, EU-Mexico FTA. See Kriebaum (n 33) 478.

standard of foreign property protection.[38] Nevertheless, their wording clearly aims to heighten the threshold required for the emergence of the host state's responsibility. Indeed, the host state's responsibility under such clauses is engaged in case of a 'fundamental' violation of the due process,[39] or in case of manifestly arbitrary conduct.[40] Moreover, these clauses seek to circumscribe the legal protection afforded to investors' expectations. Indeed, arbitral tribunals *may* – ie, they are under no obligation to – take into account such expectations when the investors have received specific host state's representations.[41] Thus, investors' expectations merely serve as a subsidiary constitutive element of the FET clause and have a limited scope of application.[42] In this respect, it is also worth noting that the EU-Mexico FTA also adds that 'the mere fact that a Party takes or fails to take an action that may be inconsistent with an investor's legitimate expectations does not constitute a breach of this Article, even if there is loss or damage to the covered investment as a result'.[43]

The provisions restating that the exercise of the host state's power to regulate cannot frustrate investors' expectations further restricts the scope of application of this doctrine.[44] In the case of CETA, adjudicators should also take into consideration the joint interpretative instrument of 2017 when deciding whether investor's expectations deserve to be protected.[45] This interpretative declaration, which may qualify as a 'subsequent agreement' under Article 31(3) lett. a) VCLT, stipulates that 'governments may change their laws, regardless of whether this may negatively affect an investment or investor's expectations of profits'.[46]

EU IIAs and investment chapters also limit the relevance of investors' expectations in case of withdrawal of subsidies and other forms of financial support. Notably, they stipulate that, in the absence of clear and unequivocal assurances, the mere abrogation of a subsidy is not sufficient to trigger the host

[38] S Hindelang and C Sassenrath, 'The Investment Chapters of the EU's International Trade and Investment Agreements in a Comparative Perspective' [2015] *European Parliament-Directorate General for External Policies* 140; Titi (n 8) 657. Yet, it has been argued that these clauses 'appear generally to reflect standards that already exist in customary international law'. Tietje and Crow (n 17) 103.

[39] It is not entirely clear whether this requirement refers to the character of the norm violated or to the gravity of the violation. Kriebaum (n 33) 474.

[40] The language of this provision is somewhat evocative of the customary international law rule on the protection of alien property. Kriebaum (n 34) 475–476. See, eg, *Glamis Gold v United States of America*, Award (8 June 2009), UNCITRAL, para 616; *International Thunderbird Gaming Corporation v Mexico*, Award (26 January 2006), UNCITRAL Rules (NAFTA), para 194.

[41] Art 8.10 CETA, Art 2.4 EUSIPA, Art 2.5 EUVIPA.

[42] See S El Boudouhi, 'Le chapitre sur les investissements de l'ALENA: le retour de l'Etat?' (2019) 123 *Revue générale de droit international public* 865, 892; Kriebaum (n 33) 478. See also Valenti (n 16) 2.

[43] Art 15, ch 17, EU-Mexico FTA.

[44] Art 8.9 CETA; Art 2.2, EUVIPA; Art 2.3, EUSIPA.

[45] Joint Interpretative Instrument on the Comprehensive Economic and Trade Agreement (CETA) between Canada and the European Union and its Member States.

[46] ibid, para 6.

State's responsibility.[47] This provision may probably be regarded as a response to the large number of claims challenging EU Member States' decisions to repeal subsidies supporting renewable energy generation.[48]

In sum, it is possible to conclude that the EU sought to clarify and circumscribe the substantive content of the FET clauses included in its IIAs and investment chapters.[49]

B. The Umbrella Clause

i. The Nebulous Umbrella Clause in Investment Treaty Practice

The umbrella clause is a treaty provision under which the breach of contractual undertakings results in a violation of the applicable IIA.[50] This product of legal craftsmanship first appeared in international contractual practice[51] and soon became an important feature of the investment protection regime.[52] Umbrella clauses generally provide that '[e]ach Contracting State shall fulfil any other obligations it may have entered into with regard to investments in its territory by investors of the other Contracting State'.[53] Other umbrella clauses adopt a less peremptory language. For instance, the Australia-Poland BIT states that '[a] Contracting Party shall, subject to its law, do all in its power to ensure that a written undertaking given by a competent authority to a national of the other Contracting Party with regard to an investment is respected'.[54]

[47] Art 8.9 CETA; Art 2.2 EUVIPA; Art 2.2 EUSIPA; Art 15, ch 17, EU-Mexico FTA.

[48] Tietje and Crow (n 17) 97.

[49] ibid 96.

[50] This rule derogates from the principle of customary international law that the breach of a contract does not constitute per se a violation of international law. R Jennings and A Watts, *Oppenheim's International Law* (Longman, 1992) 927. See also K Lipstein, 'The Place of Calvo Clause in International Law' (1945) 22 *British Yearbook of International Law* 130, 134. Umbrella clauses constitute an example of internationalisation of contracts. See E Paasivirta, 'Internationalisation and Stabilisation of Contracts versus State Sovereignty' (1989) 40 *British Yearbook of International Law* 315, 316.

[51] Its origins can be traced back to the dispute arising out of the nationalisation of the Anglo-Iranian Oil Company (AIOC). The counsel of the AIOC, sir Elihu Lauterpacht, devised an umbrella clause to reinforce the obligations stemming from a settlement agreement. See JB Potts, 'Stabilizing the Role of Umbrella Clauses in Bilateral Investment Treaties: Intent, Reliance, and Internationalisation' (2011) 51 *Virginia Journal of International Law* 1005, 1009–1010; AC Sinclair, 'The Origins of the Umbrella Clause in the International Law of Investment Protection' (2004) 20 *Arbitration International* 411, 413–14. See also R Dolzer and C Schreuer, *Principles of International Investment Law* (Oxford University Press, 2012) 166; T Wälde, 'The 'Umbrella' Clause in Investment Arbitration-A Comment on Original Intentions and Recent Cases' (2005) 6 *Journal World Investment and Trade* 183, 187.

[52] Art II Abs-Shawcross Draft Convention on Foreign Investment.

[53] Art 8 Germany Model BIT; Art 8 Austria-Algeria BIT; Art 2 Belize-UK BIT; Art 8 Burundi-Germany BIT. See also for a slightly different formulation Art 2 Italy-Jordan BIT.

[54] Art 10 Australia-Poland BIT.

These clauses have raised a panoply of interpretative questions. First, it is unclear which contractual obligations fall within the scope of application of the umbrella clause.[55] Second, divergent views have emerged as to whether only sufficiently grave violations of contractual obligations may amount to a violation of the umbrella clause.[56] Thirdly, although it is generally accepted that the umbrella clause does not come into play with respect to purely commercial disputes that do not involve the exercise of governmental authority, there is still much debate on how to draw a line between sovereign and purely commercial acts.[57]

Further interpretative problems are also associated with unilateral acts of the host state.[58] The view that the umbrella clause does not cover such acts is now predominant in arbitral case law.[59] However, it should be noted that some degree of uncertainty on this issue persists.[60]

Due to these lingering questions,[61] umbrella clauses have become less popular over time and consequently many IIAs do not feature such clauses anymore.[62]

ii. The Umbrella Clause in EU IIAs and Investment Chapters

EU IIAs and investment chapters do not always feature umbrella clauses.

The Council's negotiating Directives mandated the Commission to incorporate such a provision in the agreements with Singapore, Canada, India, and

[55] S Lemaire, 'La mystérieuse 'umbrella clause' (Interrogations sur l'impact de la clause de respect des engagements sur l'arbitrage en matiére d'investissements)' (2009) *Revue de l'Arbitrage* 479, 485–486; J Cazala, 'La clause du respect des engagements' in C Leben (ed), *Droit international des investissements et de l'arbitrage transnational* (Pedone, 2015) 317–318.

[56] *SGS Société Générale de Surveillance S.A. v Philippines*, Decision of the tribunal on objections to Jurisdiction (29 January 2004), ICSID Case No ARB/02/6, para 128; *Noble Ventures, Inc. v Romania*, Award (12 October 2005), ICSID Case No ARB/ 01/11, para 52; *cf Joy Mining Machinery Ltd v Egypt*, Award on jurisdiction (6 August 2004), ARB/03/11, para 81; *SGS Société Générale de Surveillance S.A. v Pakistan*, ICSID case No ARB/01/13, Decision on jurisdiction (6 August 2003), para 166. See also Y Nouvel, 'La compétence matérielle: contrat, traité et clauses parapluie' in C Leben (ed), *La procédure arbitrale relative aux investissements internationaux* (Anthemis-L.G.D.J., 2008) 27–28.

[57] Wälde (n 51) 235; Lemaire (n 55) 487.

[58] Cazala (n 55) 319–320. Lemaire (n 55) 488.

[59] *Continental Casualty Company v Argentina*, Award (5 September 2008), ICSID Case No ARB/03/9, para 300. See also *CMS Gas Transmission Company v Argentina*, Decision of the ad hoc Committee on the application for annulment of the Argentine Republic (25 September 2007), ICSID Case No ARB/01/8, para 95.

[60] *SGS Société Générale de Surveillance S.A. v Pakistan*, Decision of the tribunal on objections to jurisdiction (6 August 2003), ICSID Case No ARB/01/13, para 166; *LG&E Energy Corp., LG&E Capital Corp., and LG&E International, Inc. v Argentina*, Decision on Liability (3 October 2006), ICSID Case No ARB/02/1, para 175.

[61] It has been noted that these clauses have created more problems than they have solved. See P Mayer, 'Contract claims et clauses juridictionnelles des traités relatifs à la protection des investissements' (2009) *Journal du Droit International* 71, 78. See also Nouvel (n 57) 30. J Gill, M Gearing and G Birt, 'Contractual Claims and Bilateral Investment Treaties' (2004) 21 *Journal of International Arbitration* 397, 408; ME Footer, 'Umbrella Clauses and Widely-Formulated Arbitration Clauses: Discerning the Limits of ICSID Jurisdiction' (2017) 16 *The Law and Practice of International Courts and Tribunals* 87, 107.

[62] See, eg, Cambodia-Turkey BIT; Israel-Japan BIT; TPP; Iran-Slovak Republic BIT.

the US.[63] Accordingly, the early versions of CETA included an umbrella clause. The leaked draft agreement of 21 November 2013 provided that: '[e]ach Party shall observe any specific written obligation it has entered into with regard to an investor of the other Party or an investment of such an investor'.[64] Therefore, only the violation of specific written commitments could give rise to a violation of the umbrella clause.[65] The leaked draft of 4 April 2014 added that the violation of a previous commitment is relevant under the umbrella clause provided that it results from 'the exercise of governmental powers'.[66] Despite these refinements, Canada eventually refused to include the umbrella clause in the final version of CETA.[67]

By contrast, the EUSIPA and EUVIPA contain umbrella clauses with rather narrow scopes of application. Article 2.4 EUSIPA stipulates that:

> [w]here a Party [...] had given a specific and clearly spelt out commitment in a contractual written obligation towards a covered investor of the other Party with respect to the covered investor's investment or towards such covered investment, that Party shall not frustrate or undermine the said commitment through the exercise of its governmental authority either: (a) deliberately; or (b) in a way which substantially alters the balance of rights and obligation in the contractual written obligation unless the Party provides reasonable compensation to restore the covered investor or investment to a position which it would have been in had the frustration or undermining not occurred.

The unequivocal language of this provision indicates that only contractual obligations fall within the scope of application of the umbrella clause. Thus, the repudiation of previous unilateral commitments cannot give rise to host state responsibility thereunder. Furthermore, such contractual obligations must be agreed upon in writing by the host state, namely the central government, regional or local government, or non-governmental bodies exercising powers delegated by public bodies, and the foreign investor.[68] In a footnote, the EUSIPA further clarifies that the umbrella clause covers only binding agreements providing for an exchange of rights and obligations between the parties. This explanation arguably precludes investors from invoking such a clause in case of breach of non-binding understandings or agreements between the investor and the host state.

Article 2.4(6) EUSIPA also clarifies that only contractual breaches linked to the exercise of sovereign powers can trigger the host state's responsibility.

[63] C Titi, *The Right to Regulate in International Investment Law* (Hart Publishing-Nomos, 2014), 50.

[64] Art X, CETA Draft (2013).

[65] A De Luca, 'Umbrella Clauses and Transfer Provisions in the (Invisible) EU Model BIT' (2014) 15 *Journal of World Investment and Trade* 506 (2014) 516.

[66] Art X CETA Draft (2014).

[67] PJ Kuijper, I Pernice, S Hindelang, M Schwarz and M Reuling, 'Investment Protection Agreements as Instruments of International Economic Law' [2014] *Study for the European Parliament* 18.

[68] J Crawford, 'Treaty and Contract in Investment Arbitration' (2008) 24 *Arbitration International* (2008) 351.

Thus, the mere failure to perform a contractual obligation, which is devoid of any connection with host states' sovereign acts, falls outside its purview. Last, the host state responsibility under the umbrella clause may be triggered insofar as the breach of a contractual obligation is deliberate and modifies significantly the balance between rights and obligations without providing compensation.[69]

Likewise, Article 2.5 EUVIPA contains a long and detailed umbrella clause that only covers written contracts that imply an exchange of rights and obligations.[70] Additionally, it only applies to contracts without an international arbitration clause to prevent forum shopping and parallel proceedings. The scope of application of this umbrella clause is further limited by the provision, under which a contractual breach results in a violation of the umbrella clause insofar as the commitments incorporated in the relevant contract persuaded the investor to invest in the territory of the host state.[71]

In conclusion, the wording of such clauses limits the circumstances under which the host states may violate the umbrella clause. Nonetheless, they might eventually hand back a great deal of discretion to adjudicators when assessing the deliberate nature of the host State's breach of contract or the intensity of interference with the balance of rights and obligations set forth in a given contract.

C. The Protection against Illegal Expropriation

i. The Expropriation Clause in Investment Treaty Practice

The protection against illegal expropriation is another key element of the treaty-based investment protection regime. Loosely based on the customary

[69] See Tietje and Crow (n 17) 101.

[70] Art 2.5 reads as follows '[w]here a Party has entered into a written agreement with investors of the other Party or their investments referred to in Article 13 [Scope of section II Investment Protection] that satisfies all of the following conditions, that Party shall not breach the said agreement through the exercise of governmental authority. The conditions are:

(i) the written agreement is concluded and takes effect after the date of entry into force of this Agreement;
(ii) the investor relies on that written agreement in deciding to make or maintain an investment referred to in article in Article 13. 1 (i) [Scope of section II Investment Protection] other than the written agreement itself and the breach causes actual damages to that investment;
(iii) the written agreement creates an exchange of rights and obligations in connection to the said investment, binding on both parties; and
(iv) the written agreement does not contain a clause on the settlement of disputes between the parties to that agreement by international arbitration'.

[71] 'For greater certainty, a written agreement that is concluded and takes effect after the date of entry into force of this Agreement does not include the renewal or extension of an agreement in accordance with the provisions of the original agreement, and on the same or substantially the same terms and conditions as the original agreement, which has been concluded and entered into force before the date of entry into force of this Agreement'. Footnote 1, Art 2.5 EUVIPA.

international rule on property protection,[72] it stipulates that the direct or indirect expropriation of aliens' property is legal insofar as the host state: (i) pursues public interest goals; (ii) in a non-discriminatory and non-arbitrary manner; and (iii) pays compensation. The requirements sub (i) and (ii) have generally been quite uncontested. Although IIAs generally do not contain a definition of 'public interest',[73] there has generally been little controversy about it.[74] Similarly, the principle of non-discrimination has not been nearly as debated as in other contexts.[75] More problematic has been the determination of the standard of compensation. This vexed question first arose with respect to the customary international rules on property protection.[76] Capital-importing countries have traditionally rejected the traditional western view, under which the expropriation of foreign property should be compensated in a 'prompt, adequate and effective' manner (the so-called Hull rule),[77] for this rule made the taking of foreign property remarkably more expensive.[78] IIAs often adopt the Hull rule[79] or equivalent expressions, such as 'immediate, full, and effective compensation',[80] 'reasonable and fair compensation',[81] or 'prompt and adequate compensation'.[82] Other IIAs refer to 'just compensation',[83] 'adequate compensation',[84] 'real value',[85] 'fair value',[86] 'genuine value' or 'full and genuine value',[87] 'fair market value' or 'market value'.[88]

[72] I Seidl-Hohenveldern, *International Economic Law* (Kluwer Law International, 1999) 132–135; D Carreau and P Juillard, *Droit international économique* (Dalloz, 2010) 556; A De Nanteuil, *L'expropriation indirecte en droit international des investissements* (Pedone, 2014) 138–143.

[73] MR Mauro, *Gli accordi di promozione e protezione degli investimenti* (Giappichelli, 2003) 274; U Kriebaum, 'Expropriation' in M Bungenberg, J Griebel, S Hobe and A Reinisch (eds), *International Investment Law* (C.H. Beck-Hart-Nomos, 2015) 1018–1019.

[74] ibid. PM Dupuy and Y Radi, 'Le droit de l'expropriation directe et indirecte' in C Leben, *Droit international des investissements et de l'arbitrage transnational* (Pedone, 2015) 408.

[75] Kriebaum (n 753) 1025.

[76] G Sacerdoti, 'Nascita, affermazione e scomparsa del Nuovo Ordine Economico Internazionale' in A Ligustro and G Sacerdoti (eds), *Problemi e tendenze del Diritto internazionale dell'economia – Liber amicorum in onore di Paolo Picone* (Editoriale Scientifica, 2011) 130; G Ladreit de Lacharrière, *L'influence de l'inegalité de développement des Etats sur le Droit International* (Collected Courses of the Hague Academy of International Law, 1973) 243; A Lowenfeld, *International Economic Law* (Oxford University Press, 2009) 473–484.

[77] ibid, 475–482.

[78] This prevented the emergence of a customary international rule requiring 'prompt, adequate and effective' compensation. M Sornarajah, *The International Law on Foreign Investment* (Cambridge University Press, 2010) 414–418.

[79] Art 13 Energy Charter Treaty; Art 7 Austria Model BIT; Art 5 Denmark-Bolivia BIT.

[80] Art 5 Italy Model BIT.

[81] Art 4 Finland-Morocco BIT.

[82] Art 5 France Model BIT.

[83] Art 4 Netherlands-Oman BIT; Art 4 Hungary-Spain BIT.

[84] Art 7 Austria Model BIT.

[85] Art 4 BLEU-Hungary BIT; Art 5 Colombia-Spain BIT.

[86] Art 5 Panama-UK BIT.

[87] Art 7 Argentina-Netherlands BIT; Art 5 Lithuania-Netherlands; Art 5 UK model BIT.

[88] Art 5 Czech Republic-Ireland BIT; Art 4 Czech Republic-Croatia BIT; Art 6 Poland-UAE BIT; Art 5 Italy-Russia BIT.

More recent IIAs often include detailed calculation methods to determine the amount of compensation.[89]

Another thorny question raised by the expropriation clause is that of indirect expropriation. As noted above, such clauses cover both direct and indirect expropriation, namely expropriation through regulatory means. However, drawing a clear line between indirect expropriation and legitimate, hence non compensable, host states' regulation is not a simple exercise,[90] not least because IIAs have generally provided little guidance in this respect.[91] Expropriation clauses often refer to 'measures having equivalent effect' to expropriation,[92] measures 'tantamount to an expropriation'[93] and 'measures having the effect of dispossession'.[94] To fill the vacuum left by the rather vague wording of expropriation clauses,[95] investment tribunals have identified several criteria.[96]

According to the 'sole effects' doctrine, a regulatory measure amounts to an expropriation when it seriously affects a foreign investment.[97] In line with this approach, the *El Paso* tribunal[98] stated that '[i]t is generally accepted that the decisive element in an indirect expropriation is the 'loss of control' of a foreign investment, in the absence of any physical taking'.[99] Similarly, the *Tokio Tokelés* tribunal[100] held that a regulatory measure amounts to an indirect expropriation if it deprives 'the investor of a 'substantial' part of the value of the investment'.[101]

[89] The 'fair market value' is determined through slightly different calculation methods. See Art 13(2) PACER Plus; Art 9.8 CPTPP, Art 10 Israel-Japan BIT. See A Newcombe and L Paradell, *Law and Practice of Investment Treaties – Standards of Treatment* (Kluwer Law International, 2009) 387.

[90] For a critical take on this dichotomy see R Higgins, *The Taking of Property: Recent Developments in International Law* (Collected courses of The Hague Academy of International Law, 1983) 331.

[91] L Yves Fortier and SL Drymer, 'Indirect Expropriation in the Law of International Investment: I Know it When I See it, Or *Caveat Investor*' 9(2004) *ICSID Review-Foreign Investment Law Journal* 293, 297.
C Yannaca Small, 'Indirect expropriation' and the 'right to regulate' in international investment law' (2004) OECD Working Papers on International Investment, 9.

[92] Art 5, Italy Model BIT.

[93] Art 4 Germany Model BIT; Art 1110, NAFTA.

[94] Art 5 France Model BIT.

[95] Newcombe and Paradell (n 89) 341–363; Dupuy and Radi (n 74) 387.

[96] They heavily drew on the Iran-US Claims Tribunal and of the Permanent International Court of Justice.

[97] U Kriebaum, 'Regulatory Takings: Balancing the Interests of the Investor and the State' (2007) 8 *Journal of World Investment Trade* 717, 724. *Pope & Talbot Inc. v Canada*, Interim Award (26 June 2000), UNCITRAL para 102; *Charanne and Construction Investments v Spain* (n 27) para 465.

[98] *El Paso Energy International Company v Argentina*, Award (31 October 2011), ICSID Case No ARB/03/1.

[99] ibid, para 245. See also *SD Myers Inc v Canada*, Partial Award (13 November 2000), UNCITRAL, para 283.

[100] *Tokios Tokelés v Ukraine*, Award (26 July 2007), ICSID Case No ARB/02/18.

[101] ibid, para 120. See also *Occidental Petroleum Corporation and Occidental Exploration and Production Company v Ecuador* (n 28) para 85; *Waste Management Inc. v Mexico*, ICSID Case No ARB(AF)/00/3, Award (30 April 2004), para 143; *Alpha Projektholding GmbH v Ukraine*, Award (8 November 2010), ICSID Case No ARB/07/16, para 408.

Similarly, the *Telenor* tribunal[102] held that an indirect expropriation occurs when a host state's measure deprives the investor of the 'economic value, use or enjoyment of its investment'.[103]

This method clearly focuses on the effects of the regulatory measures on the investment,[104] while the purpose and the context in which the measure was adopted play a marginal role.[105] The pursuit of public interest objectives only constitutes a condition of legality, but not a criterion to discern indirect expropriations from legitimate regulation.[106] As the *Santa Elena* tribunal put it,[107] 'where property is expropriated, even for environmental purposes, whether domestic or international, the State's obligation to pay compensation remains'.[108]

In some cases, investment tribunals deployed the legitimate expectations criterion – a concept identical to that emerged in the context of the fair and equitable treatment clause[109] – to distinguish indirect expropriation from the legitimate exercise of regulatory powers.[110] Under this approach, a host state's regulatory measure constitutes indirect expropriation when it frustrates investors' expectations, ie, the expectation to exercise the rights crystallised in tangible or intangible assets acquired under the host state law.[111] Investors' expectations serve as a proxy for the economic impact of a given regulatory measure on the investment. The downside of this method lies in the fact that it tends to enlarge the scope of protection afforded to investors,[112] as evidenced by

[102] *Telenor Mobile Communications A.S. v Hungary*, Award (13 September 2006), ICSID Case No ARB/04/15.

[103] ibid, para 65; See also *Archer Daniels Midland Company and Tate & Lyle Ingredients Americas, Inc. v Mexico*, Award (21 November 2007), ICSID Case No ARB (AF)/04/5, para 242; *Marvin Roy Feldman Karpa v Mexico*, Award (16 December 2002), ICSID Case No ARB(AF)/99/1, para 59; *Electrabel S.A. v Hungary* (n 26) para 6.62; *Sempra Energy International v Argentina*, Award (28 September 2007), ICSID Case No ARB/02/16, para 285.

[104] It is still unclear whether the effects may concern the single assets or the investment as a whole. Recently, an arbitral tribunal took the view that the answer depends on the set of facts under examination. See *Philip Morris Brands Sàrl, Philip Morris Products S.A. and Abal Hermanos S.A. v Uruguay*, Award (8 July 2016), ICSID Case No ARB/10/7, para 280.

[105] R Dolzer, 'Indirect Expropriation: New Developments?' (2003) 11 *New York University Environmental Law Journal* 64, 79; Kriebaum (n 97) 724; B Mostafa, 'Sole Effects Doctrine, Police Powers and Indirect Expropriation Under International Law' (2008) 15 *Australian Journal of International Law* 267, 279–280.

[106] Yves Fortier and Drymer (n 91) 309.

[107] *Compañia del Desarrollo de Santa Elena S.A. v Costa Rica*, Award (17 February 2000), ICSID Case No ARB/96/1.

[108] ibid, para 72.

[109] J Cazala, 'La protection des attentes légitimes de l'investisseur dans l'arbitrage international' (2009) 23 *Revue Internationale de Droit Economique* 5, 20–24.

[110] This criterion focuses on the investor rather than on the investment.

[111] Newcombe and Paradell (n 89) 351.

[112] A De Luca, 'Indirect Expropriation and Regulatory Takings: What Role for the 'Legitimate Expectations' of Foreign Investors' in G Sacerdoti, P Acconci, M Valenti and A De Luca (eds), *General Interests of Host States in International Investment Law* (Cambridge University Press, 2014) 63.

the large number of awards where arbitral tribunals have found that a violation of investors' expectations resulted in expropriation.[113]

A third instrument to distinguish indirect expropriation from non-compensable regulation is the 'police powers' doctrine, according to which regulatory measures adopted to pursue public interest objectives do not qualify as expropriation.[114] Under this approach, the pursuit of a public purpose objective serves not only as a condition of the legality of the expropriation, but also as a criterion for discerning non-compensable regulation from indirect expropriation. As the *Methanex* tribunal put it,

> as a matter of general international law, a non-discriminatory regulation for a public purpose, which is enacted in accordance with due process and, which affects, *inter alia*, a foreign investor or investment is not deemed expropriatory and compensable unless specific commitments had been given by the regulating government to the then putative foreign investor contemplating investment that the government would refrain from such regulation.[115]

Unlike the previous criteria, the police powers doctrine gives prominence to the purposes pursued by the expropriating state.[116]

The existence of a public purpose objective, however, is not enough. When applying such a method, arbitral tribunals generally assess whether the host state acted in a proportional and non-discriminatory manner.[117] For instance, the *Chemtura* tribunal[118] found that, regardless of its effect, a measure can be considered as a legitimate manifestation of the host state's regulatory power insofar as it pursues public policy objectives in a non-discriminatory manner.[119]

In a similar vein, the *Total* tribunal[120] stated that host state's regulation does not constitute expropriation if it pursues a public policy objective in a proportionate manner.[121] Whether a measure is proportionate is to be ascertained

[113] See, eg, *Técnicas Medioambientales Tecmed S.A. v Mexico* (n 28) para 149; *Metalclad Corporation v Mexico*, Award (30 August 2000), ICSID Case No ARB(AF)/97/1, para 103; *Antoine Goetz et consorts v Burundi*, Award (10 February 1999), ICSID Case No ARB/95/3, para 124; *CME Czech Republic B.V. v Czech Republic*, Partial Award (13 September 2001), UNCITRAL, paras 607–609; *ADC Affiliate Limited and ADC & ADMC Management Limited v Hungary*, Award (2 October 2006), ICSID Case No ARB/03/1, paras 423–424. *cf* Yves Fortier and Drymer (n 91) 307.

[114] Kriebaum (n 97) 725–726. Mostafa (n 105) 273.

[115] *Methanex Corporation v United States of America*, Final award of the tribunal on jurisdiction and merits (3 August 2005), UNCITRAL, Part IV – ch D – para 7; see also *Waste Management Inc. v Mexico* (n 101) para 144.

[116] Kriebaum (n 97) 726. It has been noted that this method might end up hollowing out the protection against expropriation. See Mostafa (n 105) 274.

[117] This assessment inevitably grants large discretion to investment tribunals. See C Leben, 'La liberté normative de l'Etat et la Question de l'Expropriation Indirecte' in C Leben, *Le contentieux arbitral relatif à l'investissement* (LGDJ, 2006) 179; A Asteriti, 'Regulatory Expropriation Claims in International Investment Arbitrations' in K Sauvant (ed), *Yearbook on International Investment Law and Policy* (Oxford University Press, 2013) 468.

[118] *Chemtura Corporation v Government of Canada*, Award (2 August 2010), UNCITRAL.

[119] ibid, para 266.

[120] *Total S.A. v Argentina* (n 25).

[121] ibid, para 197.

considering the factual context. It follows that such an assessment should be carried out on a case-by-case basis and inevitably grants large discretion to investment tribunals.

What emerges from the preceding analysis is that, due to the variety of approaches adopted by arbitral tribunals, it is hard to outline a coherent definition of 'indirect expropriation'.[122] Consequently, the distinction between regulation and indirect expropriation remains an extremely unsettled issue. Faced with this uncertainty, some states have agreed not to include expropriation clauses in IIAs or to limit them to direct expropriation. For instance, the Brazil-Malawi BIT clearly stipulates that '[s]ubject to its laws and regulations, a Party shall not directly nationalize or expropriate covered investments by this Agreement'.[123] More frequently, however, IIAs seek to clarify the concept of indirect expropriation by adopting two main drafting techniques. First, they codify, in a somewhat restrictive manner, the criteria adopted by arbitral case law to distinguish indirect expropriation from the legitimate exercise of the host state's regulatory power. These include the impact on the economic value of the investment, the character of the measure and the legitimate expectations of the investor.[124] Second, they expressly exclude the application of the expropriation clause to genuine regulatory measures.[125] For instance, Article 6 of the Colombia-UK BIT provides that

> non-discriminatory measures that the Contracting Parties take for reasons of public purpose or social interest (which shall have a meaning compatible with that of 'public purpose') including for reasons of public health, safety, and environmental protection, which are taken in good faith, which are not arbitrary, and which are not disproportionate in light of their purpose, shall not constitute indirect expropriation.[126]

Finally, the notion of indirect expropriation raises specific problems when applied to IPRs. Since IPRs normally qualify as 'investment',[127] they would in principle enjoy the protection afforded by the expropriation clause.[128] However, distinguishing between legitimate regulation and indirect expropriation is even

[122] M Wagner, 'Regulatory Space in International Trade Law and International Investment Law' (2014) 36 *University of Pennsylvania Journal of International Law* 1, 42; G Van Harten, *Investment Treaty Arbitration and Public Law* (Oxford University Press, 2007) 93.

[123] Art 8 Brazil-Malawi BIT; See also Art 4 Morocco-Serbia BIT; Art 8 ASEAN-India Investment Agreement.

[124] Annex I Benin-Canada BIT; Annex 12 Australia-Japan EPA; Art 9 BLEU-Colombia BIT; Art 6 Colombia-UK BIT; Art 8.7 Colombia-Korea FTA; Annex 2 ASEAN Comprehensive Investment Agreement.

[125] Y Nouvel, 'Classification cursive des régles de fond issues des traits bilateraux d'investissements' (2015) 69 *Révue Générale de Droit International Public* 7, 18.

[126] Art 6 Colombia-UK BIT; Art 5 India Model BIT; Annex 2 ASEAN Comprehensive Investment Agreement; Annex B 2012 US Model BIT.

[127] See C Correa and JE Viñuales, 'Intellectual Property Rights as Protected Investments: How Open are the Gates?' (2016) 19 *Journal of International Economic Law* 91, 95–115.

[128] B Mercurio, 'Awakening the Sleeping Giant: Intellectual Property Rights in International Investment Agreements' (2012) 15 *Journal of International Economic Law* 871, 882–907.

more difficult when it comes to intangible assets.[129] Moreover, arbitrators may not always have the necessary expertise to adjudicate such claims.[130] Last, but not least, it is often problematic to coordinate investment protection rules with the TRIPS Agreement, which establishes minimum standards of protection for a variety of IPRs.[131]

Therefore, due to the peculiarities of IPRs, IIAs often establish a specific regime for them. More specifically, they generally shield the issuance of compulsory licences in relation to IPRs or other measures limiting or restricting IPRs from expropriation claims insofar such measures are consistent with TRIPS or other IP-related treaties.[132]

ii. The Expropriation Clause in EU IIAs and Investment Chapters

EU IIAs and investment chapters also contain long and detailed expropriation clauses. These treaties clearly set the standard of compensation. In particular, the compensation should be 'prompt, adequate and effective' and reflect the fair market value before the expropriation plus market-based interests.[133] The fair market value is in turn calculated by taking into account, inter alia, the going concern value and the asset value, including the declared tax value.[134]

With respect to the compensation for land expropriation, the EUVIPA and the EUSIPA stipulate that the fair market value should be determined in accordance with the domestic legislation of the contracting states.[135] The establishment of a specific regime for the compensation of land expropriation arguably seeks to accommodate the specific characteristics of two economies (such as those of Singapore and Vietnam) characterised by a high degree of state intervention.

When it comes to the definition of indirect expropriation, EU IIAs contain a non-exhaustive list of criteria to distinguish indirect expropriation from the exercise of regulatory powers. These include the economic impact, the degree of interference and the character of the measure.[136] CETA contains a further criterion, namely the interference with investment-backed expectations.[137] Although it is still unclear how these criteria would interact with each other, it seems

[129] ibid, 904.

[130] B Mercurio, 'Safeguarding Public Welfare? – Intellectual Property Rights, Health and the Evolution of Treaty Drafting in International Investment Agreements' (2015) 6 *Journal of International Dispute Settlement* 252, 261–262.

[131] S Frankel, 'Interpreting the Overlap of International Investment and Intellectual Property Law' (2016) 19 *Journal of International Economic Law* 121, 133.

[132] See, eg, Art 1110 NAFTA, Art VI Canada-Armenia BIT. Such exemptions are more frequently included in recent IIAs. See Art 9.8(5) TPP, Art 9(4) Australia-Singapore FTA.

[133] Art 2.6 EUSIPA; Art 2.7 EUVIPA; Art 8.12 CETA; Art 18, ch 17, EU-Mexico FTA.

[134] ibid.

[135] Art 2.7 EUVIPA.

[136] These clauses are better understood as 'clarification' rather than as 'exceptions'. See A Keene, 'The Incorporation and Interpretation of WTO-Style Environmental Exceptions in International Investment Agreements' (2017) 18 *Journal of World Investment and Trade* 62, 84.

[137] See Annex B.13 Canada Model FIPA.

reasonable to believe that they would preclude the application of the 'sole-effect doctrine'.[138] The economic effects of an expropriatory measure are not the only criterion to determine whether an indirect expropriation occurred.[139] Moreover, two other factors circumscribe the definition of indirect expropriation. First, EU IIAs and investment chapters[140] stipulate that non-discriminatory measures adopted to protect public interest objectives do not constitute indirect expropriation unless 'the impact of a measure or series of measures is so severe in light of its purpose that it appears manifestly excessive'.[141] Second, as we shall see later in this chapter, they contain a variety of hortatory rules reaffirming the host state's power to regulate.

It thus seems that, under such treaties, only excessively intrusive measures would qualify as expropriations.[142] Having said that, it should be noted that adjudicators still enjoy a certain degree of discretion[143] in identifying public interest objectives[144] and determining whether a given measure has a manifestly excessive impact on the investment.[145]

Finally, all EU IIAs and investment chapters further narrow down the scope of application of indirect expropriation clauses by establishing a specific regime for IPRs.[146] In particular, they stipulate that such expropriation clauses do not apply to the issuance of compulsory licences in relation to IPRs and, more generally, to measures limiting the enjoyment of IPRs on condition that the latter are consistent with the TRIPS Agreement or other IP-related international obligations.[147] In addition, CETA also contains a provision further restricting the application of the expropriation clause to IPRs. Such a mechanism was introduced upon the insistence of Canada,[148] which at the time of negotiation of CETA was still involved in an IP-related investment dispute.[149] Canada initially proposed to

[138] Titi (n 8) 655.
[139] Annex 8-A CETA; Annex 1 EUSIPA; Annex 4 EU-Vietnam IPA.
[140] ibid.
[141] See Titi (n 8) 655.
[142] L Cotula, 'Expropriation Clauses and Environmental Regulation: Diffusion of Law in the Era of Investment Treaties' (2015) 24 *Review of European Community and International Environmental Law* 278, 286.
[143] It is worth noting that the TTIP Draft Proposal expressly mentioned the principle of proportionality. See TTIP-EU Draft Proposal on Trade in Services, Investment, and E-Commerce, 2 July 2013.
[144] Asteriti (n 117) 469.
[145] Kriebaum (n 33) 466. The initial proposal of the EU explicitly mentioned the proportionality principle. See N Bernasconi-Osterwalder, 'Commentary to the draft investment ch of the Canada-EU Comprehensive Economic and Trade Agreement (CETA)', International Institute for Sustainable. Development, 2014, 21–23.
[146] IPRs fall within the scope of application of EU IIAs. See Art 8.1 CETA; Art 2.1 EUSIPA; Art 1.2 EUVIPA.
[147] Art 2.7 EUVIPA; Art 18, ch 17, EU-Mexico FTA; Art 8.12 CETA.
[148] H Grosse Ruse-Khan, 'Challenging Compliance with International Intellectual Property Norms in Investor–State Dispute Settlement' (2016) 19 *Journal of International Economic Law* 241, 271.
[149] See *Eli Lilly and Company v The Government of Canada*, Final award (16 March 2017), UNCITRAL, ICSID Case No UNCT/14/2.

introduce a provision stipulating that the expropriation clause 'does not apply to a decision by a court, administrative tribunal, or other governmental intellectual property authority, limiting or creating an intellectual property right, except where the decision amounts to a denial of justice or an abuse of right'.[150] The preference for such a specific formulation can be explained by the fact that the abovementioned investment dispute originated from the judicial invalidation of patents.[151] However, Canada's initial proposal was eventually replaced by the current Article 8.12(6) CETA, under which 'a determination that these measures are inconsistent with the TRIPS Agreement or Chapter Twenty (Intellectual Property) does not establish an expropriation'.[152] The EUSIPA features an identically worded provision.[153]

D. Redefining the Relationship between General Interest Objectives and Investment Protection Rules: Clarificatory Rules, Hortatory Rules, Exception and Carve-out Mechanisms

i. The Integration of Public Interest Objectives into IIAs: Recent Trends in Investment Treaty Practice

IIAs have traditionally been quite short and simple instruments containing investment protection rules, investor-state and state-to-state dispute settlement mechanisms. However, this way of conceiving foreign investment protection has gradually become outdated. Recent IIAs not only contain more detailed investment protection rules, but also provide for a variety of instruments governing the interaction between investment protection and non-investment interests.[154]

First, they contain clarificatory and hortatory rules safeguarding the host state's power to regulate. These rules include, for example, the 'non-lowering standards' clauses stating that it is inappropriate to attract foreign investment by weakening domestic environmental or social regulation.[155] Designed to avert the 'race to the bottom' of environmental and labour standards, these provisions are devoid of preceptive content. However, they may come into play in the contextual and purposive interpretation of investment protection rules pursuant

[150] Quoted by Grosse Ruse-Khan (n 148) 271.

[151] The claimant contended that the invalidation of such patents constituted a violation of Arts 1105 and 1110 NAFTA.

[152] Grosse Ruse-Khan (n 148) 271.

[153] Annex 3 EUSIPA.

[154] Footer (n 11) 46. This can be also regarded as a specific manifestation of a broader evolution of international law. See JB Auby, 'Public Goods and Global Administrative Law' in JB Auby and J Morrison (eds) *Values in Global Administrative Law* (Hart Publishing, 2011) 243.

[155] Art 15 Canada-Moldova BIT; Art 15 Canada-Guinea BIT; Art 12 US-Rwanda BIT.

to Article 31 VCLT.[156] More specifically, they may support a restrictive reading of such rules[157] or affect the determination of the amount of compensation.[158] Within this category it is also possible to include the rules clarifying that the promotion and the protection of foreign investment will not prevent the host state from exercising its power to regulate.[159]

Second, carve-outs and exception mechanisms have also gained currency in recent IIAs. Carve-outs generally cover particularly technical domains, such as prudential regulation,[160] which has been repeatedly targeted by investors.[161]

Carve-outs are also used to protect the contracting states' policy space in sensitive domains. For instance, the trade and investment disputes on tobacco plain packaging concerning Australia[162] may probably explain the inclusion of a carve-out clause on 'tobacco control measures' in the CPTPP.[163]

Third, recent IIAs contain exception clauses that partially or totally reproduce the wording of Article XX GATT or Article XIV GATS.[164] Like their WTO counterparts, such provisions allow respondents to justify the adoption of general interest measures, which would be otherwise inconsistent with investment protection rules.

Finally, it should be noted that regional trade and investment agreements include specific chapters, often labelled as 'environment' or 'sustainable development', containing environment or labour-related hortatory mechanisms.[165]

[156] See A Asteriti, 'Waiting for the Environmentalists: Environmental Language in Investment Treaties' in R Hofmann and CJ Tams (eds) *International Investment Law and its Others* (Nomos, 2013) 130.

[157] Footer (n 11) 63.

[158] E Van der Zee, 'Incorporating the OECD Guidelines in International Investment Agreements: Turning a Soft Law Obligation Into Hard Law?' (2013) 40 *Legal Issues of Economic Integration* 33 (2013) 56.

[159] See, eg, Art 1 New Zealand-Taiwan Province of China ECA, Art 2, PACER Plus.

[160] See, eg, Art XII Canada-Ecuador BIT; Art X(4) Canada-Czech Republic BIT; Art 4 Netherlands-Laos BIT.

[161] AD Mitchell, JK Hawkins and N Mishra, 'Dear Prudence: Allowances Under International Trade and Investment Law for Prudential Regulation in the Financial Services Sector' (2016) 19 *Journal of International Economic Law* 787 (2016) 798–800.

[162] *Philip Morris Asia Limited v The Commonwealth of Australia*, Award (8 July 2016), UNCITRAL, PCA Case No 2012-12. T Ahn, 'The Utility of Carve-Out Clauses in Addressing Regulatory Concerns in Investment Treaty Arbitration' (2016) 12 *Asian International Arbitration Journal* 65, 72.

[163] Art 29.5 CPTPP.

[164] A Newcombe, 'The Use of General Exceptions in IIAs: Increasing Legitimacy or Uncertainty' in A de Mestral and C Lévesque (eds), *Improving International Investment Agreements* (Routledge, 2013) 276; S Spears, 'The Quest for Policy Space in a New Generation of International Investment Agreements' (2010) 13 *Journal of International Economic Law* 1037, 1061–1062.

[165] Chapter 20 CPTPP; chs 16 and 17 CAFTA.

ii. Clarificatory and Hortatory Rules for the Protection of Public Interest Objectives Contained in EU IIAs and Investment Chapters

EU IIAs and investment chapters largely reflect the tendencies that have emerged in recent investment treaty practice. The preambles of such instruments generally reaffirm the commitment of the contracting states to promote and protect sustainable development, labour and environmental standards and human rights and to comply with international obligations on such matters.

The bodies of the EU IIAs and investment chapters feature rules protecting the host state's policy space. For instance, Article 8.9 of CETA stipulates that

> [f]or greater certainty, the mere fact that a Party regulates, including through a modification to its laws, in a manner which negatively affects an investment or interferes with an investor's expectations, including its expectations of profits, does not amount to a breach of an obligation under this Section.[166]

CETA also stipulates that even 'significant' amendments of fiscal legislation do not constitute a violation of the FET clause.[167] Moreover, CETA should be read in light of the 2017 joint interpretative instrument, which clarifies that

> CETA preserves the ability of the European Union and its Member States and Canada to adopt and apply their own laws and regulations that regulate economic activity in the public interest, to achieve legitimate public policy objectives such as the protection and promotion of public health, social services, public education, safety, the environment, public morals, social or consumer protection, privacy and data protection and the promotion and protection of cultural diversity.[168]

A rich repository of rules reaffirming the regulatory power of the host state also lies in the 'sustainable development and trade', 'environment and trade' or 'labour and trade' chapters.[169] Such chapters reaffirm the obligation to ratify or implement labour,[170] environment,[171] and climate change-related multilateral commitments.[172] They also provide for non-lowering standards clauses ('upholding levels of protection' clauses) that are often combined with

[166] The other EU IIAs contain similar provisions. See Art 2.2 EUVIPA; Art 2.2 EUSIPA.

[167] Art 28.7 CETA.

[168] Joint Interpretative Instrument on the Comprehensive Economic and Trade Agreement (CETA) between Canada and the European Union and its Member States, para 2. The Commission has recently discussed with Germany new clarifications on CETA investment protection rules. European Commission, Statement from the Commission on clarifications discussed with Germany regarding investment protection in the context of the CETA agreement, Press release, 29 August 2022.

[169] Similar chapters already featured in pre-Lisbon EU trade and investment agreements. Chapter 13, EU-Korea FTA (n 9); chs 4 and 5 EU-CARIFORUM EPA (n 9). Human rights-related provisions are generally included in partnership agreements. See Art 2 EU-Canada Strategic Partnership Agreement; Arts 2 and 35 EU-Vietnam Framework Agreement on Comprehensive Partnership and Cooperation.

[170] See also Art 13.4 EUVIFTA; Art 12.3 EUSFTA; Art 3, ch 27, EU-Mexico FTA.

[171] Art 13.5 EUVIFTA; Art 12.6 EUSIFTA; Art 4, ch 27, EU-Mexico FTA.

[172] Art 13.6 EUVIFTA; Art 5, ch 27, EU-Mexico FTA.

provisions strengthening the obligation to enforce environmental and labour laws.[173] Once again, it is unclear whether these provisions might create binding and enforceable obligations.[174] Owing to their wording, such hortatory and clarificatory rules add little or nothing to pre-existing international obligations and do not have a direct impact on contracting states' environmental or labour policies.[175] However, they may be relevant because they promote the idea that trade and investment are not necessarily antagonistic to environmental and societal interests.[176]

That said, it is still doubtful whether such chapters could come into play when interpreting EU IIAs and investment chapters. As regards CETA, the main obstacle lies in the fact that chapters 22, 23, and 24 are unequivocally labelled 'Trade and …' and bear no mention of the word 'investment'. However, it should not be overlooked that such chapters contain 'upholding levels of protection' clauses, which expressly refer to 'investment'.[177] Thus, it seems reasonable to conclude that chapters 22, 23, and 24 of CETA may play a role in interpreting the investment protection rules laid down therein. More specifically, such chapters might be considered as relevant 'context' under Article 31(1) VCLT. This view seems to be supported by a recent arbitral decision in the *Al Tamimi* case,[178] where the tribunal referred to the 'environment' chapter of the Oman-US FTA when assessing whether the respondent had breached the minimum standard of treatment. In particular, it noted that such chapters exemplified 'the importance attached by the US and Oman to the enforcement of their respective environmental laws'.[179]

When it comes to the EUSIPA and the EUVIPA, the relevance of such chapters is less obvious because these agreements are devoid of specific chapters on environment and sustainable development. Yet, it could be argued that the chapters on environment and sustainable development included in the EUSFTA and EUVFTA should be taken into consideration when interpreting the investment protection rules under the EUSIPA and the EUVIPA. Such chapters might indeed come into play as 'relevant rules of international law applicable in the relations between the parties' pursuant to Article 31(3) lett. c) VCLT.

[173] Art 13.3(3) EUVIFTA; Art 12.6 EUSIFTA; Art 23.4 CETA.

[174] M Bronckers and G Gruni, 'Retooling the Sustainability Standards' (2021) 24 *Journal of International Economic Law* 25, 31–32.

[175] Their impact is further limited by the fact that they are enforced through state-to-state soft mechanisms: Arts 23.9–23.11; Arts 24.13–24.16, CETA; Art 13.16, EU-Vietnam FTA; Arts 12.16 and 12.17, EU-Singapore FTA.

[176] G Adinolfi, 'A Cross-Cutting Legal Analysis of the European Union Preferential Trade Agreements' Chapters on Sustainable Development' in C Beverelli, J Kurtz and D Raess (eds), *International Trade, Investment, and the Sustainable Development Goals* (Cambridge University Press, 2020) 24–25.

[177] Art 23.4 CETA; Art 13.3 EUVIPA; Art 12.12 EUSIPA.

[178] *Adel A Hamadi Al Tamimi v Sultanate of Oman*, Award (3 November 2015), ICSID Case No ARB/11/33.

[179] ibid, para 389.

iii. General Exceptions Contained in EU IIAs and Investment Chapters

EU IIAs and chapters provide for WTO-fashioned general exception mechanisms.[180] Under the EUSIPA, this mechanism may be invoked in case of violation of the NT clause.[181] By contrast, under the EUVIPA and the EU-Mexico FTA, the general exception mechanism applies, respectively, to violations of the NT and MFN obligations, and to violations of the investment liberalisation section of the treaty.[182]

Similarly, CETA contains a two-tiered general exception, which applies in case of violation of the pre-establishment and non-discrimination obligations (MFN and NT clauses).[183] The first tier incorporates a slightly broader version of Article XX GATT. More specifically, Article 28.3 CETA clarifies that the ground of justification under Article XX GATT lett. b) also covers 'environmental measures aimed to protect human, animal and plant life'. Additionally, it stipulates that Article XX lett. g) GATT also applies to 'measures for the conservation of living and non-living exhaustible natural resources'. The second tier of the general exception clause covers, amongst others, measures necessary to protect public security or public morals or maintain public order, prevent deceptive and fraudulent practices or deal with the effects of a default on contracts, and protect the privacy of individuals.

In sum, the general exception clauses included in EU IIAs and investment chapters do not apply to investment protection rules other than the MFN and the NT clauses. This choice can be arguably explained by the fact that such exceptions are difficult to reconcile with several such provisions.[184] To begin with, it is hard to imagine how these exceptions would interact with the exceptions specific to transfer clauses, which also cover a wide range of policy areas, such as the application of criminal and insolvency law.[185] More importantly, WTO-fashioned general exceptions would not sit comfortably with the provisions clarifying the definition of indirect expropriation. As regulatory measures can amount to expropriation only in 'rare circumstances', the general exception might render the application of the expropriation clause virtually impossible.[186] Much less problematic, however, would be the relationship between these exceptions and the FET clause.

That said, it remains to be seen how arbitral tribunals will interpret these clauses. Given the evident similarities with Article XX GATT, arbitral tribunals might draw on WTO jurisprudence when construing them.[187] Specifically, the

[180] *cf* Art XX lett. a), b), d), f), g) GATT. See also Spears (n 164) 1063. See also Newcombe (n 164) 279.
[181] Art 2.3, EUSIPA.
[182] Art 4.6 EUVIPA; Art XX, ch 34, EU-Mexico FTA.
[183] Art 28.3 (1) of CETA.
[184] S Di Benedetto, 'Modelli giuridici di ecceezione e integrazione di valori non commerciali: dall'esperienza del diritto GATT/OMC ai regime di protezione degli investimenti esteri' (2013) 27 *Diritto del Commercio Internazionale* 405, 435.
[185] Art 2.7 EUSIPA; Art 4.9 EUVIPA; Art 8.13 CETA.
[186] Keene (n 136) 84.
[187] ibid, 79.

influence of WTO case law might provide support for an extensive approach, particularly vis-à-vis environmental measures.[188] However, the relevance of WTO case law in the investment context cannot be taken for granted, because arbitral tribunals have often been reluctant to transpose WTO Panels and Appellate Body's findings into the investment context.[189]

iv. Mechanisms for the Protection of the Policy Space in the Economic, Fiscal and Monetary Domains Contained in EU IIAs and Investment Chapters

EU IIAs and investment chapters also safeguard the contracting states' margin of manoeuvre in particularly sensitive and technical domains.

For instance, these treaties contain carve-out clauses to exempt prudential regulation measures from investment disciplines.[190] Interestingly, CETA establishes a specific procedure for the application of such a clause.[191] According to this procedure the respondent may request the Financial Services Committee established under Article 13.18 CETA to assess whether the prudential carve-out clause applies.[192] The Committee may thus intervene, in view of the technical expertise of its members, on a matter that would normally fall within the remit of the ISDS tribunals.[193] The referral to the Committee suspends the proceedings where the carve-out clause was originally invoked.[194] The decision of the Financial Services Committee[195] only binds the adjudicators examining the dispute where the issue was raised.[196] However, it is not possible to exclude that such decisions may have 'persuasive impact' on other ISDS tribunals.

Furthermore, EU IIAs and investment chapters also contain instruments granting the host states a reasonable margin of manoeuvre in the fiscal domain. For instance, they exempt anti-tax avoidance measures from investment disciplines.[197]

[188] R Howse, 'The World Trade Organisation 20 Years on: Global Governance by Judiciary' (2016) 27 *European Journal of International Law* 7, 36–45; Newcombe (n 164) 275. For a less optimistic view on the relevance of the general exception see L Bartels, 'Human Rights, Labour Standards, and Environmental Standards in CETA' in S Griller, W Obwexer and E Vranes (eds), *Mega-Regional Trade Agreements: CETA, TTIP, and TiSA – New Orientations for EU External Economic Relations* (Oxford University Press, 2017) 212.

[189] Keene (n 136) 79–81.

[190] Art 13.16 and Annex 13-B CETA; Art 4.4 EUSIPA; Art 4.5 EUVIPA; see also Art XX.13, ch 12, EU-Mexico FTA. The wording of such clauses is akin to that of the prudential carve-outs provided for by pre-Lisbon PTAs. See Art 7.38 EU-Korea FTA; Art 154 EU-Colombia-Peru Trade Agreement. For in-depth analysis of prudential carve outs in preferential trade agreements see CM Cantore, *The Prudential Carve-Out for Financial Services Rationale and Practice in the GATS and Preferential Trade Agreements* (Cambridge University Press, 2018), 118–148.

[191] Annex 13-B CETA.

[192] Art 13.21 CETA.

[193] Art 13.18 stipulates that the Committee shall be composed of 'representatives of authorities in charge of financial services policy with expertise in the field'.

[194] Art 13.21 CETA.

[195] The same rule applies to the decisions of the CETA Joint Committee.

[196] Annex 13-B CETA.

[197] Art 4.4 EUVIPA; Art 4.6 EUSIPA; Art 28.7 CETA; Art X.4, ch 34, EU-Mexico FTA.

Worthy of note are also the rules on investment claims[198] challenging government debt restructurings.[199] Sovereign debt workouts may give rise to 'holdout problems', namely the situation in which some of the bondholders withhold their consent to restructuring in the hope of obtaining more advantageous conditions from the borrower. Sovereign bonds often contain collective action clauses to discourage such holdouts.[200] Under these clauses, a simple or qualified majority of bondholders can modify the contractual terms governing a specific class of government bonds and curtail the ability of individual bondholders to enforce their contractual rights.[201] CACs, however, may not shield the restructuring state from investment claims.[202] That is why EU IIAs seek to limit the availability of investment protection rules in case of 'negotiated restructurings', namely an amendment of government bonds made in accordance with their terms or governing law or a debt exchange or other similar solutions approved by a qualified majority of bondholders.[203] Specifically, they bar bondholders from bringing investment claims, except those based on the most favoured nation or the national treatment clauses.[204]

Finally, EU IIAs and investment chapters contain instruments governing the interplay between investment protection rules and the conduct of monetary policy. These notably include monetary policy exceptions,[205] temporary

[198] Annex 8-B CETA; Annex 5 EUVIPA; Annex 4 EUSIPA. There is a significant number of such investment claims. See, eg, *Abaclat and others v Argentina (formerly Giovanna a Beccara and others v Argentine Republic)*, Decision on jurisdiction and admissibility (4 August 2011), ICSID Case No ARB/07/5, para 361; *Ambiente Ufficio SpA and others v Argentina*, Decision on jurisdiction (8 February 2013), ICSID Case No ARB/08/9; *Postova Banka a.s. and Istrokapital SE v Greece*, Award (9 April 2015), ICSID Case No ARB/13/8.

[199] Debt restructuring can be defined 'as an exchange of outstanding sovereign debt instruments, such as loans or bonds, for new debt instruments or cash through a formal process. Sovereign debt here refers to debt issued or guaranteed by the government of a sovereign state. One can generally distinguish two main elements in a debt restructuring: debt rescheduling, defined as a lengthening of maturities of the old debt, possibly involving lower interest rates; and debt reduction, defined as a reduction in the face (nominal) value of the old instruments'. See US Das, MG Papaioannou and C Trebesch, 'Restructuring Sovereign Debt: Lessons from Recent History' in S Claessens, MA Kose, L Laeven and F Valencia (eds), *Financial Crises: Causes, Consequences, and Policy Responses* (Washington, DC, International Monetary Fund, 2014) 597.

[200] M Waibel, 'Opening Pandora's Box: Sovereign Bonds in International Arbitration' (2007) 101 *American Journal of International Law* 711, 736–737; Y Jung and SD Han, 'Sovereign Debt Restructuring Under the Investor-State Dispute Regime' (2014) 31 *Journal of International Arbitration* 75, 83; F Suescun de Roa, 'Investor-State Arbitration in Sovereign Debt Restructuring: The Role of Holdouts' (2013) 30 *Journal of International Arbitration* 131, 150.

[201] Waibel (n 200) 736.

[202] ibid 736. See also C Fang, J Schumacher and C Trebesch, 'Restructuring Sovereign Bonds: Holdouts, Haircuts and the Effectiveness of CACs' (2021) 69 *IMF Economic Review* 155, 159; G Bianco, 'European Union's Investment Agreements and Public Debt' (2017) 28 *European Business Law Review* 119, 130–131.

[203] The EUVIPA establishes a minimum approval threshold of 66% of the aggregate principal amount threshold, while CETA and EUSIPA set it at 75%.

[204] The EUSIPA only allows investors to submit claims alleging a violation of the national treatment obligation.

[205] Art 13.17 CETA; Art 4.7 EUVIPA; Art 4.7 EUSIPA.

safeguard measures and restrictions to capital movements to be triggered in case of grave difficulties in the operation of exchange rate policies and balance-of-payments problems.[206]

E. The ISDS Mechanism in the Early Versions of the EU Investment Chapters

i. ISDS: Backlash and Reform

The ISDS mechanism has become a crucial component of the international investment regime.[207] However, as the importance of this instrument grew,[208] it also came under stricter scrutiny.[209] ISDS critics have highlighted three main shortcomings. First, in their view, the ISDS system is tainted by an inherent pro-investor bias. Arbitrators are under the sway of the appointing parties and prone to espouse their views.[210] This is because the prospect of re-appointment constitutes a powerful incentive for the arbitrators to uphold the views of the appointing party.[211] The risk of 'capture' is thus even greater when it comes to arbitrators appointed by investors, because they have the exclusive power to commence arbitral proceedings.[212]

Second, investment arbitration has also come under fire because of its (alleged) inability to ensure a reasonable degree of legal certainty.[213] As a matter of fact, similarly or identically worded provisions have often been construed in

[206] Art 4.10 EUVIPA; Art 28.4 CETA; Art 4.11 EUVIPA and 28. These provisions are modelled on Art 15.9 of the EU-Korea FTA. See A Reinisch, 'The EU on the Investment Path – *Quo vadis Europe?* The Future of EU BITs and Other Investment Agreements' (2014) 12 *Santa Clara Journal of International Law* 111, 131.

[207] Only a minority of IIAs do not contain such mechanism. Congo-Switzerland BIT; Germany-Indonesia BIT; Germany-Iran BIT; Denmark-Indonesia BIT; Australia-Malaysia FTA; Angola-Brazil BIT; Brazil-Mozambique BIT; Brazil-Chile BIT.

[208] J Pauwelyn, 'At the Edge of Chaos? Foreign Investment Law as a Complex Adaptive System, how it Emerged and how it can be Reformed' (2014) 29 *ICSID Review-Foreign Investment Law Journal* 372, 396.

[209] SD Franck, 'The Legitimacy Crisis in Investment Treaty Arbitration: Privatizing Public International Law Through Inconsistent Decisions' (2005) 73 *Fordham Law Review* 1521, 1539.

[210] This phenomenon has been referred to as 'affiliation bias'. See S Puig, 'Debiasing International Economic Law' (2019) 30 *European Journal of International Law* 1339, 1348. See also Y Shany, 'Squaring the Circle? Independence and Impartiality of Party-Appointed Adjudicators in International Legal Proceedings' (2008) 30 *Loyola of Los Angeles International and Comparative Law Review* 473, 481.

[211] It has been aptly noted that '[a]s long as income-maximizing private adjudicators compete against each other in the market of private dispute resolution for their re-appointment, judicial independence cannot be ensured'. P Hainbach, 'The EU's Approach to Investor-State Arbitration in the Comprehensive Economic and Trade Agreement (CETA)' (2016) *Transnational Dispute Management* 1.

[212] ibid.

[213] C Schreuer, 'Coherence and Consistency in International Investment Law' in R Echandi and P Sauvé (eds), *Prospects in International Investment Law and Policy* (Cambridge University Press, 2013) 398; LT Wells, 'Backlash to Investment Arbitration: Three Causes' in M Waibel, A Kaushal, K Chung and C Balchin (eds), *The Backlash Against Investment Arbitration – Perceptions and Reality* (Kluwer Law International, 2010) 342.

widely divergent manners.[214] Although inconsistency is by no means peculiar to investment arbitration, the risk of incoherent arbitral decisions is higher in this context due to the piecemeal structure of the international investment regime.[215]

Third, investment arbitration has been lambasted for the lack of a general obligation to publish documents relating to arbitral proceedings[216] and the lack of rules governing the participation of third-parties in arbitral proceedings.[217]

Last, the ISDS has been criticised for its asymmetric structure,[218] which is epitomised by the lack of investors' obligations in many IIAs.[219]

The (perceived or real) shortcomings of the ISDS system did not prevent investment arbitration from thriving.[220] Yet, they gradually eroded the trust in it. Faced with the legitimacy crisis of investor-state arbitration, several states sought to address the main drawbacks of such a mechanism. The buds of reform sprang in the NAFTA context thanks to the action of the Free Trade Commission. In two subsequent Notes, the FTC indeed clarified there was no general duty of confidentiality under NAFTA[221] and set forth the admissibility test for non-disputing parties' submissions.[222]

[214] See F Spooremberg and JE Viñuales, 'Conflicting Decisions in International Arbitration' (2009) 8 *The Law and Practice of International Courts and Tribunals* 91, 94; A Nilsson and O Englesson, 'Inconsistent Awards in Investment Treaty Arbitration: Is an Appeals Court Needed?' (2013) 30 *Journal of International Arbitration* 561, 563–569.

[215] Y Banitafemi, 'Consistency in the Interpretation of Substantive Investment Rules: Is it Achievable?' in R Echandi and P Sauvé (eds), *Prospects in International Investment Law and Policy* (Cambridge University Press, 2013) 203–204; Spooremberg and Viñuales (n 215) 96. *cf* SW Schill, *The Multilateralisation of International Investment Law* (Cambridge University Press, 2009) 15–16.

[216] L. Malintoppi, N. Limbasan, 'Living in glass houses? The debate on transparency in international investment srbitration' 2 BCDR International Arbitration Review 32 (2015), 33; T. Ishikawa, 'Third party participation in investment treaty arbitration' (2010) 59 *International and Comparative Law Quarterly* 373, 406; J. Calamita, 'Dispute settlement transparency in Europe's evolving investment treaty policy: adopting the UNCITRAL Transparency rules approach' (2014) 15 *Journal of World Investment and Trade* 585, 665–667.

[217] The lack of specific rules regulating (private) third-party participation entirely left the question up to arbitral tribunals' discretion. See, eg, *Methanex Corporation v United States of America*, Decision of the tribunal on petitions from third persons to intervene as 'amici curiae' (15 January 2001), UNCITRAL, para 49–53; *Suez Sociedad General de Aguas de Barcelona S.A.and Vivendi Universal, S.A. v Argentina*, Award (19 May 2005), ICSID Case No ARB/03/19, paras 18–33.

[218] IC Popova and F Poon, 'From Perpetual Respondent to Aspiring Counterclaimant? State Counterclaims in the New Wave of Investment Treaties' (2015) 2 *BCDR Arbitration Review* 223, 229. However, it should be noted that dispute settlement clauses containing phrases like 'any dispute' or 'all disputes' may be construed as expressing consent to the submission of counterclaims. See JA Rivas, 'ICSID Treaty Counterclaims: Case Law and Treaty Evolution' in JE Kalicki and A Joubin-Bret (eds), *Reshaping the Investor-State Dispute Settlement System* (Brill, 2015), 783.

[219] D Atanasova, CA Martínez Benoit and J Ostransky, 'Counterclaims in Investor-State Dispute Settlement (ISDS) Under International Investment Agreements (IIAs)' (2012) The Graduate Institute Centre for Trade and Economic Development 39–40.

[220] On 1 January 2020, ISDS cases reached the astounding figure of 1,023. See IIA Issues Note, July 2020, UNCTAD.

[221] Malintoppi and Limbasan (n 216) 41.

[222] Under this test, arbitral tribunals shall admit such submissions insofar as: (i) they help them clarify the facts of the case or the interpretation of the applicable rules; (ii) they concern issues falling within the scope of the dispute; (iii) the party submitting them had a significant interest in the arbitration; and (iv) the decision of the case involves public interest considerations.

In 2006, the amendments of the ICSID rules also aimed to make ICSID proceedings more transparent without changing the fundamental structure of investment arbitration.[223] The publication of excerpts of arbitral decisions became compulsory, while the publication of the integral text of such decisions remained conditional upon the disputing parties' agreement.[224] Furthermore, the amendments extended to non-disputing parties the right to attend oral hearings[225] and file written submissions.[226]

Moreover the United Nations Convention on transparency in treaty-based investor-state arbitration ('Mauritius Convention on transparency') introduced similar innovations by adopting the UNCITRAL Rules on transparency.[227] Interestingly, during the negotiation of these rules, EU Member States and the Commission took rather divergent positions as to how far the reform process should go. EU Member States expressed their opposition to adopt transparency as the default rule in the conduct of UNCITRAL arbitral proceedings,[228] while the Commission decidedly pushed for this option.[229] The approved text of the UNCITRAL Rules on transparency was eventually more reflective of the Commission's views. The UNCITRAL Rules establish the duty to publish any order, decision, or award of the arbitral tribunals.[230] Additionally, they confer on non-disputing parties the power to submit written pleadings 'on issues of treaty interpretation'[231] and, under certain conditions,[232] the power to submit pleadings on other issues.

The thrust towards greater transparency has also affected the formulation of recent IIAs. Many states, spearheaded by the US and Canada, included transparency-related obligations in their IIAs.[233] These treaties granted to third-parties participatory rights[234] and introduced the obligation to make documents of the proceedings publicly available (eg the notice of arbitration, the pleadings, and the minutes of the hearings).[235]

[223] J Wong and J Yackee, 'The 2006 Procedural and Transparency-Related Amendments to the ICSID Arbitration Rules' in KP Sauvant (ed), *Yearbook on International Investment Law and Policy 2009–2010* (Oxford University Press, 2011) 268.

[224] Rule 48, Rules of procedure for arbitration proceedings.

[225] Rule 32, Rules of procedure for arbitration proceedings.

[226] Art 37, Rules of procedure for arbitration proceedings.

[227] The Convention entered into force on 18 October 2017 and applies to disputes based on treaties entered into before 1 April 2014. United Nations Convention on Transparency in Treaty-based Investor-State Arbitration. Resolution adopted by the UN General Assembly on 10 December 2014, A/RES/69/116.

[228] Calamita (n 216) 672.

[229] ibid 673.

[230] Art 3 UNCITRAL rules on transparency.

[231] Art 5 UNCITRAL rules on transparency.

[232] Art 5 and 4(3), UNCITRAL rules on transparency.

[233] Calamita (n 216) 659–661.

[234] Art 31 Canada-Cameroon BIT.

[235] Art 29 Rwanda-US BIT; Annex B Canada-Czech Republic BIT; Art 9.17, Australia-China FTA; Art 26 Colombia-Peru BIT; Art 20 Mexico-Slovak Republic BIT; Art 18 Mexico-UK; Art 27 New Zealand-Taiwan Economic Cooperation Agreement.

Recent IIAs also tackle the long-standing inconsistency problems affecting investment arbitration by introducing a variety of instruments operating both at the pre- and the post-award stage. As divergent decisions may be the product of parallel proceedings, a growing number of treaties confer on the parties the right to request the consolidation of claims arising out of the same investment or concerning similar legal or factual issues.[236] Another coherence-enhancing tool is the consultation of draft awards, whereby the arbitral tribunal may be requested, before issuing a decision, to send the draft award for comments to the disputing parties and the state of nationality of the investors.[237] The interpretation activity of arbitral tribunals is also steered through *renvoi* mechanisms, which confer on the contracting states[238] the power to interpret the provisions of the agreement.[239] Such a mechanism does not confer a new power on the contracting states, but it only 'proceduralises' and thus facilitates the adoption of binding interpretative statements.[240]

The debate about consistency-enhancing instruments has also focused on the possible establishment of an appellate mechanism. In the early 2000s, the US updated its investment policy to include the creation of such a mechanism in its negotiating objectives.[241] Accordingly, the 2004 US Model BIT envisaged the possibility for the contracting parties to US BITs to set up an appeal facility[242] or join a future multilateral agreement establishing an appeal mechanism.[243] Shortly thereafter, the ICSID Secretariat devised a detailed proposal on this issue.[244]

[236] According to the UNCTAD database, the vast majority of treaties containing such clauses were concluded after 2005. See, eg, Art 15, India-Mexico BIT; Art 28 Canada-Senegal BIT; Art 11, BLEU-Peru BIT.

[237] Art 25 Colombia-Peru BIT.

[238] Art 13 BLEU-Madagascar BIT; Art 35 Benin-Canada BIT, Art 18 Australia-Mexico BIT; Art 30 Rwanda-US BIT; Art 9.24 Korea-Vietnam FTA.

[239] Art 35 Benin-Canada BIT; Art 33 Canada-Nigeria BIT; Art 32 Canada-Côte d'Ivoire BIT; Art 9.24 Korea-Vietnam FTA.

[240] I Venzke, 'Investor-State dispute Settlement in TTIP from the Perspective of a Public Law Theory of International Adjudication' (2016) 17 *Journal of World Investment and Trade* 374, 390.

[241] Section 2102, US Trade Promotion Authority under s 2102 of the US Trade Act 2002. See AH Qureshi, 'An Appellate System in International Investment Arbitration?' in PT Muchlinski, F Ortino and C Schreuer (eds), *The Oxford Handbook of International Investment Law* (Oxford University Press, 2008) 1155.

[242] Annex D 2004 US Model BIT reads as follows: '[w]ithin three years after the date of entry into force of this Treaty, the Parties shall consider whether to establish a bilateral appellate body or similar mechanism to review awards rendered under Art 34 in arbitrations commenced after they establish the appellate body or similar mechanism'. This provision was expunged from the 2012 US Model BIT.

[243] Art 28 2004 US Model BIT stipulates that: 'If a separate, multilateral agreement enters into force between the Parties that establishes an appellate body for purposes of reviewing awards rendered by tribunals constituted pursuant to international trade or investment arrangements to hear investment disputes, the Parties shall strive to reach an agreement that would have such appellate body review awards rendered under Art 34 in arbitrations commenced after the multilateral agreement enters into force between the Parties'. Only this provision was reproduced in 2012 US Model BIT.

[244] ICSID Secretariat, 'Possible improvements of the framework for ICSID arbitration' (2004). See also G Van Harten, 'A case for an international investment court', Society of International Economic Law, Online Proceedings Working Paper No 22/08.

The proposed appellate body was designed to exercise its review powers on arbitral decisions rendered both in the ICSID and the UNCITRAL contexts, namely the majority of arbitral decisions. The grounds of appeal were potentially far-reaching, because they comprised the grounds of annulment under Article 52 ICSID Convention, 'clear error of law', and 'serious error of fact'. However, the ICSID project never came into existence also because the US changed its position about the creation of an appeal mechanism.[245]

Another crucial aspect of the ongoing reform of international investment arbitration is the introduction of mechanisms for enhancing independence and impartiality of arbitrators. Codes of conduct are a case in point. These codes seek to ensure the even-handed discharge of arbitral functions by establishing rather stringent requirements.

To begin with, they impose on arbitrators the obligation to disclose interests and relationships, which might have an adverse effect on their impartiality. For instance, Article IV of Annex B of the Japan-Australia Economic Partnership Agreement stipulates that arbitrators must disclose 'any information relevant to the matter under dispute' before the confirmation of their appointment. These include, inter alia, financial interests, professional interests, and the opinions publicly expressed which may affect or be relevant to the solution of the dispute in question.[246]

Furthermore, they reassert and flesh out impartiality and independence obligations, such as: (i) the duty not to let professional, business or family relationship, either past or current, affect its judgment; (ii) the duty not to enter into any relationship that may undermine his or her impartiality; and (iii) the duty not to accept any benefit that would affect his or her impartiality.[247]

Last, they contain post-award obligations, whereby arbitrators cannot take part in activities that might cast doubts on the impartiality of their tenure. Another important initiative in this field is the ICSID-UNCITRAL project of a multilateral code of conduct – the latest version of the draft Code of Conduct was published in July 2022.[248] The code contains a detailed set of obligations for arbitrators, which may provide additional grounds for the removal or disqualification of arbitrators.[249] These most notably include independence and impartiality obligations, limitations on multiple roles, duties of diligence and confidentiality.[250]

In conclusion, this section has shown that international investment arbitration is going through a process of change. However, such winds of reform primarily crystallised into a variety of transparency and impartiality-enhancing rules.[251]

[245] Roberts (n 1) 419.

[246] Art 4, ch 9, Section B, Code for ISDS, CPTPP.

[247] Art VI, Annex B, Australia-Japan EPA; Art 4, ch 9, Section B, Code for ISDS, CPTPP.

[248] The first two versions dated back to April 2020, May 2021 and September 2021.

[249] Art 11 Draft Code of Conduct for Adjudicators in International Investment Disputes: version four, 2022.

[250] ibid, see Arts 3, 4, 5, 7, 8.

[251] L Boisson de Chazournes and R Baruti, 'Transparency in Investor-State Arbitration: An Incremental Approach' (2015) 2 *BCDR International Arbitration Review* 59, 75. JA Maupin,

ii. Tinkering at the Margins: The ISDS Mechanism in the Early Drafts of the EU IIAs

The initial approach of the EU to investment treaty-making largely reflected the moderate reformist trends running through investment treaty practice. As clearly stated in the Commission's Communication 'Towards a comprehensive European international investment policy', the new EU international investment policy should 'arrive at state-of-the art investor state dispute settlement mechanisms'.[252] Key to the establishment of an up-to-date ISDS mechanism was, in the Commission's view, the adoption of transparency-enhancing instruments.[253] The Commission, however, was more cautious about creating permanent or quasi-permanent dispute settlement bodies and establishing appellate review mechanisms.[254]

The leaked draft of CETA, EUSFTA and TTIP fully reflected these guiding principles.[255] These treaties preserved the role of the disputing parties in the appointment of adjudicators. Under the 2014 EUSFTA Draft and the 2014 CETA Draft, each disputing party had the power to appoint one arbitrator, whilst the chairman had to be appointed by both parties.[256] External appointing authorities merely had a subsidiary role. They had the power to intervene if the parties failed to promptly appoint the arbitrators.[257]

These draft treaties included codes of conduct for arbitrators,[258] which largely reflected the content of the codes of conduct analysed above. Moreover, they also introduced transparency-enhancing rules. The 2014 EUSFTA Draft established a general duty to disclose the documents relating to arbitral proceedings, including the statement of claim and the statement of defence.[259] The 2014 CETA Draft, on the other hand, stipulated that

> [n]otwithstanding Article 2 of the UNCITRAL Rules on transparency, prior to the constitution of the tribunal, Canada or the European Union as the case may be shall make publicly available in a timely manner relevant documents pursuant to

'Transparency in International Investment Law: The Good, the Bad and the Murky' in A Bianchi and A Peters (eds), *Transparency in International Law* (Cambridge University Press, 2013) 160–166.

252 European Commission (n 12) 10. See also Council of the European Union, Conclusions on a Comprehensive European International Investment Policy, 3,041st Foreign Affairs Council Meeting, Luxembourg, 25 October 2010, para 18.

253 European Commission (n 12) 10. Similarly, the European Parliament stated that 'changes must be made to the present dispute settlement regime, in order to include greater transparency, the opportunity for parties to appeal, the obligation to exhaust local judicial remedies where they are reliable enough to guarantee due process, the possibility to use amicus curiae briefs and the obligation to select one single place of investor-state arbitration'. See European Parliament (n 12) para 31.

254 European Commission (n 12) 10.

255 CETA Draft (2014), EUSFTA Draft (2014). This section will focus on the EUSFTA and CETA, because TTIP never came into existence.

256 Art X.25 2014 CETA Draft (2014), Art 8 EUSFTA Draft (2014).

257 Art 8 EUSFTA Draft (2014); Art x-9 CETA Draft (2014).

258 Annex II EUSFTA Draft (2014).

259 Art 4, Annex III, EUSFTA Draft (2014).

> paragraph 2, subject to the redaction of confidential or protected information. Such documents may be made publicly available by communication to the repository.[260]

The early drafts of the EUSFTA and CETA also envisaged third-party participation in investment disputes through written submissions.[261] In particular, ISDS tribunals could accept or invite non-disputing parties' submissions.

Finally, such draft agreements also sought to address inconsistency problems through the establishment of specialised committees of representatives of the contracting states, which were endowed with the power to issue binding interpretations of the treaty provisions.[262] However, they did not contain appellate mechanisms – the only partial exception being the 2014 CETA Draft, which envisaged the possibility to examine the establishment of an appellate mechanism.[263]

II. THE SHIFT TOWARDS SYSTEMIC REFORM: THE INVESTMENT COURT SYSTEM

A. The Persistent Discontent about the ISDS Mechanism in EU IIAs

The EU initially adopted an incremental reform strategy,[264] which combined the recalibration of investment protection rules with an improved version of the ISDS mechanism.[265] It soon became clear, however, that this approach was not sufficient to tame criticism against the 'new generation' of EU trade and investment agreements. Since 2013, European civil society has directed greater attention to such treaties.[266] Arguably, the beginning of the talks on TTIP with the US propelled this somewhat arcane topic into the limelight.[267] Non-governmental organisations and trade unions on both sides of the Atlantic voiced their concerns about EU investment chapters and, most notably, about the dispute settlement mechanism set forth therein. The main criticism was once again that the ISDS favour, by design, corporate interests at the expense of host state's public interest.[268] Moreover, critics decried the risks of 'regulatory chilling' – namely

[260] Art X.33 CETA Draft (2014).

[261] Art 12bis, EUSFTA Draft (2014); Art x-19 CETA Draft (2014).

[262] Art 9, EUSFTA Draft (2014); Art X.27, CETA Draft (2014).

[263] Art X.42, CETA Draft (2014).

[264] Roberts (n 1) 419.

[265] This is what the Commission defined as 'state-of-the-art' rules. See European Commission (n 12) 10.

[266] S Gáspár-Szilágyi, '*Quo vadis* EU Investment Law and Policy? The Shaky Path Towards the International Promotion of EU Rules' (2018) 23 *European Foreign Affairs Review* 167, 176.

[267] The popular discontent culminated in a series of massive demonstrations against TTIP across Europe. C Johnston, 'Berlin anti-TTIP trade deal protest attracts hundreds of thousands', *The Guardian*, 10 October 2015.

[268] European Consumer Organisation, 'Canada and EU trade talks: the backdoor to ISDS endorsement', 8 May 2014; European Trade Union Confederation, 'European Trade Union calls for a fundamental rethink of Canadian and US trade deals', 17 November 2014.

the risks of inhibiting the contracting parties from pursuing public interest objectives – which is often associated with investment disciplines.[269] The online public consultation on TTIP also confirmed these concerns.[270]

The discontent brewing in European civil society eventually reached the glassy buildings hosting the EU institutions. In May 2015, the Commission sought to address these concerns by proposing a far-reaching reform of the ISDS system.[271] In July 2015, the Parliament adopted a resolution urging the Commission to replace the ISDS system with a new system 'where potential cases are treated in a transparent manner by publicly appointed, independent professional judges in public hearings and which includes an appellate mechanism, where consistency of judicial decisions is ensured'.[272]

The Commission subsequently decided to include the dispute settlement mechanism sketched out in the proposal of May 2015 in the TTIP and its future EU IIAs and investment chapters, but not in the nearly concluded agreements, such as those with Canada, Singapore, and Vietnam.[273]

The Investment Court System was eventually born.[274] This new dispute settlement mechanism immediately found the European Parliament's support, particularly in the Socialist and Democrats group. In his letter to the Trade Commissioner of 11 November 2015, the then President of the European Parliament's Commission on International Trade, Bernd Lange, praised the introduction of a new adjudication system, which, in his view, addressed many of the concerns raised by the Parliament.[275] At the same time, Martin Schultz,

[269] See, eg, Corporate Europe Observatory, 'Public services under attack through TTIP and CETA', 2015; European Green Party, Resolution adopted by the 22nd Council of the European Green Party, 2015; European Left, 'Refound Europe, create new progressive convergence', 2015, Political Document, European Left Congress, Berlin, 16–18 December 2016; European Trade Union Confederation, 'ETUC assessment on the EU-Canada Comprehensive Economic and Trade Agreement (CETA)', 20 December 2016.

[270] European Commission, Online public consultation on investment protection and investor-to-state dispute settlement (ISDS) in the Transatlantic Trade and Investment Partnership Agreement, SWD(2015) 3 final.

[271] European Commission, Investment in TTIP and beyond – the path for reform – Enhancing the right to regulate and moving from current ad hoc arbitration towards an Investment Court, Concept Paper, 2015, 11.

[272] European Parliament, Resolution of 8 July 2015 containing the European Parliament's recommendations to the European Commission on the negotiations for the Transatlantic Trade and Investment Partnership, P8_TA(2015)0252, para XV.

[273] The EU Commissioner for trade tellingly observed that: '[w]hat has clearly come out of the debate is that the old, traditional form of dispute resolution suffers from a fundamental lack of trust … We want to establish a new system built around the elements that make citizens trust domestic or international courts. I'm making this proposal public at the same time that I send it to the European Parliament and the Member States. It's very important to have an open and transparent exchange of views on this widely debated issue'. See European Commission, 'Commission proposes new Investment Court System for TTIP and other EU trade and investment negotiations', Press release, 16 September 2015.

[274] Ironically, the ICS proposal emerged when the EU-US talks were losing momentum due to the imminent end of Obama's second presidential term.

[275] Mr Lange affirmed that: 'I am happy to see that the European Parliaments' concerns have been taken on board in the Commission's new Investment Court System- proposal'. Then, he went on to

the then President of the European Parliament, publicly supported the introduction of this system in CETA.[276] This request, however, collided with the official position of the Commission. Indeed, the Trade Commissioner, Cecilia Malmström, had already made clear that the Commission would not re-open the negotiations with Canada, as this could undermine the results already achieved during the complex negotiation process.[277] Nevertheless, Canada's general election results re-opened the way for the introduction of the ICS in CETA. The new liberal government presided over by Justin Trudeau expressed its intention to make concessions on this issue.[278] Thanks to the shift in Canada's position, in December 2015 the EU Trade Commissioner stated that, although reopening the negotiations was neither viable nor desirable, it was possible to work towards the introduction of 'elements of the investment court system' in the legal scrubbing phase.[279] The ICS was subsequently included in the other EU IIAs and investment chapters, namely the EUSIPA, the EUVIPA, and the EU-Mexico FTA.

B. Seeking Systemic Reform: The Investment Court System

The creation of the ICS epitomises the EU's shift from an incremental reform strategy to a systemic reform strategy. Although it does not completely do away with the existing arbitration rules, which still partly govern its proceedings,[280] the ICS marks a clear departure from the 'classic' ISDS model. Building on the early drafts of EU investment chapters, which already featured transparency and impartiality-enhancing mechanisms, the ICS introduces the following innovations.

i. The Establishment of Permanent Adjudicatory Bodies and the Rules on Appointment of Adjudicators

EU IIAs and investment chapters establish permanent and two-tiered investment dispute settlement bodies. Unlike traditional ISDS mechanisms, the adjudicators are not appointed on an ad hoc basis, but for fixed terms ranging from four

say that: 'The newly adopted ICS-proposal, which will be tabled during the TTIP negotiations, is not only an important step forward in addressing these institutional deficiencies of the existing dispute settlement system but it is also an important first building block towards a public International Investment Court'. See B Lange, Letter to the Commissioner Cecilia Malmström, 11 November 2015.

[276] EU Trade Insights, 'Schulz and Lange push for inclusion of ICS in CETA', 17 November 2015.

[277] Parliamentary questions, 'Answer given by Ms Malmström on behalf of the Commission', 24 August 2015. The same concern was shared by Canada. See 'Canada rules out full inclusion of Investment Court System in CETA', EU Trade Insights, 9 December 2015.

[278] H Von der Burchard, 'Canada's fresh push for EU trade deal', *Politico*, 12 November 2015.

[279] European Parliament, 'EU-Canada Comprehensive Economic and Trade Agreement', Briefing, January 2016.

[280] Art 8.23 CETA; Art 3.6 EUSIPA; Art 3.33 EUVIPA; Art 7, ch 19, EU-Mexico FTA.

to eight years and are renewable once.[281] The members of the Tribunal and the Appellate Tribunal are not selected by the disputing parties, but by committees composed of contracting parties' representatives.[282] Some randomly determined members of the Tribunals remain in office longer to ensure their continuing operation pending the appointment of the new members.[283] The adjudicators are referred to as 'members', rather than 'arbitrators', to symbolically mark the difference with investment arbitration; yet they are not granted the title of 'judges'. The number of tribunal members ranges from six to 15, but the committees of contracting parties' representatives may also decide to increase or decrease their number.[284] Two-thirds of the members of the Tribunals shall be nationals of the contracting states, while the remaining third is selected among nationals of third countries.

The members of the tribunal perform their adjudicatory tasks in smaller panels. Like the WTO Appellate Body,[285] the members of the Tribunals are then assigned into divisions to hear individual cases.[286] The divisions comprise three members, including the chairman, who is selected among the nationals of third countries. When forming the divisions, the President of the Tribunal ensures the rotation of the members and the unpredictability of their composition.[287] The members of the Tribunal must satisfy specific professional requirements. First, they 'shall possess the qualifications required in their respective countries for appointment to judicial office, or be jurists of recognised competence'.[288] Second, 'they shall have specialised knowledge of, or experience in, public international law',[289] while expertise in international investment law and international trade law is only desirable. In addition, adjudicators have to comply with a wide range of 'ethics' obligations.[290]

[281] The EU-Mexico FTA does not allow for a second term of office. See Art 11, ch 19, EU-Mexico FTA.

[282] Art 8.27 CETA; Art 3.38 EUVIPA; Art 3.9 EUSIPA; Art 11, ch 19, EU-Mexico FTA. The amendment of the rules on appointment is perfectly allowed under the UNCITRAL Rules, while it is more difficult to reconcile with the ICSID Convention. Similar to any other international agreement, the ICSID Convention may be modified by subsequent agreements concluded between some of the parties of the original treaty insofar as they satisfy the requirements under Art 41 VCLT. In particular, it has been argued that the modification of the appointment rules might be regarded as being 'incompatible with the effective execution of the object and purpose of the treaty as a whole'. C Titi, 'The European Union's proposal for an international investment Court: Significance, innovations and challenges ahead', Transnational Dispute Management (2017) 24. See also Art 1 of the UNCITRAL Rules. 'Arbitration Rules, then such disputes shall be settled in accordance with these Rules subject to such modification as the parties may agree'.

[283] Art 8.27 CETA; Art 3.38 EUVIPA; Art 3.9 EUSIPA; Art 11, ch 19, EU-Mexico FTA.

[284] The EUSIPA Tribunal is composed of six members, the EUVIPA and EU-Mexico FTA Tribunal are composed of nine members, the CETA Tribunal is composed of 15 members. See Art 8.27 CETA, Art 3.39 EUSIPA, Art 3.38 EUVIPA, Art 11, ch 19, EU-Mexico FTA.

[285] Art 6.2 Working procedures for appellate review, WT/AB/WP/6.

[286] The case may be heard by a sole judge if the parties agree to do so.

[287] Art 6.2 Working procedures for appellate review (n 285).

[288] Art 3.38 EUVIPA; Art 3.10 EUSIPA; Art 8.27 CETA, Art 11, ch 19, EU-Mexico FTA.

[289] Art 3.9 EUSIPA; Art 3.38 EUVIPA; Art 8.27 CETA, Art 11, ch 19, EU-Mexico FTA.

[290] Art 8.30, Art 3.11 EUSIPA, Art 3.40 EUVIPA, Art 13, ch 19, EU-Mexico FTA.

The committees of contracting parties' representatives may also decide the remuneration to be paid to the adjudicators, which comprises a monthly retainer fee plus additional fees and expenses. However, if the committees fail to determine the amount of the fees and expenses, these should be calculated pursuant to Article 14(1) Administrative and Financial Regulations.

ii. The Appellate Review Mechanism

The decisions of the Tribunals are subject to appeal.[291] The grounds of appeal include those listed in Article 52 of the ICSID Convention, errors in the interpretation and application of the law, and manifest errors in the appreciation of facts. The language adopted for the 'error of fact' ground of review looks more demanding than that of the error of law. Consequently, appellants are required to show that the decision of the Tribunal was based on a gross misinterpretation of facts. This higher threshold was presumably set to discourage the disputing parties from invoking this ground to obtain a second and comprehensive review of the facts of the case,[292] which could be costly and time-consuming.[293]

As regards the composition of the Appellate Tribunals, the terms of appointment, and the remuneration of their members, EU IIAs and investment chapters adopted slightly different solutions. The EUVIPA, EUSIPA, and the EU-Mexico FTA directly govern these issues, while CETA devolved to the CETA Joint Committee the power to regulate them.[294]

The Appellate Tribunals are composed of six members.[295] The committees of contracting parties' representatives may nonetheless increase the number of members.[296] The EUVIPA and EUSIPA stipulate that the members should be eligible for 'highest judicial offices',[297] while the EU-Mexico FTA requires the qualifications necessary for the appointment as a judge of the ICJ.[298] In a somewhat convoluted manner, Decision 1/2021 of the CETA Joint Committee stipulates that the members of the Appellate Tribunals shall be 'able to perform

[291] Arts 3.10, 3.19 EUSIPA; Art 8.28 CETA; Art 3.39 EUVIPA; Arts 12 and 30, ch 19, EU-Mexico FTA.

[292] L Pantaleo, *The Participation of the EU in International Dispute Settlement* (The Hague, TMC Asser Press, 2019) 89.

[293] CM Brown, 'The EU's Approach to Multilateral Reform of Investment Dispute Settlement' in A Stanič and C Baltag (eds), *The Future of Investment Treaty Arbitration in the EU* (Kluwer Law International, 2020) 231.

[294] Art 8.28 CETA. On 29 January 2021, the CETA Joint Committee adopted a decision to this effect. However, the decision will be effective once the section on dispute settlement of the investment chapter enters into force, ie, after the completion of the ratification process. Decision 1/2021 CETA Joint Committee.

[295] Art 3.39 EUVIPA; Art 3.10 EUSIPA; Art 2 Decision 1/2021 CETA Joint Committee; Art 12, ch 19, EU-Mexico FTA.

[296] ibid.

[297] Art 3.39 EUVIPA; Art 3.10 EUSIPA.

[298] Art 12, ch 19, EU-Mexico FTA.

the functions set out under this Decision and under Section F (Resolution of investment disputes between investors and states) of Chapter Eight (Investment)' of CETA.[299]

Three-member divisions hear the appeals.[300] These divisions are composed of two nationals of the contracting parties and chaired by a third-country national. The terms of office of Appellate Tribunals' members correspond to those of the members of the Tribunals except for CETA. Under the CETA Joint Committee Decision, the members of the Appellate Tribunal remain in office for nine years and cannot be renewed.[301]

The members of the Appellate Tribunals receive a variable remuneration, which includes a retainer fee plus additional fees based on the days worked and other expenses. However, a future decision of the committees of contracting parties' representatives can transform these fees into a permanent salary.[302] In such an eventuality, the members of the Appellate Tribunals will be under the obligation to ensure a full-time commitment.[303]

Appellate proceedings may end either with a dismissal of the appeal or with a reversal/modification of the appealed decision.[304] When the Appellate Tribunals find that an appeal is wholly or partly founded, they may directly issue a final decision or refer the matter back to the Tribunals.[305]

iii. Coherence Through Multilateralism: Sowing the Seeds for the Creation of the Multilateral Investment Court

The establishment of appellate review mechanisms marks a clear departure from the 'classic' ISDS model. Indeed, its establishment ensures greater coherence in the interpretation of investment protection rules. But it might not be enough.[306] The inconsistency problems associated with 'classic' arbitral awards are also linked to the bilateral structure of the investment treaty regime. Therefore, an appellate tribunal based on a bilateral agreement may ensure consistency in the application of that specific IIA. Yet, it may not address the divergences in the

[299] Art 2 Decision 1/2021.

[300] Art 3.10 EUSIPA, Art 3.39 EUVIPA; Art 2 Decision 1/2021 CETA Joint Committee; Art 12, ch 19, EU-Mexico FTA.

[301] Art 2 Decision No 001/2021.

[302] Art 3.10 EUSIPA, Art 3.39 EUVIPA; Art 2 Decision 1/2021 CETA Joint Committee; Art 12, ch 19, EU-Mexico FTA.

[303] ibid.

[304] Art 3.19 EUSIPA, Art 3.54 EUVIPA, Art 30, ch 19, EU-Mexico FTA; Art 3, Decision 1/2021 CETA Joint Committee.

[305] The EUSIPA does not seem to confer on the Appellate Tribunal the power to directly decide the dispute. See Art 3.19 EUSIPA ('If the appeal is well founded, the Appeal Tribunal shall modify or reverse the legal findings and conclusions in the provisional award in whole or in part. The Appeal Tribunal shall refer the matter back to the Tribunal, specifying precisely how it has modified or reversed the relevant findings and conclusions of the Tribunal'). *cf* Art 3 Decision 1/2021 CETA Joint Committee; Art 3.54 EUVIPA.

[306] Hainbach (n 211) 34.

interpretation of analogous investment protection rules contained in different treaties. This is not to say that the current bilateral structure is totally unable to ensure a certain degree of coherence.[307] Quite the contrary, though resting upon a bilateral structure, international investment law has achieved some degree of 'multilateralisation' and cross-treaty coherence.[308] However, this de facto 'multilateralisation' cannot be equated to a full-fledged 'multilateralisation' of the international investment regime.[309] Indeed, a multilateral investment court, like the WTO Appellate Body, may create a harmonious *corpus* of jurisprudence[310] and help to harmoniously combine investment disciplines with 'relevant non-investment concerns, such as the access to basic services, the protection of health and the environment, as exceptions in case of political, social and economic turmoil'.[311]

It is arguably with these objectives in mind that the EU used its IIAs and investment chapters to pave the way to the establishment of a Multilateral Investment Court.[312] The EUVIPA stipulates that the contracting parties 'shall enter into negotiations for an international agreement providing for a multilateral investment tribunal in combination with, or separate from, a multilateral appellate mechanism applicable to disputes under this Agreement'.[313] The EU-Mexico FTA proclaims a rather vague duty for the parties to cooperate toward the creation of a multilateral investment dispute resolution mechanism.[314] Under the CETA and the EUSIPA, the contracting parties commit themselves to 'pursue' the establishment of a multilateral investment tribunal and a multilateral appellate tribunal.[315]

As the Union was laying the groundwork for the MIC, UNCITRAL also launched a new initiative for the negotiation of a multilateral investment dispute settlement mechanism. At first, the EU's response to this plan was lukewarm, for it perceived it as a possible impediment to the implementation of its own plan.[316] After a series of formal and informal talks, however, the Union took a more cooperative posture.[317] Meanwhile, UNCITRAL gave a mandate to the Working Group III 'to work on the possible reform of investor-State dispute settlement'.[318]

[307] Schill (n 215) 16.
[308] ibid.
[309] Venzke (n 240) 388–389.
[310] ibid.
[311] Acconci (n 11) 186; D McRae, 'The WTO Appellate Body: A Model for the ICSID Facility' (2010) 1 *Journal of International Dispute Settlement* 371, 376.
[312] 3.41 EUVIPA; Art 8.29 CETA; Art 3.12 EUSIPA; Art 14, ch 19, EU-Mexico FTA.
[313] Art 3.41 EUVIPA.
[314] Art 14, ch 19, EU-Mexico FTA.
[315] Art 8.29 CETA; Art 3.13 EUSIPA, Art 14, ch 19, EU-Mexico FTA.
[316] Roberts (n 1) 426.
[317] ibid.
[318] Report of the United Nations Commission on International Trade Law, Fiftieth session (3–21 July 2017), A/72/17, para 264.

More specifically, it asked the Working Group III to: (a) single out concerns about the ISDS system; (b) evaluate whether a reform of such system was desirable; and (c) develop reform proposals.[319] In carrying out such task, the Working Group III enjoyed broad discretion and should leave to 'each State the choice of whether and to what extent it wished to adopt the relevant solution(s)'.[320]

The mandate was worded in broad terms to soothe the scepticism of many UNCITRAL members,[321] which were particularly concerned about the possibility of the EU 'hijacking' the UNCITRAL process.[322]

A few months later, the European Commission adopted a recommendation for a Council decision authorising the opening of the MIC agreement talks under the auspices of UNCITRAL.[323] In March 2018, the Council endorsed the Commission's recommendation and mandated the Commission to negotiate the MIC.[324] The Council's mandate to the Commission is circumscribed to investment dispute settlement, namely it does not include substantive provisions.[325] The Commission is thus entrusted with the negotiation of an agreement establishing a two-tiered multilateral court.[326] In the context of such negotiation, the EU illustrated its reform proposal.[327] Most notably, it explained that the MIC would be established through an opt-in mechanism subjecting pre-existing or future IIAs to its jurisdiction.[328] In other words, the MIC Agreement will supersede the ISDS provisions contained in earlier IIAs pursuant to Article 30 VCLT.

Having said that, to lay the ground for the creation of the MIC is one thing, but to set it up is quite another.[329] It is indeed hard to overestimate the difficulties associated with the negotiation of such an agreement. To begin with, the Union's proposal is not the only one under discussion. Several other plans have been submitted to UNCITRAL Working Group III.[330] Moreover, despite the

[319] ibid.

[320] ibid.

[321] Roberts (n 1) 426; Brown (n 293) 225.

[322] Roberts (n 1) 428; N Lavranos, 'The first steps towards a Multilateral Investment Court (MIC)', *Efilablog*, 19 July 2017.

[323] European Commission, Recommendation for a Council Decision authorising the opening of negotiations for a Convention establishing a multilateral court for the settlement of investment disputes COM (2017) 493 final.

[324] Council of the European Union, Recommendation for a Council decision authorising the opening of negotiations for a Convention establishing a multilateral court for the settlement of investment disputes SWD (2017) 302 final; Council of the European Union, Negotiating directives for a Convention establishing a multilateral court for the settlement of investment disputes, 12981/17 ADD 1.

[325] Council of the European Union, '12981/17 ADD 1' (n 324) para 6.

[326] ibid.

[327] UNCITRAL Working Group III, 'Establishing a standing mechanism for the settlement of international investment disputes', Annex – Submission from the European Union and its Member States, A/CN.9/WG.III/WP.159.

[328] ibid. The same mechanism was adopted by the Mauritius Convention. Brown (n 296) 225.

[329] Hainbach (n 211) 33.

[330] UNCITRAL Secretariat, 'Possible reform of investor-State dispute settlement (ISDS) Multilateral instrument on ISDS reform', 16 January 2020, A/CN.9/WG.III/WP.194, 2–3.

adoption of an opt-in mechanism, the archipelagic conformation of the international investment regime might slow down the establishment of the MIC. For example, some states might be unwilling to enter into the future MIC agreement, as they would lose their direct grip on the appointment of the members of the Tribunal and the Appellate Tribunal.[331] More importantly, the MIC project has thus far failed to gather sufficient support – many states, including the US, remain sceptical about it.[332]

Last, but not least, should the EU's project gain momentum in the UNCITRAL context, the ratification of a future treaty establishing the MIC would nonetheless be subject to the lengthy mixed agreements ratification procedure under EU law.[333]

Finally, it is also worth highlighting that the MIC might ironically fall short of achieving its primary objective, namely ensuring greater consistency in the interpretation of investment protection rules.[334] As noted earlier in this paragraph, the creation of the MIC does not entail the 'multilateralisation' of substantive investment rules. Hence, contrary to the WTO Panels and Appellate Body, the MIC would not apply a single body of rules, but a plethora of IIAs.

Figure 4.1 The ICS vs the pre-ICS ISDS

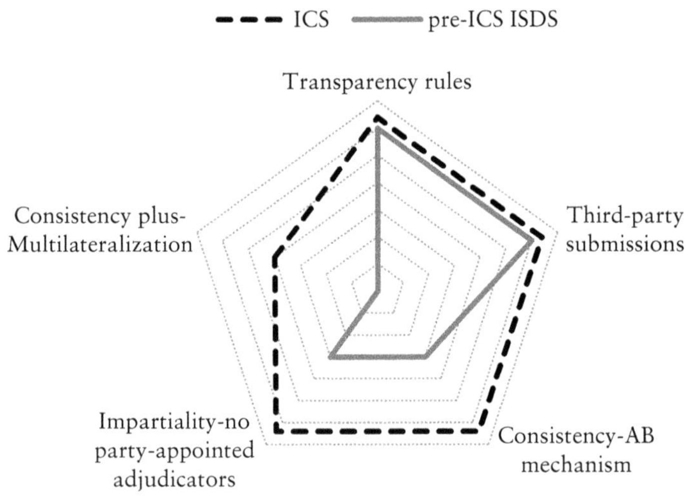

[331] ibid, 481–482.

[332] Roberts (n 1) 419.

[333] P Mengozzi, 'Les valeurs de l'Union et le règlement des différends dans le domaine des investissements internationaux' (2020) 3 *Diritto dell'Unione europea* 473, 477–478.

[334] H Lenk, 'The EU Investment Court System and its Resemblance to the WTO Appellate Body' in S Gáspár-Szilágyi, D Behn and M Langford (eds), *Adjudicating Trade and Investment Disputes – Convergence or Divergence?* (Cambridge University Press, 2020) 86.

C. Is Systemic Reform Enough? Domestic and EU Law-Based Challenges against CETA

Regardless of the outcome of the discussion on the MIC, there is little doubt that the ICS introduced relevant innovations, such as the obliteration of the disputing parties' power to appoint arbitrators and the establishment of two permanent adjudicatory bodies. Yet, it failed to defeat the mistrust and scepticism surrounding the EU IIAs and investment chapters.

This persisting discontent clearly emerged over the course of the signing and ratification process of CETA. In 2016, several individual applicants and the *Die Linke* parliamentary group filed with the German Constitutional Court an application for a preliminary injunction to prevent the German representative within the Council of the European Union from approving the signing and allowing provisional application of CETA. Stripped to its essence, the claimants' argument was that CETA undermined the functioning of German democracy and hollowed out the German Parliament's decision-making powers. CETA's incompatibility with the German Constitution stemmed primarily from the fact that the treaty covered matters falling outside the Union's competence. Another problematic aspect of CETA, in the claimants' view, was that it established a Joint Committee and several specialised committees endowed with decision-making powers.[335] These issues were further exacerbated by the fact that CETA would be applied provisionally, even before the completion of its ratification.[336]

The Court did not find that these arguments were completely unfounded. Indeed, it conceded that some components of CETA, including several provisions of the investment chapters, could fall outside the Union's competence.[337] Moreover, the establishment of a system of committees and the provisional application of the rules governing such committees might interfere with the democratic decision-making process.[338] Last, the provisional application of CETA might also, though not necessarily, result in an ultra vires act, namely a decision exceeding the Union's competence.[339] The Constitutional Court, however, eventually rejected the application, because the German Government committed to allowing the provisional application only of CETA's components falling within the Union's competence.[340]

A further domestic constitutional challenge against CETA was brought by several members of the French National Assembly.[341] The applicants once again

[335] See, in particular, ch 26, CETA.
[336] *2 BvR 1368/16, 2 BvR 1444/16, 2 BvR 1482/16, 2 BvE 3/16*, para 2.
[337] ibid, paras 51–56.
[338] ibid, paras 58.
[339] ibid, para 59. See C Calliess, 'Constitutional Identity in Germany – One for Three or Three in One?' in C Calliess and G van der Schyff (eds), *Constitutional Identity in a Europe of Multilevel Constitutionalism* (Cambridge University Press, 2019) 170–171.
[340] *2 BvR 1368/16* (n 336), paras 68–70.
[341] Decision No 2017-749 DC.

decried the possible detrimental effects of the agreement on the French constitutional system.

The CETA investment chapter was the main target of the applicants' complaints. In their view, such a chapter would impinge on France's national sovereignty (*conditions essentielles d'exercice de la souveraineté nationale*)[342] and would violate Article 88-1 of the French Constitution,[343] because it enables Canadian investors to circumvent French courts and the CJEU's jurisdiction.[344] In addition, they contended that the investor-state dispute settlement mechanism did not comply with the principle of impartiality and independence of adjudicatory bodies laid down in the French Constitution and would be inconsistent the principle of equality before the law.[345]

As a preliminary point, it should be recalled that the Constitutional Council adopted a double standard of review in scrutinising the constitutional challenges against CETA. The components of CETA falling within the shared competence of the Union and the Member States underwent full constitutionality scrutiny. By contrast, the provisions relating to matters of the EU's exclusive competence were subject to a slightly more deferential test,[346] the so-called constitutional identity review.[347]

As regards the first claim, the Constitutional Council found that the powers and the way of functioning of the investor-state dispute settlement mechanism under CETA did not impinge on the exercise of national sovereignty.[348] In reaching this conclusion, the Constitutional Council emphasised that the Tribunal and the Appellate Tribunal can award damages in case of violation of the treaty, but they cannot annul Member States' and Union's measures.[349]

As regards the second claim, it found that the codes of ethics for adjudicators and their long terms of appointment ensured their impartiality and independence.[350] The Constitutional Council also had little difficulty in

[342] F Xavier Millet, 'Constitutional Identity in France – Vices and – Above All – Virtues' in C Calliess and G Van der Schyff (eds), *Constitutional Identity in a Europe of Multilevel Constitutionalism* (Cambridge University Press, 2019) 138.

[343] Art 88-1 of the French Constitution reads as follows: '[t]he Republic shall participate in the European Union constituted by States which have freely chosen to exercise some of their powers in common by virtue of the Treaty on European Union and of the Treaty on the Functioning of the European Union, as they result from the treaty signed in Lisbon on 13 December 2007. English translation available at www.conseil-constitutionnel.fr/sites/default/files/2018-10/constitution_anglais.pdf.

[344] Decision No 2017-749 DC (n 341) para 21.

[345] ibid.

[346] ibid, paras 13–14.

[347] The Conseil Constitutionnel traditionally deployed this test to assess the constitutionality of statutes implementing EU directives. See Xavier Millet (n 342) 140–142; X Magnon, 'L'AECG devant le Conseil constitutionnel: much ado about quite nothing!' (2018) 113 *Revue française de droit constitutionnel* 173, 177; J Roux, 'La jurisprudence «IVG» fragilisée par inadvertance' (2017) 41 *Recueil Dalloz* 2378, 2379.

[348] Decision No 2017-749 DC (n 341) paras 23–29.

[349] ibid, para 23.

[350] ibid, paras 31–34.

dismissing the claim that CETA would discriminate against French (and EU) investors and favour Canadian investors. It found that this differential treatment was justified by a public interest objective, namely attracting Canadian investments in the EU and protecting French (and EU) investment in Canada.[351] Then, the tribunal also rejected the contention that the provisional application of CETA would impede the exercise of national sovereignty. In particular, it found that *only* the components of the treaty falling within the Union's exclusive competence would be provisionally applied and that the provisional application of CETA could be terminated in case of failure of the ratification process.[352]

Finally, scepticism about CETA and the ICS also emerged in the course of the Belgian ratification process. Under the Belgian Constitution, treaties with the characteristics of CETA are subject to the approval of the Federal Parliament and the regional Parliaments.[353] The Walloon Parliament refused to give the green light to CETA, thereby blocking its ratification.[354] To overcome this obstacle, Canada and the EU agreed on a joint interpretative declaration on CETA in October 2016.[355] The declaration addressed the most sensitive political issues, such as investment protection, the right to regulate, and the interplay between trade and investment disciplines and non-economic values. Moreover, the Belgian federal Government reached an agreement with its regions under which it committed, inter alia, to request an opinion on the compatibility of the ICS with the EU legal order from the CJEU.[356]

D. The Investment Court System and the EU Legal Order: Opinion 1/17

By requesting the CJEU's opinion on the compatibility of CETA with the EU Treaties,[357] the Belgian federal Government and its regions sought to solve an externally induced domestic political stalemate through the intervention of the CJEU. As a result, an inherently political question was translated into several legal questions.

[351] ibid, paras 36–39.

[352] ibid, paras 62–66.

[353] Art 167 Belgian Constitution.

[354] E Deffet, 'Ceta: pourquoi la Wallonie refuse de signer le traité', *Le soir*, 19 October 2016. This refusal prevented Belgium from ratifying CETA. See Y Lejeune, *Droit constitutionnel belge – Fondements et institutions* (Larcier, 2017) 608–616; 645–649.

[355] G Van der Loo, 'CETA's signature: 38 statements, a joint interpretative instrument and an uncertain future', CEPS Commentary, 2016, 2.

[356] Declaration of the Kingdom of Belgium on the signing of CETA (*Déclaration du Royaume de Belgique relative aux conditions de pleins pouvoirs par l'Etat fédéral et les Entités fédérées pour la signature du CETA*), 27 October 2016.

[357] Opinion 1/17, EU:C:2019:341.

i. CETA and the Autonomy of the EU Legal Order

The first question was whether the investment dispute settlement mechanism under CETA was consistent with the principle of autonomy of the EU legal order.[358] One year after its judgment in *Achmea*,[359] the Court was called upon once again to determine whether a dispute settlement body placed outside the EU judicial system was consistent with EU law.[360] However, unlike in *Achmea*, this adjudicatory body was not established by an international agreement between EU Member States but by an international agreement between, on the one hand, the EU and its Member States and, on the other hand, a non-EU state. This difference is crucial, because the relations with third states, as opposed to those between Member States, are not governed by the principle of mutual trust,[361] but by the principle of reciprocity.[362] The principle of mutual trust presupposes a 'quasi-federal' bond, which can only exist between EU members. The relationship with the outside world is governed by a less demanding principle, namely the principle of reciprocity. Accordingly, when assessing the compliance of CETA with the principle of autonomy, the Court did not follow the same path as in *Achmea*. In particular, it applied a two-tier test to assess the compatibility of CETA with EU law.

Under the first limb of the test, CETA Tribunals shall not possess the power to interpret EU law, but only the provisions of the treaty under which they are established.[363] In establishing such a requirement, the Court closely echoed its judgment in *Achmea*, where it found that the eventuality that intra-EU investment tribunals might be called upon to interpret EU law threatened the autonomy of the EU legal order.[364] CETA, at first glance, seems to comply with this requirement. Article 8.31 CETA stipulates that '[w]hen rendering its decision, the Tribunal established under this Section shall apply *this Agreement* [...] and other rules and principles of international law applicable between the Parties' (emphasis added). However, it is worth recalling that the international agreements concluded by the Union, such as CETA, are 'binding upon the institutions of the Union and on its Member States'[365] and are integral parts of the EU legal order.[366] Therefore, one could in principle argue that the CETA Tribunals interpret EU law when they interpret CETA.[367] The Court, however,

[358] ibid, para 108.
[359] *Slovak Republic v Achmea*, C-284/16, EU:C:2018:158.
[360] Opinion 1/17 (n 357) para 113.
[361] ibid, paras 127–128.
[362] ibid, para 117. M Fanou, 'The CETA ICS and the Autonomy of the EU Legal Order in Opinion 1/17 – A Compass for the Future' (2020) 22 *Cambridge Yearbook of European Legal Studies* 106, 123.
[363] ibid, para 119.
[364] *Slovak Republic v Achmea BV* (n 359) para 40.
[365] Art 216 TFEU.
[366] C Riffel, 'The CETA Opinion of the European Court of Justice and its Implications – Not that Selfish After All' (2019) 22 *Journal of International Economic Law* 503, 511.
[367] ibid, 512.

did not take this view. As a preliminary point, the Court clarified that EU international agreements did not fall within its exclusive jurisdiction.[368] Then, it found that the CETA Tribunals satisfy the first limb of the principle of autonomy test, because Article 8.31 CETA does not include the law of contracting parties, ie, domestic law and EU law, among the sources of law applicable to disputes between investors and contracting parties.[369] Relying on this finding, the Court could also distinguish the present case from that in Opinion 1/09.[370] As the reader may recall (see chapter three), one of the key concerns of the Court in Opinion 1/09 was that the ECPC could interpret and apply EU law and even review 'the validity of an act of the European Union'.[371] In the case of CETA, this concern disappeared, as CETA Tribunals are expressly precluded from reviewing 'the legality of a measure, alleged to constitute a breach of this Agreement, under the domestic law of a Party'.[372]

Furthermore, the Court found that the compatibility of CETA Tribunals with the principle of autonomy was further strengthened by the fact that CETA expressly qualifies the domestic law of the contracting parties 'as a matter of fact'.[373] This provision codifies a widely accepted principle, namely that interpreting and applying domestic law and taking it into account as a relevant fact in the context of an international dispute are two distinct hermeneutic operations (see chapter three).[374]

That said, taking domestic law into consideration as a matter of fact does not exempt CETA Tribunals from construing it. Still, the Court did not seem particularly worried about the prospect that CETA Tribunals would handle the domestic law of the contracting parties, including EU law.[375] In particular, it was reassured by Article 8.31(2), under which CETA Tribunals should follow 'the prevailing interpretation given to the domestic law by the courts or authorities of that Party' and that 'any meaning given to domestic law by the Tribunal shall not be binding upon the courts or the authorities of that Party'.[376]

The fact that the law of the contracting parties, including EU law, should only be considered as fact in the proceedings before the CETA Tribunals had two further reassuring implications for the CJEU. First, it prevented such adjudicatory bodies from ruling on the division of powers between Member States and the EU.[377] This feature of CETA Tribunals allowed the Court to distinguish

[368] Opinion 1/17 (n 357) para 116; Riffel (n 366) 513.
[369] Opinion 1/17 (n 357) paras 121 and 133.
[370] Opinion 1/09, EU:C:2011:123.
[371] ibid, para 78.
[372] Art 31.8 CETA.
[373] ibid.
[374] Fanou (n 362) 121.
[375] Opinion 1/17 (n 357) para 131.
[376] ibid.
[377] ibid, para 132.

this case from Opinion 2/13, where it found that the ECtHR threatened the preservation of the 'specific characteristics of the EU and EU law' because it could affect the division of powers through the co-respondent mechanism (see chapter three).[378] Second, it did not confer on CETA Tribunals the power to submit preliminary rulings to the CJEU.[379] In other words, the Court does not need to ensure the coherent interpretation and application of EU law, because the latter is merely a factual element in the context of investment disputes under CETA.

Having clarified this, the Court then turned to consider whether the CETA Tribunal and Appellate Tribunal could somehow prevent EU institutions from acting in accordance with EU Treaties.[380] In the Court's view, this could occur if they were to 'call into question the level of protection of a public interest' when assessing whether a given measure is consistent with the investment protection rules under CETA.[381] More specifically, the risk of affecting the level of protection of a public interest could arise if they could compel the contracting parties to amend or repeal public interest-oriented measures or award damages against the contracting parties for the adoption of such measures.[382] Here the question of compatibility with the principle of autonomy clearly overlaps with that of whether the investment dispute settlement mechanism established under CETA is capable of accommodating public interest objectives and respecting the democratic decision-making process.[383] This was arguably the most-awaited part of the CJEU's Opinion, particularly by the applicants and CETA's critics more generally.

The Court dealt with this question by shifting its focus on the substantive provisions set forth in CETA. In the Court's view, the combination of investment protection rules, exception mechanism and hortatory rules laid down in CETA prevents the CETA adjudicatory bodies from affecting the level of public interest protection set by the Union. First, the (general) exception under Article 28.3 CETA prevents them from construing the rules on non-discrimination laid down in Chapter 8 in a manner that obstructs the adoption of measures 'necessary to protect public security or public morals or to maintain public order or to protect human, animal or plant life or health'.[384] By the same token, the formulation of the main investment protection rules, ie, the expropriation and the FET clauses, as well as the hortatory rules contained in CETA Chapter 8 and the Joint

[378] ibid. See Opinion 2/13, EU:C:2014:2454, paras 233–235.

[379] Opinion 1/17 (357) paras 134–135; Mengozzi n 333) 475.

[380] Opinion 1/17 (n 357) para 137. C Contartese, 'Achmea and Opinion 1/17: why do intra and extra-EU bilateral investment treaties impact differently on the EU legal order?', ECB-Legal Working Paper Series No 19, 2019, 13–14.

[381] Opinion 1/17 (above n 357), para 148.

[382] ibid, paras 149–150.

[383] P Koutrakos, 'The Anatomy of Autonomy: Themes and Perspectives on an Elusive Principle' (ECB Legal conference, 2019) 99.

[384] Opinion 1/17 (n 357) para 152.

Interpretative Instrument on CETA of 2017 preserve the contracting parties' power to determine the appropriate level of protection of public interest.[385]

That said, one cannot rule out that, despite all the above-mentioned safeguards, the CETA adjudicatory bodies could find a public interest-oriented measure to be in breach of CETA.[386] Hence, it is not possible to exclude that, under certain circumstances, CETA may be at odds with the principle of autonomy.

Furthermore, given the Court's reliance on the wording of several CETA substantive provisions, it is hard to predict whether the Court would reach the same conclusion with any other EU investment agreement or investment chapter.[387] It is even more difficult to foresee if the future MIC would meet the requirements set out in Opinion 1/17, because there is not enough information about its structure and functioning. However, if the MIC was only to 'multilateralise' the investment dispute settlement mechanism, but not substantive provisions, its compatibility with the principle of autonomy would depend on the substantive rules applicable to a given case.[388]

ii. The Principle of Equal Treatment and Effectiveness

The second challenge directed at the CETA investment dispute settlement mechanism was based on the principles of equal treatment and effectiveness. The applicant raised the argument, which has often been used against intra-EU investment arbitration (see chapter three), that the establishment of such adjudicatory bodies would result in a discrimination against EU investors investing in the EU. In fact, while the latter are precluded from resorting to the CETA Tribunal and Appellate Tribunal, Canadian investors established in the EU can bring claims before them.[389] Belgium substantiated this argument by making a specific example – which was clearly inspired by the facts of the *Micula* case (see chapter three) – of a possible conflict between CETA and the principle of equal treatment. Such a conflict could arise if a Canadian investor, after being fined for a violation of EU competition law, would challenge this sanction before the CETA Tribunal and obtain compensation. The damages awarded by the CETA Tribunal would offset the fine, thereby treating such an investor more favourably than EU investors in similar circumstances.[390] The Court rejected both arguments. As to the first one, it found that CETA did not violate the principle of equal treatment because Canadian investors investing in the EU were not in the

[385] ibid, paras 154–158. See Joint Interpretative Instrument on the Comprehensive Economic and Trade Agreement (CETA) between Canada and the European Union and its Member States.
[386] Fanou (n 362) 127.
[387] Mengozzi (n 333) 483.
[388] Fanou (n 362) 130.
[389] Opinion 1/17 (n 357) para 53.
[390] ibid, para 54.

same situation as EU investors investing in the EU.[391] In particular, it held that Canadian investors are granted the right to resort to the CETA adjudicatory bodies because

> in their capacity as foreign investors, [they] are to have a specific legal remedy against EU measures, whereas enterprises and natural persons of the Member States who [...] invest within the Union, are not foreign investors there and will therefore not have access to that specific legal remedy and nor will they be able [...] to invoke directly the provisions contained in that agreement.[392]

This finding seems to constitute a development of the Court's case law on intra-EU IIAs. Indeed, if intra-EU IIAs are neither allowed nor necessary, then precluding the intra-EU application of EU IIAs and investment chapters cannot be deemed discriminatory.

As regards the second contention, the Court found that it is highly unlikely that a fine issued for a violation of EU competition law could be successfully challenged under CETA.[393] The Court is probably right, but it should be noted that CETA does not contain a specific exception that can be invoked in such a situation. Finally, the Court cursorily dismissed the claim that an award rendered in such circumstances could impair the effectiveness of EU competition law.[394]

iii. The Right to Access an Independent Tribunal Pursuant to Article 47 CFREU

The last question concerned the compatibility of the CETA investment dispute settlement mechanism with the right to access an independent tribunal under Article 47 CFREU.[395]

As for the accessibility question, the Court observed that CETA lacks a mechanism facilitating the access of individuals and SMEs to proceedings before the CETA Tribunal and Appellate Tribunal.[396] Article 8.39(6) of CETA only envisages the possibility of adopting instruments to reduce the financial burden on claimants.[397] However, it found that one of the statements made by the Council and the Commission at the time of the adoption by the Council of the decision authorising the signature of CETA proved the intention to implement such provision.[398]

Turning to the independence issue, the Court started by noting that, according to its well-established case law, this requirement has both an external

[391] ibid, para 180.
[392] ibid, para 181.
[393] ibid, paras 184–185.
[394] ibid, paras 187–188.
[395] ibid, paras 199–200.
[396] ibid, para 213.
[397] ibid, para 207.
[398] ibid, para 217.

dimension, ie, independence from external interferences, and an internal dimension, ie, the equidistance from the disputing parties.[399]

The assessment of external independence primarily focused on the CETA Joint Committee's power to appoint and modify the number of the CETA Tribunal and Appellate Tribunal by multiples of three. However, in the Court's view, the independence of the CETA investment dispute settlement bodies was ensured by the fact that the identity of their members and the determination of their reductions or increases were not determined in advance in the text of the treaty.[400] Moreover, the Court found that the CETA Joint Committee did not endanger the external independence of the CETA Tribunal and Appellate Tribunal, because it adopted decisions on the appointment and removal of members by mutual consent.[401] In its view, this mechanism ensured that the members of the CETA Tribunal and Appellate Tribunal would meet the professional and ethics requirement laid down therein.[402]

Additionally, the fact that the CETA Joint Committee has the power to set fees and expenses to be paid to the members of the CETA Tribunal and Appellate Tribunal did not undermine their external independence, for it does not leave the amount of such fees and expenses indeterminate.[403] Likewise, the Court rejected the view that the CETA Joint Committee's power to issue binding interpretations might undermine the external independence of the CETA dispute settlement mechanism. In particular, it found that

> [a]lthough that safeguard of no retroactive effect and no direct effect on pending cases is not expressly provided for in Article 8.31.3 of the CETA, it must again be observed that the consent of the Union to any decision specified in Article 8.31.3 of the CETA will have to comply with EU primary law and, in particular, with the right to an effective remedy enshrined in Article 47 CFREU. Accordingly, Article 8.31.3 of the CETA cannot be interpreted, having regard to Article 47, as permitting the Union to consent to decisions on interpretation of the CETA Joint Committee that would produce effects on the handling of disputes that have been dealt with or are pending.[404]

Finally, the Court had little difficulty in finding that the rules governing the composition of the CETA Tribunals and the rules on the conduct of their members ensured compliance with the internal independence requirement.[405]

[399] Opinion 1/17 (n 357) paras 202–203.
[400] ibid, para 227.
[401] ibid, para 228.
[402] ibid.
[403] ibid, para 229. The independence of the CETA Tribunal and Appellate Tribunal was further safeguarded by the rule, under which the remuneration of their members could be turned into a regular salary. ibid, para 231.
[404] ibid, para 237.
[405] ibid, para 238.

E. The Modernisation of the ECT as a Further Example of Systemic Reform?

Besides negotiating brand new IIAs and investment chapters, the EU also played a pivotal role in the process of modernisation of the ECT. The 'modernisation' process pursued multiple goals (see chapter three) – chief among them was the amendment of the ECT rules on investment protection and investment dispute settlement. In May 2020, the EU put forward its own proposal for the modernisation of the treaty.[406] The proposal largely reflected the content of its post-Lisbon IIAs and investment chapters.[407]

First, the EU redefined the main investment protection rules, such as the fair and equitable treatment clause, the expropriation clause, and the umbrella clause. The FET clause included in the EU proposal delineates more precisely the substantive content of the clause and attempts to reduce the relevance of the legitimate expectations doctrine.[408] In particular, it provides that

> [w]hen applying the above fair and equitable treatment obligation, a tribunal may take into account whether a Contracting Party made a specific representation to an investor to induce a covered investment, that created a legitimate expectation, upon which the investor relied in deciding to make or maintain the covered investment, but that the Contracting Party subsequently frustrated.[409]

As for the expropriation clause, the EU's proposal provided a definition of 'indirect expropriation' in a specific annex to the treaty.[410] More specifically, it established three criteria, namely economic impact, duration and character of the measure, to distinguish indirect expropriation from the legitimate exercise of the host state's regulatory powers. Similarly, the umbrella clause also resembles those included in the EU IIAs and investment chapters.[411] The rather broad original ECT umbrella clause is replaced by a more stringent provision, under which only a violation of a specific written commitment through the exercise of governmental authority may trigger the host state responsibility under the umbrella clause.

Second, the EU's proposal also introduced a variety of instruments to safeguard the host state's power to regulate. These included, inter alia, a specific annex governing the interplay between investment protection rules and public debt restructurings, hortatory rules reaffirming the power to regulate of the contracting parties of the ECT, and a clause limiting the application of the expropriation rules to measures pursuing public interest objectives.[412]

406 'EU text proposal for the modernisation of the Energy Charter Treaty'.
407 M Vicente, 'The European Union's Proposal for the Modernisation of the Energy Charter Treaty' (2022) 31 *European Energy and Environmental Law Review* 124, 128.
408 'EU text proposal for the modernisation of the Energy Charter Treaty', 5–6.
409 ibid.
410 ibid, 7.
411 ibid, 5–6.
412 ibid, 4–5; 7; 22.

Third, the EU proposed to include a clause allowing ECT contracting parties to opt in to the MIC.[413] The EU, however, did not dare to insert into the ECT a reference to the ICS. It thus seized the middle ground between the original ECT and the systematic reform approach adopted in designing the investment dispute settlement mechanism contained in its post-Lisbon IIAs and investment chapters.

This slightly more cautious approach can probably be explained by the fact that several contracting parties of the ECT would be unwilling to agree on such a reform strategy. Indeed, the outcome of the negotiation on the modernisation of the ECT shows that the contracting states had no appetite for systemic reform of the investor-state dispute settlement. The agreement in principle reached on 24 June 2022[414] focuses on safeguarding the contracting states' policy space by redefining the main investment protection rules and introducing specific hortatory rules in the preamble and the body of the treaty. By contrast, the agreement introduces far less innovations to the ISDS system: it only extends the application of the UNCITRAL Rules on Transparency to ECT arbitral proceedings.

III. CONCLUSION

When shaping its post-Lisbon IIAs and chapters, the EU has initially espoused an incremental reform strategy. The early versions of such agreements combined two main features. First, they contained more detailed substantive provisions, hortatory rules, exception and carve-out mechanisms to safeguard the contracting states' policy space. Second, they included a slightly amended version of the 'classic' ISDS mechanism. In particular, the early drafts of EU investment chapters inserted a variety of transparency and impartiality-enhancing provisions in the rules governing investor-state arbitration. This initial approach, however, was greeted with widespread dissatisfaction. Civil society voiced its discontent about such treaties. In response to mounting criticism, the EU, spurred by the European Parliament, relinquished its initial approach and became a vocal advocate of systemic reform of the ISDS system.[415] The ICS proposal epitomised the shift towards a systematic reform approach. The EU devised a two-tiered permanent adjudicatory body, which is more similar to an international court than to the 'classic' ISDS system. The process of 'courtification' promoted by the EU

[413] ibid, 15–16.

[414] At the time of writing, the agreement has not been published yet. Therefore, the only available source of information available at the moment is the ECT Secretariat's 'Public Communication explaining the main changes contained in the agreement in principle'. Energy Charter Secretariat, 'Public Communication explaining the main changes contained in the agreement in principle', 24 June 2022.

[415] Roberts (n 1) 419–421.

also implied a thrust towards the creation of a multilateral investment dispute settlement body. The ultimate objective of 'multilateralsation' is to replace the existing ISDS mechanisms with a newer, more balanced and 'EU-made' dispute settlement mechanism.

However, the EU-driven reform of investment dispute settlement is far from being implemented. To begin with, the EU has thus far failed to gather sufficient support around the MIC plan.[416] Moreover, the ICS and the MIC projects, however laudable, are no panacea against the persisting wariness towards international investment law and investment dispute settlement,[417] as evidenced by the slow progress of the process of ratification of EU IIAs and investment chapters. Finally, it remains to be seen whether a future multilateral investment court would comply with EU constitutional requirements.

[416] The relatively recent memory of the failure in 1998 of the OECD Multilateral Agreement on Investment, if anything, should offer a cautionary tale to the advocates of the MIC. For an exhaustive account of the debate on MAI, see P Muchlinski, 'The Rise and Fall of the Multilateral Agreement on Investment: Where Now' (2000) 34 *International Lawyer* 1033.

[417] See Columbia Center on Sustainable Development, 'Position paper in support of opinions expressed in response to the European Commission's 'Public consultation on a multilateral reform of investment dispute resolution', 2017; Rosa Luxemburg Foundation, 'A World Court for corporations: how the EU plans to entrench and institutionalize investor-State dispute settlement', 2017.

5

The External and the Internal Dimensions of the European Union's Action in the Field of Foreign Investment

I. THE EU'S AMBIVALENCE TOWARDS INTERNATIONAL INVESTMENT LAW

The previous chapters have shown that the EU has regarded international investment law with a mix of wariness and interest.

On the one hand, the Union, ie, the Commission and the CJEU, has considered intra-EU IIAs, and most notably the ISDS mechanism laid down therein, as an obstacle to the correct functioning of the internal market rather than as a further layer of protection for cross-border intra-EU investments.

On the other hand, in the post-Lisbon era, the Union has eagerly negotiated and concluded investment agreements or economic agreements containing investment protection provisions and dispute settlement mechanisms.

This ambivalent attitude towards international investment law can be explained as a side-effect of the Union's attempt to impose its own regulation model of cross-border investment both within and outside the EU internal market.

Internally, the EU has aimed to end the coexistence between EU law and intra-EU IIAs. The ultimate objective of the EU's approach ('EU law-centred approach') is to ensure the systematic prevalence of EU rules governing cross-border investment. Put differently, the application of EU internal market rules should be free from obstacles and constraints, be they domestic law or Member States *inter se* agreements. The 'EU law-centred' approach undoubtedly has the merit of simplifying the regulatory framework applicable to intra-EU cross-border investment. Yet, it may end up leaving a vacuum of protection for EU investors. This net loss in terms of protection is particularly relevant if one looks at the current state of the EU internal market for capital. It is worth reminding that, according to the 2020 single market scoreboard report, 'FDIs are unevenly distributed across EU Member States. Some small countries exhibit very high stocks of both intra-EU and extra-EU FDIs. On the contrary, certain large western European economies present comparatively lower figures, and most eastern European countries lie in the lower part of the distribution of FDI stocks.'[1] Moreover, the quality of the rule of law has dramatically deteriorated in several EU Member States.[2] The latest edition of the Rule of Law Report reiterates the Commission's concerns about the real and perceived judicial independence and impartiality, the length of judicial proceedings, and corruption in national judicial systems.[3] It is thus fair to wonder whether an additional layer of protection for intra-EU cross-border investment would be necessary in such a context.

At the external level, the Union also sought to impose its specific regulation model of foreign investment. This model combines more balanced substantive rules and a new dispute settlement body, which departs from the 'classic' ISDS system in several respects. In addition, the Union did not limit itself to including such an innovative investment dispute settlement mechanism in its post-Lisbon bilateral agreements. But it has sought and is still seeking a multilateral reform of international investment dispute settlement. In the context of the UNCITRAL Working Group III, the Union rolled out a plan for a Multilateral Investment Court. These efforts can be regarded as part of the Union's self-assigned mission to support a rule-based multilateral international legal order.[4] In this respect, it is worth recalling that the EU has also recently promoted the establishment of the Multiparty Interim Appeal Arbitration Arrangement (MPIA), which aims to overcome the forced inactivity of the WTO Appellate Body.[5] Moreover, in pursuing this strategy, the Union is arguably acting as a 'normative power', namely as an entity that wields its influence over the rest of the world through norm creation and diffusion.[6]

[1] European Commission, Foreign Direct Investment – Integration and Market Openness, Single Market Scoreboard, 2020.

[2] D Kochenov and N Lavranos, 'Achmea Versus the Rule of Law: CJEU's Dogmatic Dismissal of Investors' Rights in Backsliding Member States of the European Union' (2021) *Hague Journal on the Rule of Law* 1, 18.

[3] See, eg, European Commission, 2022 Rule of Law Report – Country Chapter on the rule of law situation in Hungary, SWD(2022) 517 final; European Commission, 2022 Rule of Law Report – Country Chapter on the rule of law situation in Poland, SWD(2022) 521 final; European Commission, 2022 Rule of Law Report – Country Chapter on the rule of law situation in Romania, SWD(2022) 523 final; European Commission, 2022 Rule of Law Report – Country Chapter on the rule of law situation in Italy, SWD(2022) 512 final.

[4] See Art 21, TEU. This objective is regularly reaffirmed in the EU's policy documents. European Commission, Global Europe: competing in the world, COM (2006) 567 final, 7; European Commission, Reflection paper on harnessing globalisation, 2017, 12.

[5] Multi-party interim appeal arbitration arrangement pursuant to Art 25 DSU, 27 March 2020.

[6] See I Manners, 'Normative Power Europe: a Contradiction in Terms?' (2002) 40 *Journal of Common Market Studies* 235; T Forsberg, 'Normative Power Europe, Once Again: A Conceptual Analysis of an Ideal Type' (2011) 49 *Journal of Common Market Studies* 1183. See also S Gáspár-Szilágyi, '*Quo vadis* EU Investment Law and Policy? The Shaky Path Towards the International Promotion of EU Rules' (2018) 23 *European Foreign Affairs Review* 167, 172–177; M Cremona, 'The Union as a Global Actor: Roles, Models and Identity' (2004) 41 *Common Market*

Beyond all this, the combination of the external and the internal dimensions of the EU's action in the field of foreign investment are arguably also instrumental in pursuing its latent 'federal aspirations'. In fact, by tightening its grip over the regulation of cross-border investment within the EU internal market and by emerging as an actor in the international treaty-making arena, the Union seeks to assert itself more as a federal state than as an international organisation.

II. THE OBSTACLES HINDERING THE FULL IMPLEMENTATION OF THE UNION'S ACTION IN THE FIELD OF FOREIGN INVESTMENT

The EU has attempted to impose both internally and externally its own model of regulation of cross-border investment. However, it did so without fully appraising the legal and political feasibility of this project. It therefore comes as no surprise that, both at the internal and the external level, its action has met with several obstacles.

A. Legal and Political Obstacles at the Internal Level

The interplay between legal and political obstacles has hindered the attempt to impose EU law as the only body of rules promoting and protecting cross-border investment within the EU internal market.[7] The 'EU law-centred approach' of the Commission and the CJEU did not play out as expected. Quite predictably, the vast majority of investment tribunals did not share this view. And even some Member States' courts sought to circumvent the CJEU's dicta on this matter. It thus became clear that the obliteration of intra-EU investment arbitration required the intervention of EU Member States. With the conclusion of the 2020 TA and the agreement in principle on the modernisation of the ECT, the EU and its Member States precisely sought to achieve such a goal.

However, both instruments suffer relevant limitations. In particular, it remains to be seen whether the TA will produce immediate effects or its impact will be diluted by the sunset clauses contained in intra-EU BITs. The agreement in principle on the modernisation of the ECT, on the other hand, might be in theory capable of ending intra-EU arbitration under the ECT once and for all. However, the ratification process of such an agreement might not be smooth sailing because the ECT is increasingly perceived as an obstacle to the implementation of climate change policies.

Law 553, 557–558; J Larik, 'Shaping the International Order as an EU Objective' in D Kochenov and F Antembrink (eds), *The European Union's Shaping of the International Legal Order* (Cambridge University Press, 2013) 78–85.

[7] For the sake of completeness, it should be noted that Art 1 of Protocol No 1 of the European Convention on Human Rights may also be invoked against measures harming intra-EU investment.

B. Legal and Political Obstacles at the External Level

The shift to the lengthier and more burdensome mixed agreements ratification procedure inevitably affected the development of the ambitious EU investment agenda,[8] as evidenced by the slow progress of the ratification procedures of the EU IIAs. As already observed (see chapter two), the main stumbling block lies in the completion of the Member States' ratification procedures. At present, 16 Member States ratified CETA; eight Member States completed the procedure for the ratification of EUSIPA; 11 Member States ratified the EUVIPA.[9] CETA, the EUSIPA, and the EUVIPA have been signed respectively in 2016, 2018 and 2019, while the EU-Mexico FTA has not been signed yet, albeit an 'agreement in principle' on the text of the agreement was reached in 2018. It is hard to predict if and when these treaties will be fully ratified. However, it is already possible to say that their ratification processes have exceeded the average length of ratification of EU mixed agreements.[10]

This is not surprising if one looks at the European public opinion about EU trade and investment agreements. A Eurobarometer survey[11] shows that the support for the defunct (at least for the moment) TTIP steadily declined between 2014 and 2016.[12] Furthermore, a 2019 survey conducted upon request of the European Commission[13] candidly acknowledged that the general public's opinion about the signed EU trade and investment agreements were 'mixed'.[14]

These surveys should be taken with a pinch of salt for they were about a specific agreement (ie, the TTIP) and implied an overall evaluation of comprehensive economic agreements, which include both the trade and investment components. Yet, they nonetheless strengthen the impression that the investment components of such agreements somehow increase their contentiousness. As repeatedly noted throughout this book, investment protection rules and investment arbitration remain unpalatable for many. The ongoing process of

[8] See L Biffi, *Too Complex or Too Ambitious: Exploring Hurdles in the Enforcement of EU Free Trade Agreements* (Graduate Institute Publications, 2021) 8.

[9] See CETA-Ratification details, available at www.consilium.europa.eu/en/documents-publications/treaties-agreements/agreement/?id=2016017; EUSIPA-Ratification details, available at www.consilium.europa.eu/en/documents-publications/treaties-agreements/agreement/?id=2018027&DocLanguage=en; EUVIPA-Ratification details, available at www.consilium.europa.eu/en/documents-publications/treaties-agreements/agreement/?id=2019015&DocLanguage=en.

[10] The average length is 30 months. C Tovo, 'Mixed Agreements in the Italian legal Order' in I Govaere and M Chamon (eds), *EU External Relations Post-Lisbon – The Law and Practice of Facultative Mixity* (Brill, 2020) 354.

[11] Cited in S Meunier and C Roederer-Rynning, 'Missing in Action? France and the Politicisation of Trade and Investment Agreements' (2020) 8 *Politics and Governance* 312, 315.

[12] ibid 315–316.

[13] European Commission, Europeans' attitude on Trade and EU trade policy (Summary), Special Eurobarometer 491, 18 May 2019.

[14] ibid, 59–62.

reform of the international investment regime has assuaged but not completely extinguished discontent. The development of an autonomous EU international investment policy is inevitably affected by the current state of the international investment regime. Despite the inclusion of state-of-the-art investment protection standards and, above all, despite the effort made in giving an original contribution to the reform of the dispute settlement mechanism, EU IIAs and investment chapters have thus far failed to win the heart and minds of EU citizens and of their representatives in national Parliaments. Whatever one may think about such agreements, it is ironic that, while these agreements raised a great deal of clamour, civil society did not mobilise so vehemently against the existing EU Member States' IIAs, which generally are 'old generation' treaties. That is to say, treaties that are particularly intrusive on the host state's regulatory space. It is not easy to understand why EU civil society had such different attitude toward new EU IIAs and existing Member States' IIAs. Perhaps the great emphasis placed by the Commission on some of such treaties, notably the TTIP and CETA, drew an exceptional amount of public scrutiny to them. The publication of Council's negotiating mandates and other EU preparatory documents further propelled them into the limelight. It has also been argued that the opposition to these agreements is often ideological.[15] This kind of remark has been frequently used against opponents of trade and investment treaties and, more generally, against the critics of globalisation. Although it may well be true in some instances, it has too often been used to hastily dismiss well-founded concerns. More crucially, those playing the 'ideologisation card' in this debate – whether consciously or not – are also often under the spell of some other kind of ideology. Last, one cannot rule out the possibility that these agreements were contested because they were perceived as a 'EU product'. After all, the trust in the European integration project has been anything but unwavering over the last decade.[16]

Whatever explanation one may prefer, it is a matter of fact that the bumpy ratification processes at the Member State level are delaying and may compromise the entry into force of the EU IIAs and of CETA investment chapter.

III. CONCLUSION

The evolution of the external and the internal dimensions of the Union's action in the field of foreign investment clearly illustrates the tendency of the Union to reassert its state-building ambitions and to shape the international economic order. This approach, however, overlooks the variety of legal and political

[15] L Biffi, *Too Complex or Too Ambitious? Exploring Hurdles in the Enforcement of EU Free Trade Agreements* (Graduate Institute Publications, 2021).

[16] See Annex Eurobarometer 94, 2021.

obstacles and risks affecting the action of a complex and hybrid entity such as the EU. In a way, this is probably a further illustration of what has aptly been labelled as 'a political culture of total optimism', which systematically ignores legal and political constraints.[17]

Furthermore, the EU has paid insufficient attention to how the external and the internal dimensions would interact with each other. Quite paradoxically, the choice to terminate all intra-EU IIAs – regardless of whether it will be fully achieved – without replacing them with an EU-wide investment agreement might well undermine the credibility of the Union as a negotiator of IIAs with third countries.[18]

The final takeaway of this book is that the stubborn pursuance of an 'ever closer' integration and the adoption of one-size-fits-all solutions may be ultimately detrimental to the European integration process.[19] Thus, this book closes with the hope that in the future EU institutions will pay more heed to this simple but extremely relevant fact.

[17] G Majone, *Rethinking the Union of Europe Post-Crisis – Has Integration Gone Too Far* (Cambridge University Press, 2014) 58–65.

[18] See 'Intra-EU Investment Treaties- Non-Paper from Austria, Finland, France, Germany and the Netherlands', 2016, paras 5–6.

[19] See G Majone, *Dilemmas of European Integration – The Ambiguities and Pitfalls of Integration by Stealth* (Oxford University Press, 2005) 219–221.

*Postscript**

SINCE SUBMITTING THE final version of this book, some important developments have affected both the internal and external dimensions of the EU's action in the field of foreign investment.

The ratification of the modernised ECT is proving to be as difficult as was warned in chapter five. Spain, France, Germany, the Netherlands, Luxembourg and Slovenia have recently announced their intention to leave the ECT[1] on the grounds that the latter impedes the implementation of climate change policies and the achievement of the Paris Climate Agreement goals. Poland is also set to withdraw from the treaty, although for a different reason, namely, solving once and for all the incompatibility between the ECT and EU law.[2]

Such unilateral withdrawals are unlikely to free immediately the withdrawing states from ECT obligations. Indeed, the so-called sunset clause under Article 47 ECT stipulates that the ECT provisions on investment protection continue to apply for 20 years from when the withdrawal became effective. In other words, the abovementioned EU Member States will be exposed to investment claims under the ECT for the next 20 years,[3] unless all the ECT contracting parties agree on the termination of the treaty.

Having said that, these unilateral initiatives have had immediate repercussions on the modernisation process. In view of the growing opposition among EU Member States to the ECT, the Commission has requested a postponement of the ECT Conference's vote on the adoption of the modernised text of the treaty.[4] Following this request, the ECT Conference has scheduled an ad hoc meeting in April 2023 to finalise the discussion on the matter.[5]

* 2nd December 2022.

[1] S Moody, 'Germany latest to quit ECT', *Global Arbitration Review* (11 November 2022); T Fisher, 'Spain announces withdrawal from ECT', *Global Arbitration Review* (13 October 2022); C Hodgson, A Hancock and L Abboud, 'France withdraws from Energy Charter Treaty', *Financial Times* (21 October 2022); 'Netherlands to pull out of treaty protecting energy investments', *Reuters* (19 October 2022); J Ballantyne, 'Luxembourg at ECT exit door', *Global Arbitration Review* (18 November 2022); T Fisher, 'Slovenia joins European exodus from ECT', *Global Arbitration Review* (10 November 2022).

[2] This justification does not appear to be entirely convincing because the modernised text of the ECT specifically addressed the issue of the intra-EU application of the ECT. W Sadowski, 'Poland to Withdraw from the ECT: Who Does It Benefit?', *Kluwer Arbitration Blog* (27 September 2022).

[3] Against this backdrop, the ECT Secretariat has issued a statement that clearly aims to discourage parties from invoking Art 62 VCLT to circumvent the sunset period provided for by Art 47 ECT. ECT Secretariat, 'Sunset Clause (Article 47 of the ECT) in relation to Article 62 of the Vienna Convention on the Law of Treaties' (VCLT), (3 November 2022).

[4] A Hancock, 'EU fails to pass revamped Energy Charter Treaty', *Financial Times* (19 November 2022).

[5] Decision of the Energy Charter Conference, 22 November 2022, CCDEC 2022 32 NOT.

Moreover, on 24 November 2022, the European Parliament has adopted a resolution calling on 'the Commission and the Member States to start preparing a coordinated exit from the ECT and an agreement excluding the application of the sunset clause between willing contracting parties'.[6]

Turning to the external dimension of the EU's action, it is worth mentioning that on 11 November 2022, the Irish Supreme Court issued a judgment on the compatibility of CETA with the Irish Constitution. The applicant, a member of the lower house (*Dáil Éireann*) of the Irish Parliament constitutional challenges, directed the bulk of his constitutional challenges towards the investor-state dispute settlement mechanism established under CETA. In his view, this system curtails the legislative sovereignty of Ireland under Articles 5 and 15 of the Irish Constitution and affects the functioning of its judiciary as protected under Article 34 of the Irish Constitution.

A majority of five judges found that CETA Tribunals do not undermine the legislative sovereignty of Ireland.[7] As to the second constitutional complaint, the Court, by a majority decision, held that the power of CETA Tribunals to issue awards that can be enforced in the Irish courts may be inconsistent with Article 34 of the Constitution.[8] However, according to the majority of the Court, this constitutional violation can be removed by conferring on national courts, through an amendment of the Irish Arbitration Act, the power to refuse the enforcement of awards threatening Ireland's constitutional identity and the effectiveness of EU law.[9] The main implication of such a decision is that Ireland will be able to complete the ratification of CETA only after the amendment of the Arbitration Act.

In conclusion, the combination of these recent events indicates once again that the Union's action in the field of foreign investment is fraught with legal and political obstacles and that its full implementation remains far from being achieved.[10]

[6] European Parliament, Resolution of 24 November 2022 on the outcome of the modernisation of the Energy Charter Treaty, P9_TA(2022)0421.

[7] Judgment of Mr Justice O'Donnell, Chief Justice, 11 November 2022, para 163; Judgment of Mr Justice John MacMenamin, 11 November 2022, paras 117–120; Judgment of Ms Justice Elizabeth Dunne, 11 November 2022, paras 187–193; Judgment of Ms Justice Baker, 11 November 2022, paras 72–77; Judgment of Ms Justice Power, 11 November 2022, paras 65–68.

[8] Judgment of Ms Justice Elizabeth Dunne (n 7) para 247; Judgment of Mr Justice Gerard Hogan, 11 November 2022, para 236; Judgment of Ms Justice Baker (n 7) para 39; Judgment of Mr Justice Peter Charleton, 11 November 2022, para 52.

[9] Judgment of Mr Justice Gerard Hogan (n 8) para 233.

[10] This might allow EU Member States to regain a significant role in this field. See M Bungenberg and B Bohme, 'Under the Radar – The Return of Member States in EU Investment Policy' (2022) *Journal of International Economic Law* 1, 15–16.

Bibliography

BOOKS

Acconci, P, 'The Integration of Non-Investment Concerns as an Opportunity For the Modernisation of International Investment Law: Is a Multilateral Approach Desirable?' in G Sacerdoti, P Acconci, M Valenti and A De Luca (eds), *General Interests of Host States in International Investment Law* (Cambridge University Press, 2014).

Adinolfi, G, 'A Cross-Cutting Legal Analysis of the European Union Preferential Trade Agreements' Chapters On Sustainable Development' in C Beverelli, J Kurtz and D Raess (eds), *International Trade, Investment, and the Sustainable Development Goals* (Cambridge University Press, 2020).

Asteriti, A, 'Regulatory Expropriation Claims in International Investment Arbitrations' in K Sauvant (ed), *Yearbook on International Investment Law and Policy* (Oxford University Press, 2013).

—— 'Waiting For the Environmentalists: Environmental Language in Investment Treaties' in R Hofmann and CJ Tams (eds), *International Investment Law and Its Others* (Nomos, 2013).

Auby, JB, 'Public Goods and Global Administrative Law' in JB Auby and J Morrison (eds), *Values in Global Administrative Law* (Hart Publishing, 2011).

Aust, A, *Modern Treaty Law* (Cambridge University Press, 2013).

Balchin, C, Chung, K, Kaushal, A and Waibel, M, (eds), *The Backlash Against Investment Arbitration: Perceptions and Reality* (Kluwer Law International, 2010).

Baltag, Ca d Dudas, S, '*Achmea*, Arbitral Tribunals and the ECT: Modernisation or Regression?' in A Stanič and C Baltag (eds), *The Future of Investment Treaty Arbitration in the EU: Intra-EU Bits, the Energy Charter Treaty, and the Multilateral Investment Court* (Kluwer Law International, 2020).

Bandelj, N, *From Communists to Foreign Capitalists: The Social Foundations of Foreign Direct Investment in Postsocialist Europe* (Princeton University Press, 2011).

Banitafemi, Y, 'Consistency in the Interpretation of Substantive Investment Rules: Is it Achievable?' in R Echandi and P Sauvé (eds), *Prospects in International Investment Law and Policy* (Cambridge University Press, 2013).

Barents, R, *The Autonomy of Community Law* (Kluwer Law International, 2004).

Bartels, L, 'Human Rights, Labour Standards, and Environmental Standards in CETA' in S Griller, W Obwexer and E Vranes (eds), *Mega-Regional Trade Agreements: CETA, TTIP, and Tisa – New Orientations for EU External Economic Relations* (Oxford University Press, 2017).

Basedow, JR, *The EU in the Global Investment Regime* (Routledge, 2017).

Beck, G, *The Legal Reasoning of the Court of Justice* (Hart Publishing, 2021).

Ben Hamida, W, 'La clause relative au respect des engagements dans les traités d'investissement' in C Leben (ed), *Le contentieux arbitral transnational relative à l'investissement* (Anthemis, 2006).

Biffi, L, *Too Complex or Too Ambitious? Exploring Hurdles in the Enforcement of EU Free Trade Agreements* (Graduate Institute Publications, 2021).

Bogojevic, S, 'Climate Change Law and Policy in the European Union' in KR Gray, R Tarasofsky and C Carlarne (eds), *The Oxford Handbook of International Climate Change Law* (Oxford University Press, 2016).

Bosse-Platière, I, 'Les instruments juridiques des relations extérieures de l'Union européenne après le Traité de Lisbonne' in AS Lamblin-Gourdin and E Mondielli (eds), *Le droit des relations extérieures de l'Union européenne après le Traité de Lisbonne* (Bruylant, 2013).

Broberg, M amd Fenger, N, *Broberg and Fenger on Preliminary References to the European Court of Justice* (Oxford University Press, 2021).

Brown, CM, 'The EU's Approach to Multilateral Reform of Investment Dispute Settlement' in A Stanič and C Baltag (eds), *The Future of Investment Treaty Arbitration in the EU* (Kluwer Law International, 2020).

Bufffard, I, 'Une relecture de la théorie des sous-systèmes en droit international' in I Buffard, J Crawford, A Pellet and S Wittich (eds), *International Law Between Universalism and Fragmentation* (Brill, 2009).

Bugarič, B, 'The Populist Backlash Against Europe' in F Bignami (ed), *EU Law in Populist Times* (Cambridge University Press, 2019).

Bungenberg, M, 'Going Global? – The EU Common Commercial Policy after Lisbon' in C Herrmann, M Krajewski and J Terhechte (eds), *European Yearbook of International Economic Law* (Springer, 2010).

Burgess, M, *Federalism and the European Union: The Building of Europe 1950–2000* (Routledge, 2002).

Calliess, C, 'Constitutional Identity in Germany – One for Three or Three in One?' in C Calliess and G Van der Schyff (eds), *Constitutional Identity in a Europe of Multilevel Constitutionalism* (Cambridge University Press, 2019).

Cantore, CM, *The Prudential Carve-Out for Financial Services Rationale and Practice In the GATS and Preferential Trade Agreements* (Cambridge University Press, 2018).

Cardwell, PJ and French, D, 'The European Union as a Global Investment Partner: Law, Policy and Rhetoric in the Attainment of Development Assistance and Market Liberalisation?' in C Brown and K Miles (eds), *The Evolution in Investment Treaty Law and Arbitration* (Cambridge University Press, 2011).

Carreau, D and Juillard, P, *Droit International économique* (Dalloz, 2010).

Cazala, J, 'La clause du respect des engagements' in C Leben (ed), *Droit international des investissements et de l'arbitrage transnational* (Pedone, 2015).

Ciurtini, H, 'Paradoxes of (Sovereign) Consent: on the Uses and Abuses of a Notion in International Investment Law' in C Baltag (ed), *ICSID Convention after 50 Years: Unsettled Issues* (Kluwer Law International, 2016).

Conforti, B, 'Consistency Among Treaty Obligations' in E Cannizzaro (ed), *The Law of Treaties Beyond the Vienna Convention* (Oxford University Press, 2011).

Contartese, C and Pantaleo, L, 'Division of Competences, EU Autonomy and the Determination of the Respondent Party: Proceduralisation as a Possible Way-Out?' in E Neframi and M Gatti (eds), *Constitutional Issues of EU External Relations Law* (Nomos, 2018).

Craig, P, *EU Administrative Law* (Oxford University Press, 2012).

Crawford, J and Koskenniemi, M, 'Introduction' in J Crawford and M Koskenniemi (eds), *The Cambridge Companion to International Law* (Cambridge University Press, 2012).

Cremona, M, 'Disconnection Clauses in EU Law and Practice' in C Hillion and P Koutrakos (eds), *Mixed Agreements Revisited: The EU and its Member States in the World* (Bloomsbury Publishing, 2010).

Das, US, Papaioannou, MG and Trebesch C, 'Restructuring Sovereign Debt: Lessons From Recent History' in S Claessens, MA Kose, L Laeven and F Valencia (eds), *Financial Crises: Causes, Consequences, and Policy Responses* (International Monetary Fund, 2014).

De Baere, G, *Constitutional Principles of EU External Relations* (Oxford University Press, 2008).

De Brabandere, E, *Investment Treaty Arbitration as Public International Law Procedural Aspects and Implications* (Cambridge University Press, 2014).

De Luca, A, 'Indirect Expropriation and Regulatory Takings: What Role for the 'Legitimate Expectations' of Foreign Investors' in G Sacerdoti, P Acconci, M Valenti and A De Luca (eds), *General Interests of Host States in International Investment Law* (Cambridge University Press, 2014).

De Nanteuil, A, *L'expropriation indirecte en droit international des investissements* (Pedone, 2014).

De Vries, CE, *Euroscepticism and the Future of European Integration* (Oxford University Press, 2018).

De Witte, B, 'A selfish Court? The Court of Justice and the Design of International Dispute Settlement Beyond the European Union' in M Cremona and A Thies (eds), *The European Court of Justice and External Relations Law* (Hart Publishing, 2014).

Devuyst, Y, 'The Constitutional and Lisbon Treaties' in E Jones, A Menon and S Weatherill (eds), *The Oxford Handbook of the European Union* (Oxford University Press, 2012).

Diaz-Candia, H, 'The Role of Municipal Laws in Investment Arbitration' in A Bjorklund (ed), *Yearbook on International Investment Law and Policy 2012–2013* (Oxford University Press, 2014).

Dimopoulos, A, 'Creating an EU Investment Policy: Challenges for the Post-Lisbon Era of External Relations' in PJ Cardwell (ed), *EU External Relations Law and Policy in the Post-Lisbon Era* (TMC Asser Press – Springer, 2012).

Dolzer, R and Schreuer, C, *Principles of International Investment Law* (Oxford University Press, 2012).

Dubuisson, F, 'Article 59' in O Corten and P Klein (eds), *The Vienna Convention on the Law of Treaties – A Commentary* (Oxford University Press, 2011).

Dumberry, P, *The Fair and Equitable Treatment Standard – A Guide to NAFTA Case Law on Article 1105* (Kluwer Law International, 2013).

Dupuy, PM and Radi, Y, 'Le droit de l'expropriation directe et indirecte' in C Leben (ed), *Droit international des investissements et de l'arbitrage transnational* (Pedone, 2015).

Eckes, C, *EU Powers Under External Pressure: How the EU's External Actions Alter its Internal Structures* (Oxford University Press, 2019).

Eulalio Do Nascimento e Silva, G, *Le facteur temps et les traités* (Collected Courses of the Hague Academy of International Law, 1977).

Fečak, T, *International Investment Agreements and EU Law* (Kluwer Law International, 2016).

Gardiner, R, *Treaty Interpretation* (Oxford University Press, 2015).

Giegerich, T, 'Article 54' in O Dörr and K Schmalenbach (eds), *Vienna Convention on the Law of Treaties – A commentary* (Springer, 2012).

—— 'Article 59' in O Dörr and K Schmalenbach (eds), *Vienna Convention on the Law of Treaties – A commentary* (Springer, 2012).

Happ, R and Bischoff, JA, 'Role and Responsibility of the European Union under the Energy Charter Treaty' in G Coop (ed), *Energy Dispute Resolution: Investment Protection, Transit and The Energy Charter Treaty* (Juris Publishing, 2011).

Hepburn, J, *Domestic law in International Investment Arbitration* (Oxford University Press, 2017).

Higgins, R, *The Taking of Property by the State: Recent Developments in International Law* (Collected Courses of the Hague Academy of International Law, 1982).

Hindelang, S, *The Free Movement of Capital and Foreign Direct Investment: The Scope of Protection in EU Law* (Oxford University Press, 2009).

Hofmann, HCH, Rowe, GC and Turk, AH, *Administrative Law and Policy of the European Union* (Oxford University Press, 2011).

Hope, J and Åkerlund, T, 'All Eyes on Sweden: Swedish Challenge Cases Post-Achmea' in A Stanič and C Baltag (eds), *The Future of Investment Treaty Arbitration in the EU: Intra-EU Bits, the Energy Charter Treaty, and the Multilateral Investment Court* (Kluwer Law International, 2020).

Johnson, L and Sachs, L, 'International Investment Agreements, 2011–2012: A Review of Trends and New Approaches' in A Bjorklund (ed), *Yearbook on International Investment Law & Policy* (Oxford University Press, 2014).

Johnson, L, Sachs, L and Coleman, J, 'International Investment Agreements, 2014: A Review of Trends and New Approaches' in A Bjorklund (ed), *Yearbook on International Investment Law and Policy* (Oxford University Press, 2016).

Jordan, A and Rayner, T, 'The Evolution of Climate Policy in the European Union: An Historical Overview' in AD Jordan, H Huitema, T van Asselt, T Rayner and F Berkhout (eds), *Climate Change Policy in the European Union* (Cambridge University Press, 2011).

Juillard, P, 'The Law of International Investment-Can the Balance be Redressed?' in KP Sauvant (ed), *Yearbook of International Investment Law and Policy* (Oxford University Press, 2009).

Kellerbauer, M, 'Article 75' in M Kellerbauer, M Klamert and J Tomkin (eds), *The EU Treaties and the Charter of Fundamental Rights: A Commentary* (Oxford University Press, 2019).

Klabbers, J, *Treaty Conflict and the European Union* (Cambridge University Press, 2008).

Klamert, M, *The Principle of Loyalty in EU Law* (Oxford University Press, 2014).

Kohen, M, 'Keeping Subsequent Agreements and Practice in Their Right Limits' in G Nolte (ed), *Treaties and Subsequent Practice* (Oxford University Press, 2013).

Krajewski, M, 'The Reform of the Common Commercial Policy' in A Biondi, P Eeckhout and S Ripley (eds), *EU Law After Lisbon* (Oxford University Press, 2012).

Kriebaum, U, 'Expropriation', in M Bungenberg, J Griebel, S Hobe and A Reinisch (eds) *International Investment Law* (C.H. Beck-Hart-Nomos, 2015).

Ladreit de Lacharrière, G, *L'influence de l'inegalité de développement des Etats sur le Droit International* (Collected Courses of the Hague Academy of International Law, 1973).

Lampo, G, 'The Relationship Between Intra-EU Investment Arbitration Under the Energy Charter Treaty and the Lisbon Treaty in Light of Article 41 of the Vienna Convention on the Law of Treaties' in G Pascale and S Tonolo (eds), *The Vienna Convention on the Law of Treaties – the Role of the Treaty on Treaties in Contemporary International Law* (Edizioni Scientifiche Italiane, 2022).

Langford, M, Behn, D and Fauchauld, OK, 'Backlash and State Strategies in International Investment Law' in T Aalberts and T Gammeltoft-Hansen (eds), *The Changing Practices of International Law* (Cambridge University Press, 2018).

Le Bouthillier, Y, 'Article 32' in O Corten and P Klein (eds), *The Vienna Convention on the Law of Treaties – A commentary* (Oxford University Press, 2011).

Leben, C, 'La liberté normative de l'Etat et la Question de l'Expropriation Indirecte' in C Leben (ed), *Le Contentieux Arbitral Relatif à l'Investissement* (LGDJ, 2006).

Lejeune, Y, *Droit constitutionnel belge – Fondements et institutions* (Larcier, 2017).

Lenk, H, 'The EU Investment Court System and its Resemblance to the WTO Appellate Body' in S Gáspár-Szilágyi, D Behn and M Langford (eds), *Adjudicating Trade and Investment Disputes – Convergence or Divergence?* (Cambridge University Press, 2020).

Lowenfeld, A, *International Economic Law* (Oxford University Press, 2009).

Majone, G, *Rethinking the Union of Europe Post-Crisis: Has Integration Gone Too Far?* (Cambridge University Press, 2014).

Mathy, D, 'Article 25' in O Corten and P Klein (eds), *The Vienna Convention on the Law of Treaties – A Commentary* (Oxford University Press, 2011).

Maupin, JA, 'Transparency in International Investment Law: The Good, the Bad and the Murky' in A Bianchi and A Peters (eds), *Transparency in International Law* (Cambridge University Press, 2013).

Mauro, MR, *Gli accordi di promozione e protezione degli investimenti* (Giappichelli, 2003).

Maydell, N, 'The European Community's Minimum Platform on Investment or the Trojan Horse of Investment Competence', in A Reinisch and C Knahr (eds), *International Investment Law in Context* (Eleven Publishing, 2007).

Mills, A, 'The Public-Private Dualities of International Investment Law and Arbitration' in K Miles and C Brown (eds), *Evolution in Investment Treaty and Arbtiration* (Cambridge University Press, 2011).

Müller-Graff, PC, 'The Common Commercial Policy Enhanced by the Reform Treaty of Lisbon?' in A Dashwood and M Maresceau (eds), *Law and Practice of EU External Relations: Salient Features of a Changing Landscape* (Cambridge University Press, 2011).

Munro, J, *Emissions Trading Schemes Under International Economic Law* (Oxford University Press, 2018).

Newcombe, A, 'The Use of General Exceptions in IIAs: Increasing Legitimacy Or Uncertainty' in A de Mestral and C Lévesque (eds), *Improving International Investment Agreements* (Routledge, 2013).

Newcombe, A and Paradell, L, *Law and Practice of Investment Treaties: Standards of Treatment* (Kluwer Law International, 2009).

Nouvel, Y, 'La compétence matérielle: contrat, traité et clauses parapluie' in C Leben (ed), *La procédure arbitrale relative aux investissements internationaux* (Anthemis-L.G.D.J., 2008).
Nowrot, K, 'Termination and Renegotiation of International Investment Agreements' in S Hindelang and M Krajewski (eds), *Shifting Paradigms in International Investment Law* (Oxford University Press, 2016).
Öberg, M, *The Boundaries of the EU Internal Market Law* (Cambridge University Press, 2020).
Odendahl, K, 'Article 41' in O Dörr and K Schmalenbach (eds) *Vienna Convention on the Law of Treaties – A commentary* (Springer, 2012).
Odermatt, J, *International Law and the European Union* (Cambridge University Press, 2021).
Orakhelashvili, A, 'Article 30' in O Corten and P Klein (eds), *The Vienna Convention on the Law of Treaties – A commentary* (Oxford University Press, 2011).
Ortino, F and Eeckhout, P, 'Towards an EU policy on Foreign Direct Investment' in A Biondi, P Eeckhout and S Ripley (eds), *EU Law After Lisbon* (Oxford University Press, 2012).
Pantaleo, L, *The Participation of the EU in International Dispute Settlement* (TMC Asser Press, 2019).
Paparinskis, M, *The International Minimum Standard and Fair and Equitable Treatment* (Oxford University Press, 2013).
Parlett, K., *The Individual in the International Legal System* (Cambridge University Press, 2011).
Pauwelyn, J, *Conflict of Norms in Public International Law: How WTO Law Relates to Other Rules of International Law* (Cambridge University Press, 2003).
Pellet, A, *Les fondements juridiques internationaux du droit communautaire* (Collected Courses of the Academy of European Law, 1997).
Perdikis, N, 'Trade Agreements: Depth of Integration' in JD Gaisford and WA Kerr (eds), *Handbook on International Trade Policy* (Edward Elgar, 2007).
Perfetti, A, 'Ensuring the Consistency of the EU Investment Policy Within the EU External Action: The Relevance of Non-Trade Values' in G Sacerdoti, P Acconci, M Valenti and A De Luca (eds), *General Interests of Host States in International Investment Law* (Cambridge University Press, 2016).
Pescatore, P, 'La Cour de justice des Communautées européennes et la Convention européenne des droits de l'homme' in F Matscher and H Petzold (eds), *Protecting Human Rights: The European Dimension* (Heymann, 1988).
Picone, P, *L'applicazione in via provvisoria degli accordi internazionali* (Jovene, 1973).
Quast Mertsch, A, 'Provisional Application of Treaties and the Internal Logic of the 1969 Vienna Convention' in MJ Bowman and D Kritsiotis (eds), *Conceptual and Contextual Perspectives on the Modern Law of Treaties* (Cambridge University Press, 2018).
Qureshi, AH, 'An Appellate System in International Investment Arbitration?' in PT Muchlinski, F Ortino and C Schreuer (eds), *The Oxford Handbook of International Investment Law* Oxford University Press, 2008).
Reinisch, A, 'The Division of Powers Between the EU and its Member States "After Lisbon"' in M Bungenberg, J Griebel and S Hindelang (eds), *European Yearbook of International Economic Law – Special Issue: International Investment Law and EU Law* (Springer, 2011).
Reinisch, A and Schreuer, C, *International Protection of Investments: The Substantive Standards* (Cambridge University Press, 2020).
Reisman, WM and Arsanjani, MH, 'Applicable Law Under the ICSID Convention: The Tortured History of the Interpretation of Article 42' in MN Kinnear, GR Fischer, J Minguez Almeida, LF Torres Arias and MU Bidegain (eds), *Building International Investment Law – The first 50 years of ICSID* 3 (Kluwer Law International, 2015).
Rivas, JA, 'ICSID Treaty Counterclaims: Case Law and Treaty Evolution' in JE Kalicki and A Joubin-Bret (eds), *Reshaping the Investor-State Dispute Settlement System* (Brill, 2015).
Roe, T and Happold, M, *Settlement of Investment Disputes under the Energy Charter Treaty* (Cambridge University Press, 2011).

Rosas, A, 'The European Union and Mixed Agreements' in A Dashwood and C Hillion (eds), *The General Law of EC External Relations* (Sweet & Maxwell, 2000).

Sacerdoti, G, 'Havana Charter' in R Wolfrum (ed), *Max Planck Encyclopedia of International Law* (Oxford University Press, 2013).

—— 'Nascita, affermazione e scomparsa del Nuovo Ordine Economico Internazionale' in A Ligustro and G Sacerdoti (ed), *Problemi e tendenze del diritto internazionale dell'economia –* Liber amicorum *in onore di Paolo Picone* (Editoriale Scientifica, 2011).

Salacuse, JW, 'The Energy Charter Treaty and the Bilateral Investment Treaty Regimes' in T Wälde (ed), *The Energy Charter Treaty: an East-West Gateway for Investment and Trade* (Kluwer Law International, 1996).

Sasson, M, 'The Applicable Law and the ICSID Convention' in A Stanič and C Baltag (eds), *The Future of Investment Treaty Arbitration in the EU: Intra-EU BITs, the Energy Charter Treaty, and the Multilateral Investment Court* (Kluwer Law International, 2020).

Schill, SW, *The Multilateralisation of International Investment Law* (Cambridge University Press, 2009).

Schreuer, C, 'Coherence and Consistency in International Investment Law' in R Echandi and P Sauvé (eds), *Prospects in International Investment Law and Policy* (Cambridge University Press, 2013).

Schreuer, C, Malintoppi, L, Reinisch, A and Sinclair, A, *The ICSID Convention: a Commentary* (Cambridge University Press, 2009).

Schütze, R, *Foreign Affairs and the EU Constitution – Selected Essays* (Cambridge University Press, 2014).

Schütze, R and Tridimas, T, *Oxford Principles of European Union Law: The European Union Legal Order* (Oxford University Press, 2018).

Schwarzenberger, G, *The Frontiers of International Law* (Stevens & Sons, 1962).

Seidl-Hohenveldern, I, *International Economic Law* (Kluwer Law International, 1999).

Selivanova, Y, 'The Energy Charter and the International Energy Governance' in Y Selivanova (ed), *Regulation of Energy in International Trade Law: WTO, NAFTA, and Energy Charter* (Kluwer Law International, 2011).

Snell, J, 'Free Movement of Capital: Evolution as a Non-Linear Process' in P Craig and G De Burca (eds), *The Evolution of EU Law* (Oxford University Press, 2021).

Sornarajah, M, *Resistance and Change in International Law on Foreign Investment* (Cambridge University Press, 2015).

—— *The International Law on Foreign Investment* (Cambridge University Press, 2010).

Stanič, A, 'Enforcement of Awards and Other Implications of *Achmea*' in A Stanič and C Baltag (eds), *The Future of Investment Treaty Arbitration in the EU: Intra- EU Bits, the Energy Charter Treaty, and the Multilateral Investment Court* (Kluwer Law International, 2020).

Strik, P, *Shaping the Single European Market in the Field of Foreign Direct Investment* (Hart Publishing, 2014).

Tietje, C and Crow, K, 'The Reform of Investment Protection Rules in CETA, TTIP, and Other Recent EU FTAs: Convincing?' in S Griller, W Obwexer and E Vranes (eds), *Mega-Regional Trade Agreements: CETA, TTIP, and TiSA – New Orientations for EU External Economic Relations* (Oxford University Press, 2017).

Titi, C, *The Right to Regulate in International Investment Law* (Hart Publishing-Nomos, 2014).

Tovo, C, 'Mixed Agreements in the Italian Legal Order' in I Govaere and M Chamon (eds), *EU External Relations Post-Lisbon the Law and Practice of Facultative Mixity* (Brill, 2020).

Toye, R, 'The International Trade Organisation' in M Daunton, A Narlikar and RM Stern (eds), *The Oxford Handbook on the World Trade Organisation* (Oxford University Press, 2012).

Treves, T, *The Expansion of International Law* (Collected Courses of the Hague Academy of International Law, 2015).

Valenti, M, 'The Protection of General Interests of Host States in the Application of the Fair and Equitable Treatment Standard', in G Sacerdoti, P Acconci, M Valenti and A De Luca (eds), *General Interests of Host States in International Investment Law* (Cambridge University Press, 2014).

—— *Gli standard di trattamento nell'interpretazione dei trattati in materia di investimenti stranieri* (Giappichelli, 2009).
Van Harten, G, *Investment Treaty Arbitration and Public Law* (Cambridge University Press, 2008).
Van Rossem, JW, 'The Autonomy of EU Law: More is Less?' in R Wessel and S Blockmans (eds), *Between Autonomy and Dependence: The EU Legal Order Under the Influence of International Organisations* (Asser Press-Springer, 2013).
Vandevelde, JK, *The First Bilateral Investment Treaties: U.S. Postwar Friendship, Commerce and Navigation Treaties* (Oxford University Press, 2017).
Villiger, ME, *Commentary on the 1969 Vienna Convention on the Law of Treaties* (Martinus Nijhoff, 2009).
Wells, LT, 'Backlash to Investment Arbitration: Three Causes' in M Waibel, A Kaushal, K Chung and C Balchin (eds), *The Backlash Against Investment Arbitration – Perceptions and Reality*, (Kluwer Law International, 2010).
Wong, J and Yackee, J, 'The 2006 Procedural and Transparency-Related Amendments to the ICSID Arbitration Rules' in KP Sauvant (eds) *Yearbook on International Investment Law and Policy* (Oxford University Press, 2011).
Xavier Millet, F, 'Constitutional identity in France – Vices and – above all – virtues' in C Calliess and G van der Schyff (eds), *Constitutional Identity in a Europe of Multilevel Constitutionalism* (Cambridge University Press, 2019).
Yotova, R, 'The New EU Competence in Foreign Direct Investment and Intra-EU Investment Treaties: Does the Emperor Have New Clothes?' in F Baetens (ed), *Investment Law Within International Law – Integrationist Perspectives* (Cambridge University Press, 2013).

ARTICLES

Abbott, KW, Keohane, RO, Moravcsik, A, Slaughter, A and Snidal, D., 'The Concept of Legalisation' (2000) 54 *International Organisation* 401.
Alvarez, GM, 'Redefining the Relationship Between the Energy Charter Treaty and the Treaty of Functioning of the European Union: From a Normative Conflict to Policy Tension' (2018) 33 *ICSID Review–Foreign Investment Law Journal* 560.
Alvarez, JE, 'The Return of the State' (2011) 20 *Minnesota Journal of International law* 223.
Andersen, T and Hindelang, S, 'The Day After: Alternatives to Intra-EU BITs' (2016) 17 *Journal of World Investment and Trade* 984, 993.
Atanasova, D, Martínez Benoit, CA and Ostransky, J, 'Counterclaims in Investor-State Dispute Settlement (ISDS) Under International Investment Agreements (IIAs)', Trade and Investment Law Clinic Papers 2012.
Baratta, R, 'La politica commerciale comune dopo il trattato di Lisbona' (2012) 26 *Diritto del Commercio Internazionale* 403.
Basedow, JR, 'A Legal History of the EU's International Investment Policy' (2016) 17 *Journal of World Investment and Trade* 734.
—— 'The *Achmea* Judgment and the Applicability of the Energy Charter Treaty in Intra-EU Investment Arbitration' (2020) 23 *Journal of International Economic Law* 271.
Bernasconi-Osterwalder, N, 'Commentary to the Draft Investment Chapter of the Canada-EU Comprehensive Economic and Trade Agreement (CETA)', International Institute for Sustainable Development, 2014.
Bianco, G, 'European Union's Investment Agreements and Public Debt' (2017) 28 *European Business Law Review* 119.
Binder, C, 'A Treaty Law Perspective on Intra-EU BITs' (2016) 17 *Journal of World Investment and Trade* 964.
Bischoff, JA, 'Just a Little Bit of Mixity? The EU's Role in the Field of Foreign Investment Protection Law' (2011) 48 *Common Market Law Review* 1527.

Boisson de Chazournes, L and Baruti, R, 'Transparency in Investor-State Arbitration: An Incremental Approach' (2015) 2 *BCDR International Arbitration Review* 59.

Bondar, K, 'Annulment of ICSID and non-ICSID Investment Awards: Differences in the Extent of Review' (2015) 32 *Journal of International Arbitration* 621.

Borgen, C, 'Resolving Treaty Conflicts' (2005) 37 *George Washington International Law Review* 573.

Briguglio, A, '*Achmea* and the Day After *Achmea*' [2018] *Rivista dell'Arbitrato* 504.

Bungenberg, M and Böhme, B, 'Under the Radar – The Return of Member States in EU Investment Policy', (2022) *Journal of International Economic Law* (forthcoming).

Burgstaller, M, 'European Law and Investment Treaties' (2009) 26 *Journal of International Arbitration* 181.

Calamita, J, 'Dispute Settlement Transparency in Europe's Evolving Investment Treaty Policy: Adopting the UNCITRAL Transparency Rules Approach' (2014) 15 *Journal of World Investment and Trade* 585.

Cappiello, B, 'Il mantenimento in vigore dei BITs intra europei e la legittimità della clausola compromissoria negli accordi bilaterali e multilaterali di investimento alla luce della sentenza Achmea' [2019] *Giurisprudenza commerciale* 258.

Cazala, J, 'La protection des attentes légitimes de l'investisseur dans l'arbitrage international' (2009) 23 *Revue Internationale de Droit Economique* 5.

Cellerino, C, 'EU Common Commercial Policy in Context: Opportunities and Challenges of a Changing Landscape' (2105) 29 *Diritto del Commercio Internazionale* 783.

Ceyssens, J, 'Towards a Common Foreign Investment Policy? – Foreign Investment in the European Constitution' (2005) 32 *Legal Issues of Economic Integration* 259.

Contartese, C, '*Achmea* and Opinion 1/17: Why do intra and extra-EU bilateral investment treaties impact differently on the EU legal order?', ECB-Legal Working Paper Series No 19, 2019.

—— 'The Autonomy of the EU Legal Order in the ECJ's External *Relations Case Law: From the "Essential" to the "Specific Characteristics" of the Union and Back Again*' (2017) 54 *Common Market Law Review* 1627.

Contartese, C and Andenas, M, 'EU Autonomy and Investor-State Dispute Settlement Under *Inter Se* Agreements Between EU Member States: *Achmea*' (2019) 56 *Common Market Law Review* 157.

Correa, C and Viñuales, JE, 'Intellectual Property Rights as Protected Investments: How Open are the Gates?' (2016) 19 *Journal of International Economic Law* 91.

Cortez Pimentel, M, 'Distortion of the Common Market? Analysis and Perspective of the MFN Clause Within EC Law' (2005) 34 *Intertax* 485.

Cotula, L, 'Expropriation Clauses and Environmental Regulation: Diffusion of Law in the Era of Investment Treaties' (2015) 24 *Review of European Community and International Environmental Law* 278.

Crawford, J, 'Treaty and Contract in Investment Arbitration' (2008) 24 *Arbitration International*.

Cremona, M, 'Shaping EU Trade Policy Post-Lisbon: Opinion 2/15 of 16 May 2017' (2018) 14 *European Constitutional Law Review* 231.

Dahlquist, J, Lenk, H and Rönnelid, L, 'The Infringement Proceedings Over Intra-EU Investment Treaties – an Analysis of the Case against Sweden', Swedish Institute for European Policy Studies, European Policy Analysis No 4 (2016).

De Groot, IM, 'Member States Must Apply Most Favoured Nation Treatment Under EU Law' (2014) 42 *Intertax* 405.

Di Benedetto, S, 'Modelli giuridici di ecceezione e integrazione di valori non commerciali: dall'esperienza del diritto GATT/OMC ai regime di protezione degli investimenti esteri' (2013) 27 *Diritto del Commercio Internazionale* 405.

Dimopoulos, A, 'The Common Commercial Policy after Lisbon: Establishing Parallelism Between Internal and External Economic Relations?' (2008) 4 *Croatian Yearbook of European Law and Policy* 101.

—— 'The Involvement of the EU Investor-State Dispute Settlement: A Question of Responsibility' (2014) 51 *Common Market Law Review* 1671.

Dolzer, R, 'Indirect Expropriation: New Developments?' (2003) 11 *New York University Environmental Law Journal* 64.

Dony, M, 'Quel avenir pour la politique commerciale commune de l'Union européenne' (2017) *Revue trimestrielle de droit européen* 189.

Douglas, Z, 'The Hybrid Foundations of Investment Treaty Arbitration' (2003) 74 *British Yearbook of International Law* 151.

Eckes, C, 'EU Counter-Terrorist Sanctions against Individuals: Problems and Perils' (2012) 17 *European Foreign Affairs Review* 113.

Eeckhout, P, 'Opinion 2/13 on EU Accession to the ECHR and Judicial Dialogue: Autonomy or Autarky' (2015) 38 *Fordham International Law Journal* 955.

Eilmansberger, T, 'Bilateral Investment Treaties and EU Law' (2009) 46 *Common Market Law Review* 383.

El Boudouhi, S, 'Le chapitre sur les investissements de l'ALENA: le retour de l'Etat?' (2019) 123 *Revue générale de droit international public* 865.

Fang, C, Schumacher, J and Trebesch, C, 'Restructuring Sovereign Bonds: Holdouts, Haircuts and the Effectiveness of CACs' (2021) 69 *IMF Economic Review* 155.

Fanou, M, 'Intra-European Union Investor-State Arbitration Post-*Achmea*: RIP?' (2019) 26 *Maastricht Journal of European and Comparative Law* 316.

—— 'The CETA ICS and the Autonomy of the EU Legal Order in Opinion 1/17 – A Compass for the Future' (2020) 22 *Cambridge Yearbook of European Legal Studies* 106.

Fischer-Lescano, A and Teubner, G, 'Regime-Collisions: The Vain Search for Legal Unity in the Fragmentation of Global Law' (2004) 25 *Michigan Journal International Law* 999.

Footer, ME, 'BITs and Pieces: Social and Environmental Protection in the Regulation of Foreign Investment' (2009) 18 *Michigan State Journal of International Law* 33.

—— 'Umbrella Clauses and Widely-Formulated Arbitration Clauses: Discerning the Limits of ICSID Jurisdiction' (2017) 16 *The Law and Practice of International Courts and Tribunals* 87.

Franck, SD, 'The Legitimacy Crisis in Investment Treaty Arbitration: Privatizing Public International Law Through Inconsistent Decisions' (2005) 73 *Fordham Law Review* 1521.

Frankel, S, 'Interpreting the Overlap of International Investment and Intellectual Property Law' (2016) 19 *Journal of International Economic Law* 121.

Gaillard, E, 'The Myth of Harmony in International Arbitration' (2019) 34 *ICSID Review-Foreign Investment Law Journal* 553.

Gaja, G, 'The Diverse Legal Effects of the Provisional Application of Treaties' (2022) 105 *Rivista di Diritto di Internazionale* 753.

Gáspár-Szilágyi, S, '*Quo vadis* EU Investment Law and Policy? The Shaky Path Towards the International Promotion of EU Rules' (2018) 23 *European Foreign Affairs Review* 167.

Gill, J, Gearing, M and Birt, G, 'Contractual Claims and Bilateral Investment Treaties' (2004) 21 *Journal of International Arbitration* 397.

Govaere, I, 'Setting the International Scene: EU External Competence and Procedures Post-Lisbon Revisited in the Light of Opinion 1/13' (2015) 52 *Common Market Law Review* 1277.

Grosse Ruse-Khan, H, 'Challenging Compliance with International Intellectual Property Norms in Investor-State Dispute Settlement' (2016) 19 *Journal of International Economic Law* 241.

Guarin Duque, GA, 'The Termination Agreement of Intra-EU Bilateral Investment Treaties: A Spaghetti-Bowl with Fewer Ingredients and More Questions' (2020) 37(5) *Journal of International Arbitration* 798.

Hainbach, P, 'The CJEU's Opinion 2/15 and the Future of EU Investment Policy and Law-Making' (2018) 45 *Legal Issues of Economic Integration* 199.

Harrison, J, 'The Life and Death of BITs: Legal Issues Concerning Survival Clauses and the Termination of Investment Treaties' (2012) 13 *Journal of World Investment and Trade* 928.

Hess, B, 'The fate of Investment Dispute Resolution after the Achmea Decision of the European Court of Justice', MPILux Research Paper 2018 (3).

Hindelang, S and Sassenrath, C, 'The investment chapters of the EU's international trade and investment agreements in a comparative perspective', European Parliament-Directorate General for External Policies, 2015.

Hobér, K, 'Investment Arbitration and the Energy Charter Treaty' (2010) 1 *Journal of International Dispute Settlement* 153.

Horng, D, 'Reshaping the EU's FTA policy in a Globalized Economy: The Case of the EU-Korea FTA' (2012) 46 *Journal of World Trade* 301.

Ishikawa, T, 'Third Party Participation in Investment Treaty Arbitration' (2010) 59 *International and Comparative Law Quarterly* 373.

Istvan Nagy, C, 'Intra-EU Bilateral Investment Treaties and EU Law After *Achmea*: Know Well What Leads You Forward and What Holds You Back' (2018) 19 *German Law Journal* 981.

Jadeau, F and Gélinas, F, 'CETA's Definition of the Fair and Equitable Treatment Standard: Toward a Guided and Constrained Interpretation' [2016] *Transnational Dispute Management*.

Jenks, W, 'The Conflict of Law-Making Treaties' (1953) 30 *British Yearbook of International Law*.

Jung, Y and Han, SD, 'Sovereign Debt Restructuring under the Investor-State Dispute Regime' (2014) 31 *Journal of International Arbitration* 75.

Keene, A, 'The Incorporation and Interpretation of WTO-Style Environmental Exceptions in International Investment Agreements' (2017) 18 Journal of World Investment and Trade 62.

Klamert, M and Maydell, N, 'Lost in Exclusivity: Implied Non-Exclusive External Competences in Community Law' (2008) 13 *European Foreign Affairs Review* 493.

Kleimann, D and Kübek, G, 'The Signing, Provisional Application, and Conclusion of Trade and Investment Agreements in the EU: The Case of CETA and Opinion 2/15' (2018) 45 *Legal Issues of Economic Integration* 13.

Kleinheisterkamp, J, 'European Policy Space in International Investment Law' (2012) 27 *ICSID Review – Foreign Investment Law Journal* 416.

—— 'Investment Protection and EU Law: The Intra-EU and Extra-EU Dimension of the Energy Charter Treaty' (2012) 15 *Journal of International Economic Law* 85.

Kochenov, D and Lavranos, N, '*Achmea* Versus the Rule of Law: CJEU's Dogmatic Dismissal of Investors' Rights in Backsliding Member States of the European Union' [2021] *Hague Journal on the Rule of Law*.

Korom, V, 'Jurisprudence *Achmea*: la fin de l'arbitrage d'investissement au sein de l'Union européenne?' (2018) 36 *Recueil Dalloz* 2005.

Koutrakos, P, 'The Autonomy of EU Law and International Investment Arbitration' (2020) 88 *Nordic Journal of International Law* 41.

—— 'The Anatomy of Aautonomy: Themes and Perspectives on an Elusive Principle', ECB Legal conference, 2019.

Krajewski, M, 'External Trade Law and the Constitution Treaty: Towards a Federal and More Democratic Common Commercial Policy?' (2005) 42 *Common Market Law Review* 91.

Kriebaum, U, 'FET and Expropriation in the (invisible) EU Model BIT' (2014) 15 *Journal of World Investment and Trade* 454.

—— 'Regulatory Takings: Balancing the Interests of the Investor and the State' (2007) 8 *Journal of World Investment Trade* 717.

Kuijper, PJ, Pernice, I, Hindelang, S, Schwarz, M and Reuling, M, 'Investment protection agreements as instruments of international economic law', Study for the European Parliament, 2014.

Kulick, A, 'Case comment- *Electrabel S.A. v Hungary*' (2014) 15 *Journal of World Investment and Trade* 273.

Lavranos N., 'The *MOX Plant* and *Ijzeren Rijn* disputes: which court is the supreme arbiter?' 19 Leiden Journal of International Law 223 (2006).

Lavranos, N and Singla, T, 'Achmea: Groundbreaking or Overrated?' (2018) 6 *SchiedsVZ – German Arbitration Journal* 348.

Łazowski, A and Wessel, RA, 'When Caveats Turn into Locks: Opinion 2/13 on Accession of the European Union to the ECHR' (2015) 16 *German Law Journal* 179.

Leczykiewicz, D, 'Common Commercial Policy: The Expanding Competence of the European Union in The Area of International Trade' (2005) 6 *German Law Journal* 1673.
Leinarte, E, 'The Principle of Independent Responsibility of the European Union and its Member States in the International Economic Context' (2018) 21 *Journal of International Economic Law* 171.
Lemaire, S, 'La mystérieuse 'umbrella clause' (Interrogations sur l'impact de la clause de respect des engagements sur l'arbitrage en matiére d'investissements)' [2009] *Revue de l'Arbitrage* 479.
Lipstein, K, 'The Place of Calvo Clause in International Law' (1945) 22 *British Yearbook of International Law* 130.
Magnon, X, 'L'AECG devant le Conseil constitutionnel: Much Ado About Quite Nothing!' (2018) 113 *Revue française de droit constitutionnel* 173.
Malintoppi, L and Limbasan, N, 'Living in Glass Houses? The Debate on Transparency in International Investment Arbitration' (2015) 2 *BCDR International Arbitration Review* 32.
Maupin, J, 'Where Should Europe's Investment Path Lead? Reflections on August Reinisch, "*Quo Vadis Europe?*"' (2014) 12 *Santa Clara Journal of International Law* 183.
Mayer, P, 'Investissements internationaux – Contract claims et clauses juridictionnelles des traités relatifs à la protection des investissements' [2009] *Journal du Droit International* 71.
McLachlan, C, 'The Principle of Systemic Integration and Article 31(3)(c) of the Vienna Convention' (2005) 54 *International and Comparative Law Quarterly* 279.
McRae, D, 'The WTO Appellate Body: A Model for the ICSID Facility' (2010) 1 *Journal of International Dispute Settlement* 371.
Mengozzi, P, 'Les valeurs de l'Union et le règlement des différends dans le domaine des investissements internationaux' (2020) 3 *Diritto dell'Unione europea* 473.
Mercurio, B, 'Awakening the Sleeping Giant: Intellectual Property Rights in International Investment Agreements' (2012) 15 *Journal of International Economic Law* 871.
—— 'Safeguarding Public Welfare? – Intellectual Property Rights, Health and the Evolution of Treaty Drafting in International Investment Agreements' (2015) 6 *Journal of International Dispute Settlement* 252.
Meunier, S, 'Integration by Stealth: How the European Union Gained Competence Over Foreign Direct Investment', EU Working Papers, RSCAS 2014/66.
Meunier, S and Roederer-Rynning, C, 'Missing in Action? France and the Politicisation of Trade and Investment Agreements' (2020) 8 *Politics and Governance* 312.
Mitchell, D, Hawkins, JK and Mishra, N, 'Dear Prudence: Allowances under International Trade and Investment Law for Prudential Regulation in the Financial Services Sector' (2016) 19 *Journal of International Economic Law* 787.
Mostafa, B, 'Sole Effects Doctrine, Police Powers and Indirect Expropriation under International Law' (2008) 15 *Australian Journal of International Law* 267.
Neframi, E, 'Article 216(1) TFEU and the Union's Shared External Competence in the Light of Mixity: *Germany v Council (COTIF)*' (2019) 56 *Common Market Law Review* 489.
Nilsson, A and Englesson, O, 'Inconsistent Awards in Investment Treaty Arbitration: Is an Appeals Court Needed?' (2013) 30 *Journal of International Arbitration* 561.
Nouvel, Y, 'Affaire Achmea – commentaire' [2018] *Journal du Droit International*.
—— 'Classification cursive des régles de fond issues des traits bilateraux d'investissements' (2015) 69 *Révue Générale de Droit International Public* 7.
—— 'Les mesures équivalant à une expropriation dans la pratique récente des tribunaux arbitraux' (2002) 106 *Revue générale de droit international public* 79.
Orakhelasvili, A, 'The Normative Basis of the "Fair and Equitable Treatment": General International Law on Foreign Investment' (2008) 46 *Archiv des Völkerrechts* 74.
Ortolani, P, 'Intra-EU Arbitral Awards vis-à-vis Article 107 TFEU: State Aid Law as a Limit to Compliance' (2015) 6 *Journal of International Dispute Settlement* 118.
Paasivirta, E, 'Internationalisation and Stabilisation of Contracts versus State Sovereignty' (1989) 40 *British Yearbook of International Law* 315, 316.

Palchetti, P, 'The Allocation of International Responsibility in the Context of Investor-State Dispute Settlement Mechanisms Established by EU International Agreements' (2017) 28 *European Business Law Review* 185.

Pauwelyn, J, 'At the Edge of Chaos? Foreign Investment Law as a Complex Adaptive System: How it Emerged and How it can be Reformed' (2014) 29 *ICSID Review-Foreign Investment Law Journal* 372.

Pescatore, P, 'Opinion 1/94 on "Conclusion" of the WTO Agreement: is There an Escape from a Programmed Disaster' (1999) *36 Common Market Law Review* 387.

Pigeon, N, 'La *soft law* dans la construction de la politique européenne en matière d'investissements internationaux' (2014) 577 *Revue de l'Union Européenne* 201.

Pohl, JH, 'Intra-EU Investment Arbitration after the *Achmea* Case: Legal Autonomy Bounded by Mutual Trust?' (2018) 14 *European Constitutional Law Review* 767.

Popova, IC and Poon, F, 'From Perpetual Respondent to Aspiring Counterclaimant? State Counterclaims in the New Wave of Investment Treaties' (2015) 2 *BCDR Arbitration Review* 223.

Potts, JB, 'Stabilizing the Role of Umbrella Clauses in Bilateral Investment Treaties: Intent, Reliance, and Internationalisation' (2011) 51 *Virginia Journal of International Law* 1005.

Puig, S, 'Debiasing International Economic Law' (2019) 30 *European Journal of International Law* 1339.

Radicati di Brozolo, LG, 'Controllo del lodo internazionale e ordine pubblico' [2006] *Rivista dell'arbitrato* 629.

Regan, E, 'The Role of the Principles of Mutual Trust and Mutual Recognition in EU Law' (2018) 2 *Diritto dell'Unione europea* 231.

Reinisch, A, 'The EU on the Investment Path – *Quo vadis Europe*? The Future of EU BITs and Other Investment Agreements' (2014) 12 *Santa Clara Journal of International Law* 111.

Reuter, A, 'Taking Investors' Rights Seriously: The *Achmea* and *CETA* Rulings of the European Court of Justice do not Bar Intra-EU Investment Arbitration' (2020) 80 *Zeitschrift für ausländisches öffentliches Recht und Völkerrecht* 379.

Riffel, C, 'The CETA Opinion of the European Court of Justice and its implications – Not that Selfish After All' (2019) 22 *Journal of International Economic Law* 503.

Roberts, A, 'Clash of Paradigms: Actors and Analogies Shaping the Investment Treaty System' (2013) 107 *American Journal of International Law* 45.

—— 'Incremental, Systemic, and Paradigmatic Reform of Investor-State Arbitration' (2018) 112 *American Journal of International Law* 410.

Rosas, A, 'The Status in EU Law of International Agreements Concluded by EU Member States' (2011) 34 *Fordham International Law Journal* 1304.

Rousseau, C, 'De la compatibilité des normes juridiques contradictoires dans l'ordre international' (1932) 39 *Revue générale de droit international public* 132.

Roux, J, 'La jurisprudence «IVG» fragilisée par inadvertance' (2017) 41 *Recueil Dalloz* 2378.

Ruggie, J, 'International Regimes, Transactions, and Change: Embedded Liberalism in the Postwar Economic Order' (1982) 36 *International Organisation* 379.

Salacuse, JW, 'The Treatification of International Investment Law' (2007) 13 *Law and Business Review of the Americas* 155.

Salacuse, JW, Sullivan and NP, 'Do BITs Really Work: An Evaluation of Bilateral Investment Treaties and their Grand Bargain' (2005) 46 *Harvard International Law Journal* 67.

Sbragia, AM, 'The European Community: A Balancing Act' (1993) 23 *Journal of Federalism* 23.

Shan, W, 'Towards a Common European Community Policy on Investment Issues' (2001) 2 *Journal of World Investment* 603.

Shan, W and Zhang, S, 'The Treaty of Lisbon: Half Way Toward a Common Investment Policy' (2011) 21 *European Journal of International Law* 1049.

Shany, Y, 'Squaring the Circle? Independence and Impartiality of Party-Appointed Adjudicators in International Legal Proceedings' (2008) 30 *Loyola of Los Angeles International and Comparative Law Review* 473.

Sinclair, AC, 'The Origins of the Umbrella Clause in the International Law of Investment Protection' (2004) 20 *Arbitration International* 411.

Snodgrass, E, 'Protecting Investors' Legitimate Expectations: Recognizing and Delimiting a General Principle' (2006) 21 *ICSID Review-Foreign Investment Law Journal* 1.

Sørensen, KE, 'The Most-Favoured Nation Principle in EU Law' (2007) 34 *Legal Issues of Economic Integration* 315 (2007).

Spears, S, 'The Quest for Policy Space in a New Generation of International Investment Agreements' (2010) 13 *Journal of International Economic Law* 1037.

Spiermann, O, 'The Other Side of the Story: An Unpopular Essay on the Making of the European Community Legal Order' (1999) 10 *European Journal of International Law* 766.

Spooremberg, F and Viñuales, JE, 'Conflicting Decisions in International Arbitration' (2009) 8 *The Law and Practice of International Courts and Tribunals* 91.

Suescun de Roa, F, 'Investor-State Arbitration in Sovereign Debt Restructuring: The Role of Holdouts' (2013) 30 *Journal of International Arbitration* 131.

Suse, A and Wouters, J, 'Exploring the Boundaries of Provisional Application: The EU's Mixed Trade and Investment Agreements' (2019) 53 *Journal of World Trade* 395.

Titi, C, 'International Investment Law and the European Union: Towards a New Generation of International Investment Agreements' (2015) 26 *European Journal of International Law* 639.

—— 'The European Union's Proposal for an International Investment Court: Significance, Innovations and Challenges Ahead' *Transnational Dispute Management* (2017).

Tjetje, C, Ruff, D and Schmitt, M, 'Final Countdown in EU Investment Protection Law: Does the ECJ's Komstroy Ruling also Apply in Intra-EU ICSID Proceedings?' [2022] *Institut für Wirtschaftsrecht*.

Touscoz, J, 'The Role of the European Union in the Framework of the Energy Charter Treaty' (1997) 2 *European Foreign Affairs Review* 23.

Tropper, J and Reinisch, A, 'The 2020 Termination Agreement of Intra-EU Bits and its Effect on Investment Arbitration in the EU – A Public International Law Analysis of the Termination Agreement' (2022) 16 *Austrian Yearbook on International Arbitration* 301.

Van der Loo, G, 'CETA's Signature: 38 Statements, a Joint Interpretative Instrument and an Uncertain Future', CEPS Commentary, 2016.

—— 'Less is more? The role of national parliaments in the conclusion of mixed (trade) agreements', CLEER Papers, 2018/1.

Van der Loo, G and Wessel, R, 'The Non-Ratification of Mixed Agreements: Legal Consequences and Solution' (2017) 54 *Common Market Law Review* 735.

Van der Zee, E, 'Incorporating the OECD Guidelines in International Investment Agreements: Turning a Soft Law Obligation into Hard Law?' (2013) 40 *Legal Issues of Economic Integration* 33.

Van Elsuwege, P, 'EU External Action after the Collapse of the Pillar Structure: In Search of a New Balance Between Delimitation and Consistency' (2010) 47 *Common Market Law Review* 987.

Van Harten, G, 'A case for an international investment court', Society of International Economic Law, Online Proceedings Working Paper No 22/08.

Venzke, I, 'Investor-State Dispute Settlement in TTIP from the Perspective of a Public Law Theory of International Adjudication' (2016) 17 *Journal of World Investment and Trade* 374.

Vicente, M, 'The European Union's Proposal for the Modernisation of the Energy Charter Treaty' (2022) 31 *European Energy and Environmental Law Review* 124.

Vignes, D, 'Une notion ambiguë: la mise en application provisoire des traités' (1962) 18 *Annuaire française de droit international* 181.

Voon, T, Mitchell, A and Munro, J, 'Parting Ways: The Impact of Mutual Termination of Investment Treaties on Investor Rights' (2014) 29 *ICSID Review – Foreign Investment Law Journal* 451.

Vranes, E, 'The Definition of 'Norm Conflict' in International Law and Legal Theory' (2006) 17 *European Journal of International Law* 395.

Wagner, M, 'Regulatory Space in International Trade Law and International Investment Law' (2014) 36 *University of Pennsylvania Journal of International Law* 1.

Waibel, M, 'Opening Pandora's Box: Sovereign Bonds in International Arbitration' (2007) 101 *American Journal of International Law* 711 (2007).

Wälde, T, 'International Investment under the 1994 Energy Charter Treaty – Legal, Negotiating and Policy Implications for International Investors within Western and Commonwealth of Independent States/Eastern European Countries' (1995) 29 *Journal of World Trade* 5 (1995).

—— 'Investment Arbitration under the Energy Charter Treaty – From Dispute Settlement to Treaty Implementation' (1996) 12 *Arbitration International* 429.

—— 'The 'Umbrella' Clause in Investment Arbitration – A Comment on Original Intentions and Recent Cases' (2005) 6 *Journal World Investment and Trade* 183.

Waleson, J, 'Corporate Social Responsibility in EU Comprehensive Free Trade Agreements: Towards Sustainable Trade and Investment' (2015) 40 *Legal Issues of Economic Integration* 143.

Wehland, H, 'The Enforcement of Intra-EU BIT Awards: *Micula v Romania* and Beyond' (2016) 17 *Journal of World Investment and Trade* 942.

Yannaca Small, C, 'Indirect Expropriation' and the 'Right to Regulate' in International Investment Law' (2004) OECD Working Papers on International Investment.

Yves Fortier, L and Drymer, SL, 'Indirect Expropriation in the Law of International Investment: I know It when I see it, or *Caveat Investor*' (2004) 9 *ICSID Review-Foreign Investment Law Journal* 293.

Ziegler, KS, 'Beyond Pluralism and Autonomy: Systemic Harmonisation as a Paradigm for the Interaction of EU Law and International Law' (2016) 35 *Yearbook of European Law* 667.

NEWSPAPER ARTICLES, ONLINE SOURCES, ETC

'Canada rules out full inclusion of Investment Court System in CETA', *EU Trade Insights*, 9 December 2015.

Bray, D and Kapoor S, 'Agreement on the termination of intra-EU BITs: sunset in stone?', 4 November 2020, Kluwer arbitration blog.

Davoise, M and Burgstaller, M, 'Another one BIT the Dust: is the Netherlands' termination of intra-EU Treaties the latest symptom of a backlash against investor-State arbitration?', 11 August 2020, Kluwer arbitration blog.

Deffet, E, 'Ceta: pourquoi la Wallonie refuse de signer le traité', Le soir, 19 October 2016.

European Commission, 'Commission presents EU-Vietnam trade and investment agreements for signature and conclusion', Press release, 17 October 2018.

—— 'Commission proposes new Investment Court System for TTIP and other EU trade and investment negotiations', Press release, 16 September 2015.

—— 'EU and Japan finalise Economic Partnership Agreement', 8 December 2017, Press release.

—— 'EU and Singapore conclude investment talks', Press release, 17 October 2014.

—— 'European Commission proposes signature and conclusion of EU-Canada trade deal', Press release, 5 July 2016.

—— 'European Council endorses Commission's priorities', Press release, 29 June 2016.

—— 'Sincere cooperation and primacy of EU law: Commission refers UK to EU Court of Justice over a UK Judgment allowing enforcement of an arbitral award granting illegal State aid', Press release, 9 February 2022.

—— 'Sincere cooperation and primacy of EU law: Commission refers UK to EU Court of Justice over a UK Judgment allowing enforcement of an arbitral award granting illegal State aid', Press release, 9 February 2022.

—— 'Trade: European Commission proposes signature and conclusion of Japan and Singapore agreements', Press release, 18 April 2018.

Fisher, T, 'Spain announces withdrawal from ECT', *Global Arbitration Review*, 13 October 2022.

Hodgson, C, Hancock, A and Abboud, L, 'France withdraws from Energy Charter Treaty', *Financial Times*, 21 October 2022.

Johnston, C, 'Berlin anti-TTIP trade deal protest attracts hundreds of thousands', *The Guardian*, 10 October 2015.
Lavranos, N, 'The first steps towards a Multilateral Investment Court (MIC)', *Efilablog*, 19 July 2017.
Moody, S, 'Germany latest to quit ECT', *Global Arbitration Review*, 11 November 2022.
Sadowski, W, 'Poland to Withdraw from the ECT: Who Does It Benefit?', *Kluwer Arbitration Blog*, 27 September 2022.
Von der Burchard, H, 'Canada's fresh push for EU trade deal', *Politico*, 12 November 2015.
Yong, L, *Airbus Withdraws Treaty Claim Against Poland*, Global Arbitration Review, 22 May 2018.

EU AND OTHER DOCUMENTS

BEUC, 'Canada and EU trade talks: The backdoor to ISDS endorsement', 8 May 2014.
Canada-European Union Comprehensive Economic and Trade Agreement (CETA) – Draft Investment Chapter, 2014, available at https://www.transnational-dispute-management.com/news.asp?key=522.
Canada-European Union Comprehensive Economic and Trade Agreement (CETA) – Investor-State Dispute Settlement (ISDS) 2014, available at https://www.transnational-dispute-management.com/news.asp?key=522.
Canada-EU CETA Draft Investment Chapter – 21 November 2013, available at https://www.transnational-dispute-management.com/news.asp?key=522.
Columbia Center on Sustainable Development, 'Position paper in support of opinions expressed in response to the European Commission's 'Public consultation on a multilateral reform of investment dispute resolution', 2017.
Conclusions of the European Council, 25 and 26 June 1990.
Conference of the representatives of the governments of the Member States, CONF-UP 1788/91, 1991.
Conference on the future of Europe – Report on the final outcome, 2022.
Corporate Europe Observatory, 'Public services under attack through TTIP and CETA', 2015; European Green Party, Resolution adopted by the 22nd Council of the European Green Party, 2015.
Corporate Europe Observatory, 'Public services under attack through TTIP and CETA', 2015.
Declaration of the Kingdom of Belgium on the signing of CETA (*Déclaration du Royaume de Belgique relative aux conditions de pleins pouvoirs par l'Etat fédéral et les Entités fédérées pour la signature du CETA*), 27 October 2016.
Declaration of the Member States of 15 January 2019 on the legal consequences of the *Achmea* judgment and on investment protection.
Declaration of the Representative of the Government of Hungary of 16 January 2019 on the legal consequences of the judgment of the Court of Justice in *Achmea* and on investment protection in the European Union.
Declaration of the Representatives of the Member States of 16 January 2019 on the enforcement of the judgment of the Court of Justice in *Achmea* and on investment protection in the European Union.
Draft Investor-State Dispute Settlement (ISDS) text of the EU-negotiations with Singapore – 20 February 2014, available at https://www.transnational-dispute-management.com/news.asp?key=522.
Energy Charter Secretariat, Public Communication explaining the main changes contained in the agreement in principle, 24 June 2022.
ETUC, 'European Trade Union calls for a fundamental rethink of Canadian and US trade deals', 17 November 2014.

European Commission, 'Europeans' attitude on Trade and EU trade policy' (Summary), Special Eurobarometer 491, May 2019, 18.
—— 2022 Rule of Law Report – Country Chapter on the rule of law situation in Hungary, SWD (2022) 517 final.
—— 2022 Rule of Law Report – Country Chapter on the rule of law situation in Poland, SWD(2022) 521 final.
—— 2022 Rule of Law Report – Country Chapter on the rule of law situation in Romania, SWD(2022) 523 final.
—— 2022 Rule of Law Report – Country Chapter on the rule of law situation in Italy, SWD(2022) 512 final.
—— A balanced and progressive trade policy to harness globalisation, COM (2017) 492 final.
—— Completing the internal market: white paper from the Commission to the European Council, COM (85) 310.
—— Decision authorising the opening of negotiations for a Convention establishing a multilateral court for the settlement of investment disputes SWD (2017) 302 final.
—— Foreign Direct Investment – Integration and Market Openness, Single Market Scoreboard, 2020.
—— Global Europe: competing in the world, COM (2006) 567.
—— Investment in TTIP and beyond – the path for reform – Enhancing the right to regulate and moving from current ad hoc arbitration towards an Investment Court, Concept Paper, 2015, 11.
—— Online public consultation on investment protection and investor-to-state dispute settlement (ISDS) in the Transatlantic Trade and Investment Partnership Agreement, SWD(2015) 3 final.
—— Overview of the FTA and other negotiations, 2020.
—— Proposal for a Council Decision on the Provisional Application of CETA, COM (2016) 470.
—— Protection of intra-EU investment, COM (2018) 547 final.
—— Reflection paper on harnessing globalisation, 2017.
—— Report on the application of Regulation (EU) No 1219/2012 establishing transitional arrangements for bilateral investment agreements between Member States and third countries, COM (2020) 134 final.
—— Shared Vision, Common Action: a Stronger Europe – A Global Strategy for the European Union's Foreign and Security Policy, 2017.
—— The 2020 EU Justice Scoreboard.
—— Towards a comprehensive European international investment policy, COM (2010) 343 final.
European Consumer Organisation, 'Canada and EU trade talks: the backdoor to ISDS endorsement', 8 May 2014.
European Green Party, Resolution adopted by the 22nd Council of the European Green Party, 2015. European Left, 'Refound Europe, create new progressive convergence', 2015, Political Document, European Left Congress, Berlin, 16–18 December 2016.
European Left, 'Political Document', European Left Congress, Berlin, 16–18 December 2016.
European Parliament, Driving trade in the ASEAN region – Progress of FTA negotiations, Briefing, 2016.
—— EU-Canada Comprehensive Economic and Trade Agreement, Briefing, January 2016.
—— India and prospects for closer EU ties, Briefing, 2017.
European Trade Union Confederation, 'ETUC assessment on the EU-Canada Comprehensive Economic and Trade Agreement (CETA)', 20 December 2016.
—— 'European Trade Union calls for a fundamental rethink of Canadian and US trade deals', 17 November 2014.
ICSID Secretariat, 'Possible improvements of the framework for ICSID arbitration', 2004.
IMF, 'Balance of Payments Manual', 2010.
Intra-EU Investment treaties- Non-paper from Austria, Finland, France, Germany and the Netherlands, 2016.

Joint Declaration of the European Parliament, the Council and the European Commission on the Conference on the future of Europe – Engaging with citizens for democracy – Building a more resilient Europe, OJ C91 I.

Nolte, G, First report on subsequent agreements and subsequent practice in relation to the interpretation of treaties, A/CN.4/660, 66.

Report of the Study Group of the International Law Commission, 13 April 2006, A/CN.4/L.682.

Report of the United Nations Commission on International Trade Law, Fiftieth session (3–21 July 2017), A/72/17.

Rosa Luxemburg Foundation, 'A World Court for corporations: how the EU plans to entrench and institutionalize investor-State dispute settlement', 2017.

TTIP Draft, 26 May 2014, available at https://www.transnational-dispute-management.com/news.asp?key=522.

UNCITRAL Secretariat, 'Possible reform of investor-State dispute settlement (ISDS) Multilateral instrument on ISDS reform', 16 January 2020, A/CN.9/WG.III/WP.194, 2–3.

UNCITRAL Working Group III, 'Establishing a standing mechanism for the settlement of international investment disputes', Annex – Submission from the European Union and its Member States, A/CN.9/WG.III/WP.159.

UNCTAD, 'Bilateral investment treaties – 1959–1999', 2000.

—— Bilateral investment treaties 1995–2006: Trends in investment rule-making', 2007.

—— 'The changing landscape: new treaties and recent policy developments', IIA Issue Note, 2020.

Index

accession to the ECHR:
EU autonomy, impact on, 46–47
accession to the EU:
Grandfathering Regulation, 20
impact on pre-existing intra-EU IIAs, 4, 43–44, 52
Achmea tribunal, 56, 57, 90–91
other tribunals, 55–60
***Achmea* tribunal:**
accession to the EU, impact of, 56, 57, 90–91
Achmea objection, 51, 69–70, 72, 74, 89
arbitral awards, 65–68
arbitration clause
non-discrimination principle, consistency with, 62
preliminary reference mechanism, consistency with, 62
autonomy principle, 63–64, 65, 66–68
enlarged scope of application, 87–91
EU law, consistency with, 64–65
fair and equitable treatment, 64–65
ICDS mechanism and EU law, 62–63
impact
autonomy, 68
ECT, 70–71
ICSID awards, 70
'taking into account' EU law, 68
uncertainty, 68–70
jurisdiction, 63–65
member states' reaction to
declarations on legal consequences of judgment, 75–78
pre-*Achmea*
European Commission approach, 51–54
international law approach, 54–62
preliminary rulings, 65–66
'taking into account' EU law, 64–65
***Achmea* objection,** 51, 69–70, 72, 74, 89
advisory opinion procedure, 47
Agreement for the Termination of Bilateral Investment Treaties between Member States of the EU, *see* **Termination Agreement**
amendment of IIAs/BITs:
ECT, 95, 146
European Commission
notification and authorisation, 20–21
fair and equitable treatment clauses, 102
CETA, 117
***amicus curiae* briefs:**
European Commission, 51–54
arbitral tribunals:
EU law, relationship with, 63, 65–66
arbitration without privity doctrine, 9
Association of Southeast Asian Nations (ASEAN):
direct expropriation, 112
fair and equitable treatment clauses, 100–1
trade negotiations, 24–25
autonomy of EU law, 6, 96
Achmea judgment, 63–64, 68, 71, 87–89
CETA, relationship with, 140–41, 142–43
decision-making procedures, 44
dispute settlement mechanism
EEA Court, 45
ECHR accession, 46–47
ECT, relationship with, 87, 95
enforcement proceedings, 66–67
ECPC compatibility, 46
ICS, relationship with, 98
ISDS system, relationship with, 63
Mox Plant case, 45–46
pacta sunt servanda, 91
'taking into account' EU law, 65

bilateral investment treaties (BITs), 8–9
external BITs, 13
intra-EU IIAs, 4–5, 6
Netherlands-Slovak Republic BIT, *see Achmea* judgment
see also international investment agreements
Brexit, impact of, 2–3

Canada-United States-Mexico Agreement (CUSMA):
fair and equitable treatment clauses, 101
legitimate expectations, 101–2
carve-outs, 75, 116, 120, 147

Charter of Fundamental Rights of the European Union (CFREU), 16
legitimate expectation doctrine
ECT, 39
right to effective remedy, 144–45
clarificatory and hortatory rules:
EU IIAs and investment chapters, 117–18
investment treaty practice, 115–16
climate policy:
ECT, relationship with, 151, 155
intra-EU IIAs, relationship with, 41–42
co-respondent mechanism, 47, 141–42
collective action clauses (CACs), 121
common commercial policy (CCP):
enlargement, 12
EU competences, 17, 25, 34–35
foreign investment, 10, 12–13, 34–35
foreign direct investment, 15
Lisbon Treaty, 17–18
reform proposals, 14–15
competences, 1
CCP, 17, 25, 34–35
European Community
Opinion 1/94, 12
Opinion 2/92, 12
European Union
allocation of foreign direct investment competences, 14–18
Art. 207 TFEU, 18–19
draft Constitutional Treaty, 14–15
interpretation by European Commission, 24–26
TFEU, 16–19
interpretation of, 24–26
Opinion 2/15 (EUSFTA), 5, 26–27
direct investment, 27–28
indirect investment, 28–30
ISDS, 28–30
transition from member state BITS to EUSFTA, 30–31
competition law:
investment protection rules, 40–41
state aid, 40–41
Comprehensive and Progressive Agreement for Trans-Pacific Partnership (CPTPP):
carve-out clauses, 116
fair and equitable treatment clauses, 101
Comprehensive Economic and Trade Agreement (CETA), 26, 152–53
appellate review mechanism, 132–33
carve-out clauses, 120
compatibility with EU treaties, 139
autonomy principle, 140–43
equal treatment and effectiveness, 143–44
right to effective remedy, 144–45
compatibility with Irish Constitution, 156
challenges, 137–39
facultative mixity, 31–33
general exception, 119
indirect expropriation, 113–15
ICS, 130, 137–39
ISDS mechanism, 127–28
legitimate expectations, 103
multilateralism, 134
non-discrimination, 102
protection of public interest objectives, 117–18
umbrella clauses, 106
Court of Justice of the European Union (CJEU):
Achmea judgment, 62–63
arbitral awards, 65–68
arbitral tribunals' jurisdiction, 63–65
EU law, consistency with, 64–65
impact, 68–71
'taking into account' EU law, 64–65
arbitration of investor-state disputes, 42–43
autonomy of EU law
compatibility of CETA investment dispute (Opinion 1/17), 139–45
compatibility of ECPC (Opinion 1/09), 46, 58, 63–64
EEA Agreement (Opinion 1/91), 45
EU accession to ECHR (Opinion 2/13), 46–47, 63
European Common Aviation Area (Opinion 1/00), 45
external autonomy (Opinion 1/76), 44
compatibility of CETA investment dispute (Opinion 1/17), 139
autonomy, 140–43
equal treatment and effectiveness, 143–44
right of effective remedy, 144–45
eradication of intra-EU investment arbitration, 87–91
EU accession to ECHR (Opinion 2/13), 46–47, 63
EU compatibility of transfer clauses, 38
EUSFTA (Opinion 2/15), 5, 26–27, 35
direct investment, 27–28
indirect investment, 28–30
ISDS, 28–30
transition from member state BITS to EUSFTA, 30–31
customs union, 3–4, 9–10, 60

direct effect, 1, 6, 145

emission trading scheme:
intra-EU IIAs, relationship with, 41–42
Energy Charter Treaty (ECT), 4, 6, 13–14
amicus curiae brief, 53–54
EU judicial system and ECT ISDS mechanism
relationship between, 60–61
EU substantive law and investment protection rules
relationship between, 61–62
European Commission
amicus curiae brief, 53–54
Komstroy judgment
impact of, 91–95
legitimate expectation doctrine, 39–40
reform and the ICS, 146–47
unilateral withdrawals, 155
EU law:
autonomy principle
decision-making procedures, 44
dispute settlement mechanism, 45
EEA Court, 45
ECHR accession, 46–47
ECPC compatibility, 46
Mox Plant case, 45–46
see also autonomy of EU law
international law, relationship with, 1–3, 50–51
intra-EU IIAs, tensions with, 95–96, 52–53
adjudicatory bodies, 42–43
approaches to cross-border investment regulation, 37–38
autonomy vs primacy of EU law, 43–47
climate policy, 41–42
competition law, 40–41
EU law-centred approach, 43–47
international law-centred approach, 47–50
investment protection rules, 40–41
legitimate expectations principle, 38–40
state aide, 40–41
investment protection rules, relationship with, 51, 59–60, 61–62, 87, 91, 95
ISDS clauses compatibility, 56–57
legitimate expectation, 38–40
primacy, *see* primacy of EU law
see also Court of Justice of the EU

European and Community Patents Court (ECPC):
compatibility with EU Treaties (Opinion 1/09), 46, 58, 64, 141
European Commission:
amicus curiae briefs
EU law and intra-EU IIAs, 51–54
Art. 207 TFEU, 18–19
EU IIAs
interpretation of EU's competence, 24–26
transition to, 20–21
European Parliament, relationship with, 18
foreign direct investment competence, 18
Grandfathering Regulation, 20–21
ISDS
financial responsibility, 21–24
Opinion 1/94, 12
post-*Achmea* approach, 71–72
pre-*Achmea* approach, 51–54
European Community (EC):
developing role in foreign investment, 5–6, 8–9, 12–14, 34–35
European Convention on Human Rights (ECHR):
ECT and, 53–54
EU accession
autonomy principle, 46–47
European Council:
foreign direct investment competence, 17–18
European Court of Human Rights (ECtHR):
co-respondent mechanism, 47, 141–42
European Economic Area (EEA):
autonomy principle (Opinion 1/91), 45
European Economic Community (EEC):
developing role in foreign investment, 5–6, 8–9
European Monetary Union:
foreign investment, 10–11
European Parliament:
CCP, 17–18
ECT, 156
European Commission, relationship with, 18
foreign direct investment competence, 17–18, 25
ISDS reform and ICS, 129–30, 147–48
treaty making, 17–18
European Union (EU), 3–4
developing role in foreign investment, 5–6, 8–9, 19, 34–35
foreign direct investment competences, 17–18

involvement in investment disputes, 21–24
transition to EU IIAs, 20–21
enlargement, 4
EU IIAs
financial responsibility, 21–24
transition to, 20–21
competences, 1
direct effect, 1
external powers, 2
foreign investment, 153
developing role in, 5–6, 8–9, 19, 34–35
foreign direct investment competences, 17–18
involvement in investment disputes, 21–24
legal and political obstacles, 151–53
transition to EU IIAs, 20–21
international investment law, ambivalence towards, 149–51
intra-EU IIAs, 4–5, 6
ISDS
financial responsibility, 21–24
primacy of EU law, 1
sui generis entity, as, 1, 43–44
European Union-Singapore Free Trade Agreement (EUSFTA), 24, 26
environmental and sustainable development, 118
facultative mixity, 29–30, 34
Opinion 2/15, 5, 26–27
direct investment, 27–28
indirect investment, 28–30
ISDS, 28–30
transition from member state BITS to EUSFTA, 30–31
European Union-Singapore Investment Protection Agreement (EUSIPA), 34, 152
appellate review mechanisms, 132
environmental and sustainable development, 118
expropriation, 113, 115
general exception mechanisms, 119
ICS, 130
multilateralism, 134
umbrella clauses, 106–7
European Union-Vietnam Free Trade Agreement (EUVIFTA):
environmental and sustainable development, 118
facultative mixity, 34
European Union-Vietnam Investment Protection Agreement (EUVIPA), 34, 152
appellate review mechanisms, 132
environmental and sustainable development, 118
expropriation, 113
general exception mechanisms, 119
ICS, 130
multilateralism, 134
umbrella clauses, 106, 107
exception clauses, 116
carve-outs and exception mechanisms, 116
clarificatory and hortatory rules, 115–16, 116, 117–18
GATS-type exception clauses, 116
GATT-type exception clauses, 98–99, 116
general exceptions
EU IIAs and investment chapters, 119–20
expropriation clauses, 16, 19, 38–39, 56, 64–65
EU investment law reforms, 146
general exceptions, 119
illegal expropriation
EU IIAs and investment chapters, 113–15
investment treaty practice, 107–13

facultative mixity, 17
CETA, 31–33
EUSFTA, 29–30, 34
EUVIFTA, 34
fair and equitable treatment (FET) clauses, 9, 38–39
content and evolution
EU IIAs and investment chapters, 102–4
investment treaty practice, 99–102
financial consequences of investment disputes, 21–24
foreign direct investment (FDI), 8–9
European Community competence, 17–18
Opinion 1/94, 12
Opinion 2/92, 12
European Union competence
allocation of foreign direct investment competences, 14–18
Art. 207 TFEU, 18–19
developing role in, 5–6, 8–9, 19–24, 34–35
draft Constitutional Treaty, 14–15
foreign direct investment competences, 17–18
involvement in investment disputes, 21–24
legal and political obstacles, 151–53

TFEU, 16–19
transition to EU IIAs, 20–21
free circulation of capital, 3, 9–11, 13, 38
Treaty of Rome, 9–10
foreign indirect investment, 8–9
CETA, 33
competences, 19, 28–30
Treaty of Rome, 9–10
free circulation of capital, 3, 9–11, 13, 38
Free Trade Commission (FTC), 100, 123

General Agreement on Tariffs and Trade (GATT), 11
exception clauses, 98–99, 116, 119
General Agreement on Trade in Services (GATS), 12
exception clauses, 116
Grandfathering Regulation, 20–21

holdouts, 121

independence and impartiality:
adjudicatory bodies, 138–39
arbitrators, 126
national judicial systems, 150
right to effective remedy, 144–45
Termination Agreement, 83
indirect investment, *see* **foreign indirect investment**
infringement procedure, 21, 42–43, 52
intellectual property rights:
indirect expropriation, 112–13, 114–15
International Centre for Settlement of Investment Disputes (ICSID):
Achmea judgment, impact of, 70, 73, 74
appellate mechanism, 125–26, 132
EU law and intra-EU ICSID arbitration, 90–91
recognition and enforcement of awards, 58, 72–73, 87
transparency, 124
international investment agreements (IIAs):
EU IIAs
EU transition to, 20–21
financial responsibility, 21–24
intra-EU IIAs, 4–5, 6
see also intra-EU IIAs
external IIAs, 6–7
international investment tribunals:
EU law and intra-EU IIAs
ECT, 60–62
EU law and ISDS mechanisms, 54–59, 60–61
investment protection rules, 59–60, 61–62
see also International Centre for Settlement of Investment Disputes; Investment Court System; investor-state dispute settlement
intra-EU IIAs, 4–5, 6, 36–37
EU as a *sui generis* entity, 43–44
EU law, tensions with, 95–96
CJEU and international arbitration, 42–43
climate policy, 41–42
competition law, 40–41
investment protection rules, 40–41
state aid, 40–41
EU treaties, relationship with, 43–44
international investment tribunals
ECT, 60–62
EU law and ISDS mechanisms, 54–59, 60–61
investment protection rules, 59–60, 61–62
post-*Achmea*, 72–75
transfer clauses, 37
Investment Court System (ICS):
CETA, challenges to, 137–39
autonomy, 140–43
equal treatment and effectiveness, 143–44
Opinion 1/17, 139–45
right to access independent tribunal, 144–45
creation, 128–30
appellate review mechanism, 132–33
appointment of adjudicators, 130–31
multilateralism, 133–37
permanent adjudicatory bodies, 130–31
remuneration of adjudicators, 132
ECT, 146–47
investment protection rules:
competition law, 40–41
ECT and EU substantive law relationship between, 61–62
EU law, relationship with, 51, 59–60, 87, 91, 95
ECT, 61–62
international investment tribunals, 59–60, 61–62
intra-EU IIAs, relationship with, 40–41
investor-state dispute settlement (ISDS):
autonomy of EU law, relationship with, 63
calls for reform, 2–3, 122–28
CETA, 127–28

compatibility with EU law, 56–57
ECT, 60–61
ECT ISDS mechanism, 60–61
EU IIAs, 127–28
discontent, 128–30
EU law, compatibility with, 56–57, 60–61
European Parliament
ISDS reform and ICS, 129–30, 147–48
financial responsibility, 21–24
international investment tribunals, 54–59, 60–61
reforms, 122–28, 129–30, 147–48
treaty-making
EU reforms, 122–28
VCLT
compatibility of ISDS clauses with EU law, 56–57

***Komstroy* judgment,** 88
impact of, 89, 91–95

legitimate expectation, 38–40, 100, 101–2, 103, 110–11, 146

member states, 4–5
Achmea judgment
declarations on legal consequences of judgment, 75–78
EU IIAs
financial responsibility, 21–24
transition to, 20–21
intra-EU IIAs
role of *Achmea* declarations, 78–81
ISDS
financial responsibility, 21–24
mixity, *see* **facultative mixity**
most-favoured nation (MFN) clauses, 102, 119
Multilateral Investment Court (MIC), 98, 133–36, 148, 150

national treatment (NT) clauses, 102, 119, 121
negotiation of IIAs/BITs:
European Commission
notification and authorisation, 20
Netherlands-Slovak Republic BIT, *see* ***Achmea* judgment**
new arbitration proceedings, 83
non-discrimination, 27–28, 38
CETA, 119, 142
emission trading system, 41
general exceptions, 119, 142
investor-state arbitration, 52, 55, 58–59
public purpose objective, 111–12, 114
North American Free Trade Agreement (NAFTA):
fair and equitable treatment clauses, 100
Free Trade Commission, 123
ISDS reforms, 123

***pacta sunt servanda*,** 32, 52–53, 60, 91
pending arbitration proceedings, 83
preliminary reference procedure, 43, 52
Achmea award, 62–63, 65, 88
autonomy of EU law, 45, 46–47
CETA tribunals, 142
ECT, 39
enforcement proceedings, 66–67
Komstroy judgment, 92
primacy of EU law, 1, 43–44, 91, 93–94
pacta sunt servanda, relationship with, 52–53
see also EU law
privity doctrine, 9
proportionality, 38, 111–12
public interest objectives:
EU IIAs and investment chapters, 117–18
investment treaty practice, 115–17

Regional Economic Integration Organisation (REIO):
European Union as, 60–61, 93, 94

state aid:
investment protection rules, relationship with, 40–41, 90, 91
structured dialogue procedure, 83–84
sunset clauses, 76, 82, 85–86, 151, 155–56

Termination Agreement (TA), 82
enforcement of intro-EU arbitral decisions, 86–87
impact, 82–85
ratione materiae, 85
ratione temporis, 85–86
Trade-Related Aspects of Intellectual Property Rights (TRIPS), 113, 114–15
Trans-Pacific Partnership (TPP), 101
Transatlantic Trade and Investment Partnership (TTIP), 127, 128–29, 152–53
transfer clauses, 9, 37–38, 56, 119
treaty-making, 97–98, 147–48
EU reforms, 98–99
carve-outs and exception mechanisms, 116

clarificatory and hortatory rules, 115–16, 116, 117–18
economic, fiscal and monetary protections, 120–22
exception clauses, 116
fair and equitable treatment clauses, 99–104
general exceptions, 119–20
illegal expropriation, 107–15
ICS, creation of, 128–47
ISDS mechanism, 122–28
public interest objectives, 117–18
umbrella clauses, 104–7
Treaty of Rome:
customs union, 9–10
Treaty on the European Union (TEU):
common values, 68, 98
sincere cooperation, 31–32
see also EU law
Treaty on the functioning of the European Union (TFEU):
allocation of competences, *see* competences
Achmea judgment, 68, 75, 93
Art. 207, 15–16, 18–19
Art. 345, 16
CCP, 17
foreign direct investment competences, 17–18, 27–28
foreign indirect investment competences, 28–30
see also EU law
umbrella clauses:
EU IIAs and investment chapters, 104–7
investment treaty practice, 104–5
UNCITRAL Working Group III:
reform of international investment law, 3
United Nations Convention of the Law of the Sea (UNCLOS), 45–46

Vienna Convention on the Law of Treaties (VCLT), 32
ECT, 74, 93–94
EU law and intra-EU IIAs, relationship between, 47–48
customary *lex specialis* principle, 50
non-derogation/preservation clauses, 48–49
treaty interpretation, 48
EU law interpretation of intra-EU IIAs
conflict between approaches, 48–49, 50–51, 74, 78, 80–81, 96, 103, 115–16
ISDS clauses
compatibility with EU law, 56–58, 135
sunset clauses, 86

World Trade Organization (WTO):
exception clauses, 116
general exceptions, 119–20

www.ingramcontent.com/pod-product-compliance
Ingram Content Group UK Ltd.
Pitfield, Milton Keynes, MK11 3LW, UK
UKHW020816290926
15470UKWH00003B/1196